Remapping Memory

This book was sponsored by the Committee on International Peace and Security of the Social Science Research Council.

Remapping Memory

The Politics of TimeSpace

Jonathan Boyarin, editor

Afterword by Charles Tilly

 University of Minnesota Press

Minneapolis

London

"The Reincarnation of Souls and the Rebirth of Commodities: Representations of Time in 'East' and 'West,' " by Akhil Gupta, was previously published in *Cultural Critique* 22 (1992): 187–211. Copyright 1992 Oxford University Press. Used with permission.

An earlier version of "*Memoria de Sangre:* Fear, Hope, and Disenchantment in Argentina," by Carina Perelli, was published in *Social Research* 59, no. 2, as "Settling Accounts with Blood Memory: The Case of Argentina." Reprinted with permission of *Social Research* and the author.

Figure 1 in " 'Wan Tasbaya Dukiara': Contested Notions of Land Rights in Miskitu History," by Charles R. Hale, is reprinted from Charles R. Hale, *Resistance and Contradiction: Miskitu Indians and the Nicaraguan State, 1894–1987* (Stanford, Calif.: Stanford University Press, 1994). Copyright 1994 by the Board of Trustees of the Leland Stanford Junior University. Used by permission of the publisher. Figure 2 in " 'Wan Tasbaya Dukiara' " is used by permission of the author.

Published by the University of Minnesota Press
111 Third Avenue South, Suite 290, Minneapolis, MN 55401-2520
Printed in the United States of America on acid-free paper

Library of Congress Cataloging–in–Publication Data
Remapping Memory: the politics of TimeSpace / Jonathan Boyarin, editor.
    p.   cm.
  Includes bibliographical references and index.
  ISBN 0-8166-2452-6. — ISBN 0-8166-2453-4 (pbk.)
    1. Political culture. 2. Political anthropology. 3. Space and
time. I. Boyarin, Jonathan.
JA75.7.S69 1994
306.2 — dc20   94-9358

Contents

v

Introduction

Jonathan Boyarin

COLLECTIVE VOLUMES LIKE this one are sometimes presented as if they had dropped fully formed from the sky, needing only, perhaps, some appended acknowledgments to sponsors. They may thus seem to pretend to be the last and complete word on their given topic. This one, at least, is the result of contingent connections between specialists in widely divergent areas who took advantage of an opportunity to articulate a common agenda. The book's topic is so large, and intersects with so many fast-developing trends in cultural research, that it seems wisest to introduce it with a straightforward account of how it came to be. To some readers this bit of personal narrative may still smack of self-absorption. I trust that most will take it in the way it is intended, as an invitation to critical participation in the issues the contributors raise.

Remapping Memory: The Politics of TimeSpace grew out of two small-group workshops held in 1990 and 1991. The workshops were sponsored by the Program in International Peace and Security, which is administered by the Social Science Research Council and funded by the John D. and Catherine T. MacArthur Foundation.[1]

The very week I began my fellowship in the program, in June 1989, I flew to Mexico City to participate in the second annual fellows' conference. It was an unsettling experience. I found myself in the middle of a foreign and very poor country. Indeed, the planners had chosen the site both for pragmatic financial reasons and out of a desire to expose the fellows to non–United States realities. Yet—along with dozens of people I'd never met before—I was basically confined to the resort compound of Cocoyoc, a relic of the Spanish conquistadores' luxurious and self-aggrandizing lifestyle. Arriving at Cocoyoc during the weekend, when the place was filled with upper-middle-class residents of Mexico City, I had the unsettling feeling that the place was the Mexican equivalent of a Catskills resort. It was, perhaps, a typical case of the peculiar "time-space compression" that the geographer David Harvey describes as characteristic of postmodernity (see my first essay in this volume).

The conference was disorienting in other ways as well. I was flattered and pleased to have been granted a fellowship. Because the program was explicitly designed to promote innovative, critical, and cross-disciplinary thinking on issues of peace and security, I hoped to find much stimulation for my own project, which concerned the cultural dynamics of the Israeli-Palestinian conflict. Certainly, the fellows' presentations dealt with a wide range of regions, issues, and approaches. Yet the plenary speakers on the topic of "regional security" worked within what struck me and others as an entirely conventional and highly alienated discourse of international relations.

Still, the conference turned out to be a very important opportunity. Among the fellows were a few whose research areas were geographically far removed from my own but whose theoretical concerns were very much ones I shared. Three of these participants were Lisa Yoneyama, then a doctoral candidate in anthropology at Stanford who was just about to begin fieldwork in Hiroshima; Charles Hale, just completing a doctorate in anthropology at Stanford on the conflict between the Miskito Indians and the Sandinistas; and Carina Perelli, a sociologist from Uruguay who was working on the transition from military dictatorship to democracy in Uruguay, Brazil, and Argentina.

Shortly after the conference, all the fellows received a request for proposals for small-group workshops. Carina took the initiative, writing to me and suggesting that she and I together draft a proposal for a workshop focusing on a theme that interested all of us: the role of memory and rhetorics of collective identity in constructing and maintaining the nation-state.

As a group consisting mostly of anthropologists, we already felt somewhat outside the mainstream of the field of international relations and security studies. In our proposal, we sought language that would convey the material power of constructions of identity and history to senior scholars more accustomed to thinking of geographical borders and fire-power. Thus, in response to the item labeled "the topic and its relations to the Council's aims," we wrote:

> The workshop is intended to help destabilize "naturalistic" conceptions of the nation-state. Instead, the participants will help to share and develop ways of analyzing historical self-constructions of human groups, and their construction of the spaces which they shape and which shape them. To paraphrase Gallie, the discussion will focus on "essentially contested memories" vis-à-vis time and/or space. These theoretical forays will be both informed by and tested within the context of several profound cultural/political conflicts in various parts of the contemporary world. The workshop is ultimately intended to foster the infusion of critical humanist and social theory into the more "political science" oriented realm of peace and security studies. These considerations should yield, inter alia, a view of the state as a highly contingent artifact of groups contending for legitimacy vis-à-vis their own sense of "insider-hood," their control of positions within hierarchies, and their control of geographical territories. In terms of practical policy-making, this workshop could help promote a new conceptual language to avoid the pitfalls of thinking of states per se as individual "actors," focusing instead on the ways individual and collective human actors work in, through, despite, and against states.

The committee administering the program funded two workshops. Present at the first, in addition to Charles, Lisa, Carina, and me, were Adam Ashforth, a political scientist specializing in contemporary South Africa; Richard Ashley, a poststructuralist international relations theorist at the University of Arizona; and Charles Tilly, a historical sociologist who is director of the Center for Studies of Social Change at the New School for Social Research. We devoted most of that weekend to an exciting and nec-essarily inconclusive attempt to figure out how this combination of rela-tively ordinary words — space, time, politics, memory — could serve as an analytic rubric.

Is memory subjective or objective, or is this conventional dichotomy itself bankrupt? Is memory the residue of what "really" happened in the past, as ordinary, nonscholarly usage would have it? Is it more proper to speak of memory as a narrative constructed about the past in the present, as scholarly investigations of the shifting rhetorics about memory would suggest? If the latter is true, then how can we account for the persuasive power of such "rhetorics of memory"?

And further: What are the limits of politics? Is all human action in some ultimate sense "political," as critical scholars in many areas of the humanities and social sciences argue? Are there epistemological distinctions that must be made in analyzing the political actions of nonstate collectives versus the representatives of states?

Finally, the hardest question for a collection of nonphysicists: How can we use space and time as analytic categories, when our everyday use of these terms is so far from the meanings given to them by scientists who study them in quite precise ways? Unlike those who treat memory and "the political," who have at least made attempts to articulate critical understandings, scholars concerned with the presence of the past and with contests over terrain often rely on perfectly vernacular notions of dimensionality.

As one of the initial convenors, it fell to me to draft a theoretical essay expounding on the title of our two workshops—a task I mused, worried, and read about, and reluctantly set to writing up in the winter of 1991. Not content to deal with cultures of nationalism, I begin by considering changing theories of space and time, as a first approach to the ethnoscience of modernity. Then I discuss new technologies of transportation and communication that have profoundly altered our sense of time and space, the "reach" of power, and the possibilities of reifying and hence "preserving" images of the past. My third section emphasizes the intense interest of nation-state apparatuses in both memory and dimensionality; the fourth draws connections among identity, memory, and the current interest in the human body as an artifact. I conclude by asking that two ethics, as yet separated, be brought together: our sense of common human identification with people of the past, and our solidarity with living people everywhere.

Carina Perelli's essay details the explosively dangerous power of memories of repression during the period of military rule in Argentina, a country where "people's sense of self-worth and identity depends on what is perceived as the [country's] grand heritage and historical tradition." The phenomenon of "holes of memory" is also discussed—the willing forgetting or silencing of events of which those who witnessed them dare not speak, such as the disappearances of neighbors, coworkers, and even relatives, and the pained legacy of such breaches of human solidarity. Perelli offers a rather pessimistic appraisal of the efforts by human rights organizations to assure "Nunca más"—that this will never happen again. More important, this essay provides us with a great deal of insight into the local problems of what we might otherwise categorize, in a way at once too facile and too schematic, as "the transition to democracy."

Lisa Yoneyama's contribution on memory in contemporary Hiroshima is by turns horrifying, unsettling, and ironic. It chronicles the debates and dilemmas faced by Hiroshima's residents today over the proper way to shape their city's relation to the past and the future. Is the tendency inevitable to "tame memories," to wipe away the bloodstains and to smooth the jagged edges of the ruins of the bombed city into "clean surfaces"? What forces work to preserve a living memory of the disaster that befell Hiroshima, and how effective can they be against the forces of normality, the market, and renewed nationalism? By thus articulating memory as a counterweight to the consumerism of "lite" postmodernity, Yoneyama's essay finds its place as well within critical investigations of the link between political economies and symbolic economies.

Charles Hale brought us "Contested Notions of Land Rights in Miskitu History." Beyond documenting the various forces that go into the shaping of a new ethnic consciousness among "indigenous" peoples, Hale raises a dilemma as profound as those dealt with in Perelli's and Yoneyama's contributions: when an indigenous group claims autonomous rights to self-rule and land against the hegemonic claims of the state, is it inevitable that the indigenous claims will be cast in the same terms that legitimate state rule? Hale reveals that an attempt to resolve the contradictions between epistemology and politics by appealing to subjugated knowledges is not always successful. In a conflict between a revolutionary government bitterly opposed by the United States and a marginal group of Indians covertly supported by the United States, "there was no single 'subjugated standpoint' with which to align."

A second essay of my own, originally prepared for the first workshop, deals in a different way with the same issue of the apparent compulsion to frame claims for national identity as statebuilding projects. I find some striking parallels between aspects of Hegel's philosophy and aspects of classic Zionist ideology. These two bodies of thought, lacking a direct link in terms of intellectual history, nevertheless share key attitudes toward the philosophy of history and toward the state—toward, that is, time and space. For Hegel, history was a conflict-ridden yet necessary progress toward ever more universal harmony between world and spirit—and the state was the proper and only vehicle of such progress. Classic liberal Zionism shared this progressivism, in dismissing the solidarity with past generations that had traditionally grounded Diasporic Jewish consciousness, and likewise argued that the Jews could properly share in the progress of universal history only through creating their own state. The essay thus aims to help elucidate, within these two bodies of thought, some of the conventional notions of the politics of dimension and identity that this volume puts in question.

After both workshops were completed, we found other scholars whose work adds important complications to the perspective elaborated by our working group. Akhil Gupta's essay challenges "Western" notions of time and continuity much more directly. Gupta presents, without attempting to "explain," an everyday vignette from his fieldwork in India that reveals the common Indian belief in reincarnation. One aspect of the politics of time and space that anthropologists can no longer fail to recognize is the way in which "non-Western" peoples have been treated as objects for scientific study, their own practices and concepts studied symptomatically, the goal being a scientific account of the functions of their diversion from Western standards of logic and perception. As Gupta paraphrases, "If only they had a sense of time like ours, the logic goes, they too would be rich." Gupta, in a move that is increasingly being adopted by scholars but should become even much more common, uses the Indian belief in reincarnation as a springboard for a reexamination of the Marxist idea of commodity fetishism—revealing that circular notions of time are indeed present in the most "material" and everyday aspects of "Western" life. Rather than reformulating generalized contrasts between East and West, Gupta aims to "destabilize established orders of difference."

Jennifer Schirmer contributes a feminist perspective on the politics of urban social space. The "claiming of space" by women activists in England and Argentina disrupts the rationalized plans for ordering the modern state. Schirmer takes a forthright stance toward the question of these women's subjectivity, writing of the "imagination, conviction, and alternative perspectives" they bring to political issues. Of course, through spatial contention the women in both situations are also refusing to remain in the silence to which the state would condemn them, and thus, in the case of the mothers who have demonstrated at the Plaza de Mayo, insisting that "space" be made in public, social memory for their loss at the hands of the very state that presumes to regulate social space. In one sense Schirmer follows the lead of Michel Foucault, who calls for a renewed focus on space in social criticism. Yet the fact that what disrupts statist spatial "gridlock" is precisely a demand for the acknowledgment of memory echoes the point of my first paper in this volume, that time and space, memory, and territory are actually no more separate in the body politic than in our own organismic identity.

Daniel Segal's essay on race, class, and nation in Trinidad and Tobago details a nationalist ideology far different from those my theoretical paper claims as typical—different, that is, from those that rely on the claim of a unitary ethnic group living in and controlling its own primordial space. Segal shows how notions of cultural pluralism are employed in the "official" Trinidadian account of national identity, so that those of East Indian descent who violate Islamic laws against eating pork and drinking liquor are construed as violating their ancestral essence. Meanwhile, different chronotopes from Trinidad's history become commingled and simultaneously available—whites are naturally masters, "Africans" are slaves and hence underclass, those descended from East Indian immigrants are imported labor and hence not only underclass but also outsiders. The important theoretical point that Segal contributes concerns the way in which a selective mix of heterogeneous and anachronistic images from the past, not only the suppression of certain memories at the expense of others, can be employed in the invention of the nation and are also available to subvert the fictive community of nationhood.

Each of the three essays on Latin America displays its author's deep personal stake in the conflicts under discussion. Perelli combines a symbolic presentation of the state's investment in silence with her own contribution to the demand for testimony. Hale is careful to remain on the side of an analysis of collective rhetoric that might have some potential for resolution of conflicts, and takes care to avoid slipping into a removed critique that might delegitimize that rhetoric altogether. Schirmer attempts to identify the commonalities in the strategies for seizure of time and space employed by women in Greenham Common and the Plaza de Mayo. Meanwhile, standing a bit off from South America and at some ironic distance from the official discourse of Trinidadian pluralism that he analyzes, Segal simultaneously aims to disrupt the Eurocentric model of nationalism as an ideology of commonality.

The three remaining essays of the volume all focus in different ways on the culture of modernity and postmodernity. Starting from the perspective of a village in India, Gupta effectively limns the intense symbolic weight attached to commodities in capitalism. My study of Hegel and Zionism is likewise intended to uncover the implicit symbolic or narrative structures of modern secularist politics. Yoneyama describes the pained contest between those who insist on retaining a fresh sense of the horror at Hiroshima and those who wish to reprocess the city's past into grist for a postmodern capitalism trading in images. Finally, Charles Tilly returns us to the early modern Western European scene, where, perhaps, we may retrospectively see the notion of "resistance" first crystallizing.

Taken together, these essays should afford significant insights into the actual contexts of certain keywords in contemporary cultural theory—"anamnesia" (the failure or refusal to forget), "subjugated knowledge," "multiculturalism." Memories once evoked may be employed in infinite and unpredictable ways. The rhetoric used to justify colonialism is subject to sea changes that simultaneously infect and empower anticolonial movements. Assertions of identity grounded in contentious links to history and land may be reabsorbed into the relatively smooth integrating mechanisms of state ideology. But our goal in this book is by no means to unmask or dismantle those keywords. Rather, by focusing on personal and collective identity as the site where constructions of memory and dimensionality are tested, shaped, and effected, we hope to contribute to a more careful and subtle response to those in whose interest such keywords are invoked.

Notes

1. The first workshop, held at the University of California at Santa Barbara, was cosponsored by the university's Interdisciplinary Humanities Center. Our thanks go to the center and to its director, Paul Hernadi.

1

Space, Time, and the Politics of Memory

Jonathan Boyarin

The concept of the historical progress of mankind cannot be sundered from the concept of its progression through a homogeneous, empty time. A critique of the concept of such a progression must be the basis of any criticism of the concept of progress itself. (Benjamin 1969: 261)

It is a world where time and space have yet to be separated, where evening lies ahead and travelling is tomorrow. (Carter 1989: 77)

THE SOCIAL DIMENSIONS of time and space are the subject of numerous discourses, most notably perhaps in contemporary geography. The relations between history and memory (both "individual" and "collective") have also received increasing attention from the likes of historians, anthropologists, and literary scholars. In the past few years, "the politics of memory" has even become an object of explicit concern (Comay 1990; Rappaport 1990).[1] The French have already moved on from memory to forgetting, with a collection called *Usages de l'oubli* (Yerushalmi et al. 1988).

Links among these themes have recently emerged, in landmark critiques of ethnographic rhetoric (especially Fabian 1983); examinations of the link among the establishment of national literatures, imperial ambitions, and the geographic imagination (such as Knapp 1992); and now in several sophisticated collections of ethnographic and philosophical essays (including Bender and Wellbery 1991; Duncan and Ley 1993; Ferguson and Gupta 1992; Fox 1990; Hobsbawm and Ranger 1983; Friedland and Bowman 1994). Implicit but not often articulated in these studies is awareness of a profound paradox in scholarly thinking. On one hand, we pragmatically assume that time is a one-dimensional and irreversible phenomenon. On the other hand, our commitment to the past and its representations implies that the past affects the present in much more complex ways than the model of points on a straight line permits us to imagine (see, among a great many worthy studies, Gould 1987; Jankélévitch 1974; Reichenbach 1991). When we say "politics of memory," how many of us really mean that memory could *constitute* a politics? We aren't thinking of memory as some autonomous force that in and of itself dictates a political situation. We aren't even really thinking of memory as a distinct sphere of our daily lives that has its own political discourse, analogous to "the politics of housework" or "the politics of labor."[2] Most of us, I submit, are really referring to rhetoric about the past mobilized for political purposes.

Is it possible for us to think otherwise, as cultural actors evidently do, and conceive of "past" events being truly effective in the present—conceive of them, that is, as not really past? To try to imagine the latter possibility, I suggest, requires that we complicate the model of a one-dimensional arrow of time along which we move through or within a separate, three-dimensional "space." *I further suggest that our reified notions of objective and separate space and time are peculiarly linked to the modern identification of a nation with a sharply bounded, continuously occupied space controlled by a single sovereign state, comprising a set of autonomous yet essentially identical individuals.* Even the most sophisticated discussions of postmodernism sometimes refer to time and space as if they had an independent existence that came under challenge only in the past few years. What is called for is a simultaneous critique of epistemology and ideology. By becoming more aware of our own preconceived notions of dimensionality, I believe we can work much more effectively at the vital project of historicizing and relativizing both collective identities (see Connolly 1991), grounded as they are in temporal rhetorics of memory, and the nation-state form, grounded as it is in notions of fixed and unchanging geography.

This essay will therefore be a preliminary, and necessarily tentative and partial, attempt to articulate our changing understanding of dimensionality with our best insights into the contest and constitution of memory and with recent research into the culture of nationalism and the ethnography of the state. In covering such a vast topic in such a short space, I will necessarily have recourse to frequent quotations and summaries that cannot do justice to complex theoretical discussions. Still, I hope this paper will come to something more than a guide to further reading. Perhaps it will serve as a useful compendium of issues, all of which need further articulation, in order to facilitate a wide range of scholarship.

My discussion is divided into four main sections, which seem to correspond roughly to various foci of relevant studies. I start by discussing changing theories of space and time. Although it is a hazardous venture for someone who is neither a physicist nor a proper cognitive anthropologist, this section might be thought of as an approach to the ethnoscience of modernity (see Elkana 1988; Atran 1990). This will serve as an extended introduction to the rest of the paper, and should also help alert readers to some of the paper's implicit insights and unseen limitations. The second section might crudely be thought of as the practical counterpart of these theoretical developments. It deals with new technologies of transportation and communication that have profoundly altered our sense of time and space, the "reach" of power, and the possibilities of reifying and hence "preserving" images of the past. The third section focuses on the problem of legitimizing the vast scope and detail of power in modernity, emphasizing the intense interest of nation-state apparatuses in both memory and dimensionality. The fourth turns inward, from state and empire to the organism, asking how studies of "the body" may inform our understanding of the relation between dimensionality and identity. In conclusion I call for a new effort at synthesizing two hitherto separated ethics. The first is a sense of solidarity, of common human identification, with those who lived and died in previous generations; the other is solidarity with our living contemporaries across the planet.

The point in all this is not to transcend dimensionality or to resolve the conundrum of memory as recollection versus memory as retrospective construction. Just as the postmodern contains the modern in its name, here too the aim is rather to set all of the terms in the title at critical play, to enable us to work with the tensions inherent in them rather than to have our imagination limited by assuming that we know what they are when we say them. The kind of integrated personal universe described in Geertz's classic essay "Person, Time, and Conduct in Bali" (Geertz 1973) — a world in which the "immediatization and concretization of space-time brings the world back home" (Jackson 1989: 155) — might well have existed or still exist "there," or it might be seen as a mirror of the longing for wholeness and rest that our own fragmentation calls forth. It is not the universe we live in. Ours is the one in which, "just as the classical object has been redefined in physics, so the phenomenological subject is no longer discrete, apart from the event, but, like time and space themselves, functions of specific events and bound by their limitations" (Ermarth 1992: 8). The only place in this universe where we might feel at home is with the realization that we are not at home. If we want to retain even that, we must vigorously pursue the contingent consciousness that such realization affords us, and think carefully about the links among identity, empathy, responsibility, and action.

The Disjunctions of Changing Theory

Social scientists are aware that modern physics has challenged our commonsense notions of the changeless grid of time and space. But most of us take no more cognizance of these developments in physical theory than do most businesspeople or politicians (see Wilcox 1987: 4ff. and passim). Our deliberations usually proceed as if "culture" and "society" were played out within a Cartesian world. Fortunately some social theorists have begun to realize the need to interrogate our understandings of space and time in the human *and* physical sciences (Morin 1985), as well as the historical contingency of Cartesian thinking (Toulmin 1992). We can't all become physicists, but for now it might be appropriate to expect that we expand our peripheral vision a bit and consider some of our assumptions about time and space.

Why is it that our physics are now those of Einsteinian relativity and quantum mechanics, whereas our politics and our rhetorics still assume a world as described by Newton and Descartes? One suggestion made by postmodern political scientists is that there are close genealogical links between the "Cartesian coordinates" of space and time and the discrete, sovereign state, both associated with European society since the Renaissance (Walker 1989).[3] These links include relations of mapping, boundary setting, inclusion, and exclusion, practices in which the tradition of social research is closely involved. What Adam Ashforth (1990) has identified as the distinctively "problem-oriented" approach of Western social thought is consistent with the image of a world "out there," identifiable by its coordinates, which can be manipulated by a discrete, sovereign individual or state.

The three "spatial" dimensions to which we conventionally add time as a fourth are the basis of Euclid's geometry, and insofar as the everyday conceptions of social scientists and other educated "Westerners" are still rooted in the explorations of the Renaissance and the early modern period — the times of Galileo, Newton, Kant — our "real"[4] world is still dominated by the schemata of geometry:

> For the Greeks, space was the object of a science whose clarity and rigor were opposed to the confusion of the nascent physics, and geometry was a model which appeared to have nothing hypothetical about it. In fact, this conviction constituted the surest guide for the development of physics from the Middle Ages to the Renaissance, notably for Galileo — for whom the ideal goal was to model physics on Euclidean geometry — then for Newton and most certainly for Kant, for whom mathematics was the ideal science (in both senses of the term) and Euclidean a priori of sensibility, that is a condition of access to consciousness, therefore not susceptible to being cast in doubt or replaced by any other geometry. (Lestienne 1985: 9; my translation)

The relevant question here is not the existence of absolute space or time, irrespective of the existence of objects or events. Newton believed in such absolutes; Leibniz and Kant did not (Newton [1687] 1964; Leibniz [1716] 1964; Kant [1781] 1964). But they all implicitly agreed on the analytic distinction between time and space; all of them discussed time and space separately and sequentially. Indeed, the very terms of the dispute between, say, Newton and Kant over whether space and time exist as external absolutes or are universal a priori forms of cognition make abundantly clear that neither could imagine such categories as artifacts of human consciousness. For Kant the distinction between spatial extension and temporal succession is obvious:

> Time has only one dimension; different times are not simultaneous but successive (just as different spaces are not successive but simultaneous). These principles cannot be derived from experience, for experience would give neither strict universality nor apodeictic certainty. (Kant [1781] 1964: 110–11)

Now, to a generation of anthropologists schooled on the Sapir-Whorf hypothesis, a dilemma presents itself. Kant seems quite convincing in his argument that "space" and "time" are properties of cognition, not properties inherent in the world, and yet equally dogmatic in his positing of them as *universal* properties. The dilemma can be dealt with only by clearly recognizing the confident way in which Kant extrapolates out from a particular language, a tradition of research and reasoning, to subsume all of human cognition. His arrogation of the first-person plural pronoun, by which he makes claims for each member of the species, has the further effect of making his claims for cognition seem paradoxically "objective":

> Time is therefore a purely subjective condition of our (human)
> intuition (which is always sensible, that is, so far as we are affected
> by objects), and in itself, apart from the subject, is nothing.
> Nevertheless, in respect of all appearances, and therefore of all the
> things which can enter into our experience, it is necessarily
> objective. (113)

Kant, apparently, never spoke to anyone who denied the postulates of Euclidean geometry, or the notion that time moves in a unidirectional sequence. He thus read these presumed universally human a priori forms of intuition as "objective," in the sense that they are not subject to the vagaries of individual will or consciousness. This universalist epistemology feeds directly into Kant's universalist ethic. If the structures of phenomenal cognition are everywhere the same, adequate knowledge of another person's environment should be sufficient to, and should encourage us to, experience the world as that person does. Thus Kant's political philosophy of tolerance and his epistemology grounded in the a priori concepts of time and space were complemented by his studies and regular lectures in geography, which he regarded as the basis of all reliable knowledge about the world (see May 1970).

Kant is not unique here; he is an extraordinarily influential figure, but also indicative of his time. The precise relations among the European colonial project, individualist epistemologies, and geography remain to be explored. Yet before the world was thoroughly mapped by Europeans, geography was one of the prime ways to "make one's mark" upon the world, and thus to define oneself as an actor. It was even, as Joseph Conrad suggested, the object of some (men's?) fantasies of spatial escape from the confines of the known and civilized, "in the manner of prisoners dreaming behind bars of all the hardships and hazards of liberty dear to the heart of man" (Conrad [1924] 1970: 2). Furthermore, it seems clear that the models of spatial "diffusion" of identity, ideology, and social structure from Europe that justified the colonial project were closely analogous to models of progressive Enlightenment in time.[5] Indeed, as Bury explained earlier in this century, the notion of "progress" as taking place in time is rooted in a spatial metaphor of *stepping* forward:

> The idea of human Progress ... is based on an interpretation of history which regards men as slowly advancing—*pedetemtim progredientes*—in a definite and desirable direction, and infers that this progress will continue indefinitely. (Bury 1932: 5)[6]

Here we arrive at a significant and fruitful paradox. On one hand we have the modern postulate, which strictly differentiates between space and time. In social theory (as opposed to physics), we generally continue to work with the assumption that there are three dimensions that make up spatiality and one—a line—that describes motion in time, and that human experience "in" time and "in" space can be discussed separately. On the other hand, the very notion of "progress," of stepping forward in time, exemplifies how the metaphorical structures of our language betray that bifurcation, displaying in particular a tendency to borrow terms connoting spatial relations in our references to change over time. We have a notion of "progress" that metaphorically discusses temporal sequence in terms of spatial distancing and vice versa: we speak of distant times, and, as will be discussed, we think of long-ago places, if not in so many words.

Nor should we assume that the persistent tendency of social theorists to think in terms of a bifurcation between space and time is limited to those thinkers whom we might call "conservative." On the contrary, this can be found among those considered to be at the cutting edge of social theory. This is one of the main points in an interview given by Michel Foucault in 1980 that forms the leitmotiv for Edward Soja's recent *Postmodern Geographies* (1989). In this interview Foucault complains about the hegemony of time over space roughly from the midnineteenth to the midtwentieth century:

> A critique could be carried out of this devaluation of space that has prevailed for generations. Did it start with Bergson, or before? Space was treated as the dead, the fixed, the undialectical, the

immobile. Time, on the contrary, was richness, fecundity, life, dialectic. (Foucault 1980: 70)

Michel de Certeau concurs, noting that "the functionalist organization, by privileging progress (i.e., time), causes the condition of its own possibility—space itself—to be forgotten; space thus becomes the blind spot in a scientific and political technology" (de Certeau 1984: 95). But the plea for a critical emphasis on space is hardly universal. Ernst Bloch claimed decades ago that "the primacy of space over time is an infallible sign of reactionary language" (cited in Fabian 1983: 37). Some anthropologists likewise find it appropriate to insist that time is the most critical hinge of social life: "From a processual perspective, change rather than structure becomes society's enduring state, and time rather than space becomes its most encompassing medium" (Rosaldo 1989: 103).

The best ethnography, of course, does not rigidly choose either a spatialist or a chronological analysis, but keeps aware of the politics of dimensionality.[7] Thus Jane Nadel-Klein, writing about localism in Scotland, neither takes local identities as autochthonous givens nor relegates them to nostalgia. As she understands it, "global processes call localities into existence, but make no commitments to their continued survival. ... 'Local people' may oppose their own communal extinction" (Nadel-Klein 1991: 502). She not only celebrates local resistance but also pinpoints dimensional disenfranchisement: people identified as "local," hence nonglobal, particular, and backward, are "barred from participating in change because they are defined as incapable of sharing not only the same space but also the same time or epoch as modern society" (503).

Arguments about the priority of space and time *in theory* still need to be attended to. If Soja and Foucault are correct, and there has been a comparative overemphasis on time in critical social theory, and at the same time Rosaldo is justified in criticizing the assumption, common to anthropology of the "classic" interwar period (Kearney 1991: 64),[8] that space is society's medium and structure its most enduring state, how can this divergence be explained?

The beginning of an explanation is contained in Soja's own narrative of critical discourses on time and space in the past century and a half (see also Pred 1990). Soja claims that the emphasis on time is largely a result of Marx's reaction against Hegel's state-territorial emphasis: "In grounding the Hegelian dialectic in material life, Marx ... rejected its particularized spatial form, the territorially defined state, as history's principal spiritual vehicle" (Soja 1989: 46; see also 86). Of course Hegel was far from unique in linking geography with destiny; the ideology of British imperialism, for example, was shot through with geographical determinism (Hudson 1985). The influential German geographer Ratzel, writing in the last third of the nineteenth century, emphasized the "organic" ties between a specific land and its people (Kern 1983: 224ff.).

Furthermore, this emphasis on geography was not typical of the imperialists alone. The emancipatory claims of colonized peoples were also grounded in narratives of territorial priority. As Edward Said remarks, "if there is anything that radically distinguishes the imagination of anti-imperialism, it is the primacy of the geographical in it" (Said 1989b). That is, those whose collective consciousness was articulated in the context of a struggle against European imperialism adopted the notion that collective identity, and hence both loyalty and legitimate deployment of power, was determined by spatial relations. By the end of the nineteenth century, then, the contest was for control of space rather than its definition; social theory may have joined "common sense" in coming to see the world[9] as having been finally explored and mapped once and for all, the age of European pioneering and exploration having come to a close (Malin 1944).

In this light, it is especially revealing that Foucault complains of space being treated as "dead." We think of death as a process occurring within time rather than space (although, as I state below, death is also the spatial dissolution of an organism). In our commonsense world, what is dead is past. The "death" of space, the closure of geographical knowledge in the culmination of modern imperialism around the turn of the twentieth century, may therefore be linked to the notion that once being "fixed," *known,* it is thereby "past" (Atlan 1985). Indeed, this link between imperialism, progressive temporality, and the known has been noted by Meaghan Morris: the modern is "understood ... 'as a *known history,* something which has *already happened elsewhere,* and which is to be reproduced, mechanically or otherwise, with a local content'" (Morris 1990: 10, cited in Chakrabarty 1992b: 17; emphasis in original). To restate this rather complex point: I am suggesting (a) that in complaining that space has been treated as "dead" and time as the field of agency and struggle, Foucault is implicitly both temporalizing our sense of space and historicizing our sense of time; (b) that this "deadness" of space is related to the fact that, by the late nineteenth century, the world had been fully mapped and was therefore "known"; and (c) that the connection between points (a) and (b) can be seen if we conceive of the past as what is known and the future as what is still unknown—as the place where "evening lies ahead and travelling is tomorrow" (Carter 1989: 77).

But there is another plausible approach to Foucault's statement. The literary scholar David Lloyd has read Foucault here as if Foucault were responding directly to Kant's imperial geography. Kant, Lloyd suggests, finessed the contradiction between ethical universals and particular examples "by endowing a geography of differences with a temporal disposition" (Lloyd 1989: 36). Put more bluntly, this means that Kant identified individual examples of the universal good within Europe and posited their eventual diffusion *in time* throughout the world. This is another expression of the general idea of universal progress with Europe at the vanguard that underlies the rapidly obsolescing terminology of first, second, third, and fourth "worlds" (see also Kemp 1991, especially 158).[10] Against this justification of imperialism, Lloyd suggests that Foucault's insistence on spatializing the relation between the individual and the collective (and by extension among different collectives) "highlight[s] the geography of relations of domination" (1989: 36). Foucault is strategically reasserting the Kantian link between space and simultaneity, insisting that those elsewhere on the planet living in drastic relative deprivation are not "behind" us or temporally "backward." They are the contemporaries of the professional-managerial class in the "first world," and no amount of temporizing will enable us to deny the equal priority of their humanity. In effect, Lloyd proposes that Foucault wants to reinstate (ironically enough, given the misconceptions about Foucault's "anti-humanism") an *ethical* demand about the equality of all persons living on the planet, simultaneously in the present.[11] (The phrase "simultaneously in the present" is not a mere redundancy, as I will explain.)

Shortly before making the statement quoted above, Foucault claims that "anyone envisaging the analysis of discourses solely in terms of temporal continuity would inevitably be led to approach and analyse it like the internal transformation of an individual consciousness" (1980: 70). Doubtless this too relates back to Kant's understanding of time as constituted by the sequential ordering of events in the individual human mind. It is true as well that figures like Bacon and Pascal did conceive of the species as an individual, "continually existing and continually learning" (Bury 1932: 68). But it is certainly not the case that this is an "inevitable" consequence of an emphasis on temporal dynamics. As the critic Stéphane Mosès explains, for Walter Benjamin the powerful politics of time were grounded precisely in the inevitable reality of discontinuity and death:

> Tradition—the transmission of a collective memory from
> generation to generation—most inherently implies a break from
> time, the fracture between eras, the gaping void separating fathers
> from sons. If, for Benjamin, tradition serves as a vehicle for
> authentic historical consciousness, it is because it is founded on the
> reality of death. (Mosès 1989: 15)

This might seem simply to bear out Foucault's complaint that time is seen as the field of life and space as the field of death. But unlike Bergson's ahistorical, impersonal *durée,* Benjamin's insistence on the fragmentation of time and memory through death and the resistance to death's dissolution via tradition denies, in a sense, the very "pastness" of the past (compare Funkenstein 1989; Yerushalmi 1982). In terms of the links I outlined above among the past, the dead, and the known, the past is not unproblematically "known" for Benjamin, and as long as it remains the stakes of contention in the present, it is not dead. Fanon, complementing and extending the reach of Benjamin's purview, suggested that a people's past may be colonized as well (Said 1989b: 26). In a sense, Foucault's call for a spatialized sense of struggle and Benjamin's articulation of the past as a political field complement each other. Foucault reminds us of those living with us on the planet; that they are "distant" from us does not make them "fixed, dead, immobile," as the lingering discourses of primitivism, racism, and Orientalism would have us believe. Benjamin reminds us of the demands of our ancestors who died unjustly (compare Comay 1990); their death is, in a powerful sense, not "past," but subject to the meaning it is given through action in the present. And thus "to pretend that the past can be modified by the present, this is what most deeply shakes the trust of modern man in the irreversible nature of historical time" (Mosès 1989: 30).[12] When it is possible to contemplate the transformation of Hiroshima into a theme park of amnesiac "peace" for postmodern tourists (Yoneyama 1991), such lingering trust in the safe pastness of death certainly must be shaken.

Technology, Time, and Space

The preceding section comes no closer to particular narratives of history or other aspects of "the real world" than a passing reference to colonialism, which is itself a grand enough abstraction. But this emphasis on categories of language and thought should not be taken as an implicit attack on theories of state and empire building that deal with material "causes" (e.g., Wallerstein 1974; Tilly 1990). On the contrary, it is abundantly clear that considerations of changing consciousness cannot be separated from changes in the world that consciousness construes. The reference to memory in the atomic age made just above perfectly exemplifies how these processes are inseparably related.

The more systemic or "material" theories can be complicated and enriched in at least two ways. The first way to work against our ingrained tendency toward a dualistic analysis of consciousness and material life is to expunge our commonsense notion of technology as being restricted to *machines for operating on things outside of our bodies.* There are also technologies of knowledge and, especially relevant here, technologies of memory. They are abundantly evident today, when the storage and processing capacity of computers is called "memory" (Casey 1987: 4). Such quantified memory is referred to spatially, as when a file is designated as being "on drive C," or when we get the unfortunate message that drive C is "out of memory." But computers were long ago preceded by medieval and ancient "memory palaces" (Ong 1983; Spence 1984; Yates 1966), mnemonic schemes by which people were taught to "fix" memories in imaginary spaces and thus enable themselves to recall them more easily. Did this technology inaugurate or merely reflect a spatialized notion of memory?

Second, we should recognize that our tendency to separate technology (and the material world in general) from consciousness is justified, if it is justified at all, by the impossibility of holding everything in thought at once, rather than by a legitimate ontological duality between being and consciousness. Memory is by no means an autonomous "human" or "mental" or "cultural" sphere separate from a sphere of matter and technology. On the contrary, we can trace out relations between memory and "materialism" in the crudest sense, that of profit, or what we might call an economics of memory. Thus one scholar has suggested, in an article on "the advantages of a bad conscience," a positive link between the continuing discourse about German war guilt and the success of German manufactures exports (Baier 1988): the very fact that Germany shows itself to be morally concerned about its legacy of genocide helps smooth the way for current international commerce.[13] In a more straightforward way, of course, a commodified version of "memory" is commonly deployed to promote new technologies of tourist travel (Bommes and Wright 1982; Church 1990).

While we continue imagining ourselves in a reliably Newtonian world, new technologies of transportation and communication (such as shipping, railroads, airplanes, video, telephones, and personal computers) have changed the very conditions of our possible experiences of "proximity" and "simultaneity" (see Kern 1983; Schivelbusch 1986). David Harvey has characterized these changes as the most recent in a series of "time-space compressions":

> As space appears to shrink to a "global village" of
> telecommunications and a "spaceship earth" of economic and
> ecological interdependencies ... and as time horizons shorten to
> the point where the present is all there is (the world of the
> schizophrenic), so we have to learn how to cope with an
> overwhelming sense of *compression* of our spatial and temporal
> worlds. (Harvey 1989: 240; emphasis in original)

Although his book is called *The Condition of Postmodernity,* Harvey argues that all of the new communicative modes that enable this compression are fundamentally recycled back into the modern capitalist project of accumulation, predication, and control. But if I am right in suggesting a close and logical connection between the modern notions of absolute space and time and modern nation-statism, there still seems room to wonder whether the effect of these new technologies is merely to "compress" space and time, or rather to bend them in completely unexpected ways. If there is at least a measure of genuinely new dimensionality, as Harvey does concede, then "postmodernism" might obviate some of the constraints of modern consciousness and offer us new escape routes from the treadmill of accumulation and control—*not through the liberating force of some putative self-directed "History," but through different paradigms of identity and relation that can overcome our fearful resistance to change.*

Air travel is to me still the most striking of the new technologies; taking our bodies halfway around the world in a matter of hours is somehow more impressive than sending our image around the world instantaneously.

Because airplanes pass through a medium uncontrolled by conventional borders between nations,[14] they can serve to remind us of another area where we need to expand our peripheral vision in social studies of memory. Many of these studies focus on the relation between memory and the nation, so it is not surprising that they tend to be conducted as if the nation were in fact an effective boundary against time and space — as if all it had to control were the people inside it. This should be borne in mind in the rest of this essay, which frequently rests within the discursive boundaries of the nation-state. An exclusive concern with the nation, taken as a given, would exclude the question of the politics of *reach*.

The question of reach — which might be glossed as extraterritorial sovereignty, but only inasmuch as we are still talking about power exercised by state organizations rather than, for example, multinational corporations — has to do with the possibility of planning, "discovery," and long-distance control facilitated by technological innovations. We must not imagine that the availability of these technologies in themselves "caused" the colonizing project. It was easy enough in a pragmatic age to suppose that machines sufficed to fuel the colonial project. Gayatri Spivak has noted that the railroad train, developed in Britain as its empire was expanding, "is a widely current metonym for the unifying project of territorial imperialism" (Spivak 1989: 284, citing V. G. Kiernan); and Theodor Herzl correctly noted the close connection between technology and colonialism, but wrongly assumed a unidirectional causal relation between them (Herzl 1973; compare Helms 1988). On the contrary, it was only in tandem with an imaginative projection of the lands to be conquered, as well as with a legal apparatus that determined in advance the property to be acquired, that such colonial endeavors were conceivable. As Roberto González-Echevarría has remarked, "America existed as a legal document before it was physically discovered" (1987: 108). The legal structures that made that document an authoritative guide to action and power were technologies as well. Furthermore, by producing history as the projected justification of schemes of conquest, rather than the retrospective recording of literally contingent experiences of travel — by producing accounts of colonial exploration as imperially controlled rather than spatially experienced (see Carter 1989, introduction) — imperial technologies of legitimation collapsed and molded time and space in their own particular ways.

Meanwhile the space and time open to indigenous structures of dimensionality was being not so much "compressed" as squeezed out. New technologies of communication have had a nefarious effect on the varieties of memory: they have enabled the colonial assault on the indigenous populations, and they offer themselves as almost irresistible alternatives to indigenous modes of communication, transportation, and commemoration.[15]

We should not imagine that this is a unidirectional process, however. The "natives," in many situations, have shown themselves quite capable of reinventing their own identities in ways that are not only compatible with, but take advantage of, the new technologies. Also, the very diffusion of technology means that the withdrawal of information about indigenous cultures to "colonial" archives is not irreversible. Scholars, critics, and artists among the formerly colonized utilize both postmodern theory and new media technologies to challenge the pastness of their archived past.[16] Doubtless the idea of a species-wide "global archive" of endangered memories, presumably to be made available to the descendants of the bearers of those memories (Riffaterre 1988, responding to the critique of Price 1983 in Said 1989a), seems to avoid blithely the question of who controls the archives. Yet we cannot know what newly self-imagined peoples, using as yet uninvented means of communication, will create out of the archives of colonialism.

Mapping the Time of the Nation

Given the extension of the realm of the political that is so prevalent in contemporary critical scholarship (and so distressing to scholars who see themselves as more "traditional"), it might seem a step backward to focus on state structures in a discussion of the politics of memory. Yet there remains a powerful tendency for collective identities to be cast as national histories in the support of claims to independent statehood. Hegel's *Philosophy of History* would have us think that such assertions of *historical* identity are almost inevitably cast as claims of *national* identity, and at least one recent student of the formation of historical consciousness has suggested that this is the case: "living historically ... implies the creation of nationness and, conversely, the elaboration of the construct, 'nation,' is necessarily historical" (Malkki 1990: 34).

However, one need not accept the conflation of the historical with the national in order to agree that statist ideologies involve a particularly potent manipulation of the dimensionalities of space and time, invoking rhetorically fixed national identities to legitimate their monopoly on administrative control. The creation of state identities has largely to do with the assertion of temporal origins and spatial boundaries (Debray, quoted in Brennan 1990: 51), but these are not rigidly separate from each other. States may be said to map history onto territory. Brian Stock, a literary historian, has described this dynamic interaction of temporal and spatial discourses:

> The coalescing of a tradition often corresponds to the settlement and organization of a society within definable geographical boundaries, for which the writing down of traditions acts like a set of intellectual fenceposts. ... The hold of the past is not only legal and cultural. It is also spatial. It is expressed in land and people, who are geographically placed, and may think they are divinely ordained, to mirror a particular tradition. Churches monumentalize these relations in medieval Europe, as do temple sites in Southeast Asia, while pilgrimages ritualize relations between the centers and peripheries of religious experience. (Stock 1990: 162–63)

But Stock is primarily concerned with the interplay of text and community in the European Middle Ages. If I dwell there too long and make the Middle Ages the ground of my reflections on the space and time of the nation, I risk remaining within a nineteenth-century notion of "national identity" as rooted primarily in the narrative of historical origin, in a shared national past. Against this, Benedict Anderson, working to some extent on the basis of Walter Benjamin's insights, has stressed the centrality to modern national consciousness of the simultaneous existence of the entire population living within one's country. Anderson focuses on the effects of media such as the novel, the newspaper, and especially radio, which reduce the time needed for communication between speakers of the same language located at considerable distances from each other. These developments in communication in turn foster the implicit notion of a set of people, unknown to each other, but all working at the same time toward a common national goal (Anderson 1983).[17]

But Anderson's undifferentiated concept of the experience of "simultaneity" reveals a possible implicit assumption that the experience of nationalism is uniquely born in the West and diffuses thence in basically the same form (compare the critique of Anderson in Chatterjee 1986, and the 1991 revised edition of Anderson's book). Most recently, Robert Paine has suggested an important distinction between "simultaneity," the sense that others are doing at the same time things that are meaningfully related to your own experience, and "meanwhileness," the mere awareness that there *are* others going about their separate business at the same time as you are. As Paine summarizes, elaborating on examples Anderson himself uses, "in the mosque [at Mecca, where Berber and Malay come to pray]: simultaneity; in the American home [where Daddy relaxes with the sports section]: meanwhileness" (Paine 1992: 58).

The emphasis on "imagined communities," even with the nuances and refinements offered by such scholars as Chatterjee and Paine, suggests that the important things to look at are the consolidation of monolithic collective identities within states on one hand, and, on the other, the intrastate plurality and interstate diffusion of collectives, largely enabled by new technologies of transportation and communication.[18] Thus there is equally insightful recent research focusing on rhetorics of struggle between competing national and ethnic identities. The competition for primacy, for a prior claim to a defined territory, is especially important. Of course, the claim of having been there first is most congenial to, and hence most straightforwardly deployed by, those fighting to rid themselves of foreign overlords. But colonialists also acknowledge the authority of claims to priority by subtly and overtly combating them. South African historiography, for example, takes pains to deny autochthonous status to the black African residents of the country, while still labeling them as "native" (Ashforth 1990: 31).[19]

Of course such discursive claims to temporal priority and hence to rights over specific territory have to do with power. But if they were merely a reflection of already existing power relations, it seems they would not be necessary. That they are made even in the face of overwhelming evidence to the contrary suggests that they also have the function of convincing the dominant group of its own legitimacy and collective identity. Generally the claim to priority includes a claim of autochthony, of an origin inseparable from that very territory and free of dependence on any other group, as Pierre Vidal-Nacquet suggests: "To be autochthonous means [ideally — J.B.] not having been instructed by anyone else; the theme is fundamental" (Vidal-Nacquet 1982: 58, footnote 80).

A corollary to the struggle for priority is the continuing contest to determine how much of what has happened on a nation's territory is contained in its self-image. Ana Maria Alonso notes, for instance, that in Mexico "the nation appropriates the totality of the history enacted in its territory" (Alonso 1988: 41). But the inclusion of all the "peoples" of Mexico within the official historiography is wrongly taken by many social scientists as a sign that "Mexico's is 'an inclusionary authoritarianism'"; these scholars "unwittingly [reproduce] the view of power and society artic- ulated by official ideology. For this inclusion of subordinated groups and classes is above all imagined" (44). Other states work equally vigorously, not to create an "imagined" but illusory inclusiveness of their entire pop- ulation, but to reshape both geography and chronology in the image of the dominant collective (see, for example, Benvenisti 1986 on Israel, and Kapferer 1988 on the contrast between Australia and Sri Lanka). Does a greater variety of sanctioned pasts tend to correlate with greater toleration of diversity in the present, or is it simply mobilized for legitimation of hi- erarchy in a different manner — through hierarchical inclusion rather than the exclusion of a constructed "Other"? This is, of course, a heuristic ques- tion, and hence not susceptible to a simple yes or no answer. The example of the United States — where place names both evoke a buried Native American presence and hearken back to ancestral homes in Europe, and homogenization is carried out in the name of "pluralism" — shows that the contrast between the two types of integrative strategies is itself found almost nowhere in pure form. Furthermore, the relations between "hier- archy" and "diversity" are not only always colored by our prejudices but always more complex than our formulations of them.

Whether the vexing problem of cultural differences within an ideally homogeneous nation-state (McNeill 1986) is dealt with through hierar- chical inclusion or egalitarian exclusion, it is inseparable from the vital importance of symbolic as well as legal state/nation boundaries (Ashley 1989; Walker 1989; Sahlins 1989).[20] Threats from "outside" the state, such as guerrilla fighters in bases across the border, come to take on a "de- monic" and uncanny image, even though they originate within the state from which they have been effectively expelled (Kapferer 1988: 85). When a new national identity is being asserted, groups that do not conform to that identity may be symbolically expelled in public rituals. Thus in early Norwegian celebrations of national folk life,

at the culmination of the nationalist celebration stands a ritualized
expulsion of the "Gypsies" from the consecrated folkloric space of
patrimony. When a national culture stops to celebrate and take
stock of itself, it is only the "Gypsies" who keep moving and who
persist as interlopers. (Trumpener 1992: 846)

Once established, the geographical boundaries of memory may need
shoring up from time to time. France in the 1980s witnessed an ambitious
and well-publicized project called *Les lieux de la mémoire,* documenting
not only historical monuments but all of those places and material sites
that give rise to the idea of the national patrimony, the sense of "French-
ness" (Nora 1989). The politics of this project seem ambiguous. On one
hand, who can be against "memory"? Everything is to be gained from a
nuanced awareness of patterns of experience in the past, selective as such
awareness must always be. On the other hand, it is all too easy to suspect
that the slogan and the multivolume project on "places of memory" work
to reinvent "la France profonde" as a defense against the onslaught within
France of Others making claims for their own collective rights and identities (see Leveau and Kipel 1988).

Indeed, while "les lieux de la mémoire" seems at first to be a characteristically French poetic turn of phrase, in fact it is consistent with an altogether common tendency, particularly among contemporary scholars, to
speak of the past in territorial and national metaphors. David Lowenthal's
The Past Is a Foreign Country (1984) both marks this tendency and perpet-
uates it. In the introduction to a recent special journal issue, James Brow
likens memory to an agricultural crop: "Almost everywhere, it seems, the
sense of belonging together is nourished by being cultivated in the fertile
soil of the past" (Brow 1990: 2–3). Spreading time out in space has even
been adopted as an organizing scheme for the planning of tourist landscapes. In a recent planning document for the Shetland Islands tourist
commission, there is

a review of the important themes of Shetland's natural and social
history which should be developed for interpretation. These themes
are broken down as: The Life of Prehistoric Peoples; Iron Age to
Viking Age; The Development of Trade; Mines, Quarries and Oil
Wells; Work and the Land; Work and the Sea; The Air and the Sky;
Shetland at War. The plan correlates these particular themes to areas

of Shetland where they may be best expressed. ... What is so
remarkable about this plan is that under the authorization of
culture, all of history can be thematized and spatially spread out in
the present. (Church 1990: 41, footnote 9)

Even so abstract a concept as "civil society," which relates to the state
in ways touched on below, is discussed in the spatial metaphors of "the public sphere"[21] and "public space." Memory erupts into and shapes "public
space" in various and often ambiguous ways, as in monumental public art.
The erection of monuments is a central means of shaping memory. Usually we think of monuments like the Arc de Triomphe as bulwarks of national identity, but, as with the "Goddess of Liberty" erected in Tiananmen-
men Square, they may also contest state power (Mitchell 1990; Boyarin
1992). Other recent monuments have been explicitly designed to counter
the tendency to congeal living memory (Young 1992). Space for memory
is also contested through ephemeral demonstrations against forgetting,
such as those of the Plaza de Mayo Madres in Argentina (Taussig 1990). In
one sense, we might think of these women as monumentalizing themselves, constituting themselves as living memorials to their "disappeared"
children. As memorials, they still "bore" their now grown but invisible
children within their own older but still visible bodies. The act is especially resonant because of the furtive way in which the disappearances
were carried out and the fearful way in which neighbors and friends refused to acknowledge them (Perelli 1991).

Embodied Memory

The jury of physicists still seems to be out on the question of whether
space and time are "really" separate dimensions, and, if so, which has ontological priority. The geographers are busy trying to complicate the relation between the two but still tend to speak about "time and space" rather
than "temporalizing and spatializing discourses." I seem to have much less
faith in any objective distinction between space and time than do even the
postmodern geographers or the historians of consciousness (e.g., Kern
1983). My sense, contra Kant, is that this suspicion is grounded in my
own embodied experience, and that the bifurcation between space and
time actually belies "the inseparability of conceptual and bodily activity"

(Jackson 1989: 153). To the extent that we do (inescapably "here" and "now") continue to speak of time and space as distinct realms within which bodies exist and events take place, we must at least acknowledge that organisms exist not only in space but in time as well (Holquist 1989). We move "through time" as much as we move "through space," and this motion is not separated into spatial sequences on one hand and temporal sequences on the other. However, this does not mean that the distinction between time and space is entirely arbitrary. Indeed, a focus on the organism and the sense of a bounded self that is congruous with it might give us the clue to understanding any claim time and space have to being "cultural" universals:

> The interaction of such binaries as resemblance/difference [and] figure/ground have at their heart the master distinction of self/other. In cognition even more than in the physical world, two bodies cannot occupy the same space at the same time. As subject, I must not share the time/space of an object. (Holquist 1989: 15)

Something else, that is, can be where I am later or before, or somewhere else now, but not where I am now. Cognitive anthropologists would have to answer whether this sensibility can be detected even in languages that do not strictly differentiate between "here and there" and "then and now." Holquist at any rate does not rely on "the body" as some bedrock of prelinguistic Being, but insists that the body, too, is culturally constructed and furthermore systemically "resorts to storytelling" in order to maintain itself. Although his title refers to the "chronobiological basis of narrative," he actually suggests that the communicative patterns that characterize narrative are also essential to the ways in which organisms both reproduce and maintain themselves. The body is structured, then, not just synchronically in space, but diachronically as well. And, of course, the organism cannot exist only in space or only in time. Thus we can call the body a "rubric" in which spatiality and temporality coexist indissolubly, in which their necessary unity is most clearly shown. When you die in time you dissolve in space.

Holquist's distinctly postmodern notion that the body "remembers" itself as it tells itself (genetic) stories is closely analogous to the biophilosopher Henri Atlan's description of the Rabbinic Jewish conception of memory as "genitive." Atlan argues that in the view of the Babylonian Talmud, "one conceives a memory as one conceives an idea and as one conceives a child" (Atlan 1987: 189). Perhaps we could further gloss this as the notion that memory is neither something preexistent and dormant in the past nor a projection from the present, but a potential for creative collaboration between present consciousness and the experience or expression of the past.[22] In any case, the analogy between memory and the body recalls Holquist's idea of bodily organization through genetic narrative. Memory and the organism share the characteristic of reinventive resistance to an oblivion that will always ultimately overwhelm them. Thus it is inappropriate to align memory with some ideal realm over against our animal nature, as when Stanislaw Baranczak calls on us "to help Memory recover its proper place, a place among the instruments of humane understanding rather than animal hatred" (Baranczak 1992: 14).

This link between memory and the organism, then, is connected to the peculiar relation between life and the universe. The irreversibility of sequence that we perceive as an existential condition, which is indeed (Kant was apparently right here) inseparable from the very possibility of sentience, is linked to the universal vector of transformation from order into disorder, posited by the second law of thermodynamics (Hawking 1988). On the other hand, the "self-organization of the living" paradoxically represents a local reversal of the general tendency toward entropy described by the second law of thermodynamics (Atlan 1985: 28). So too memory is not only constantly disintegrating and disappearing but constantly being created and elaborated.

Perhaps the most obvious link between memory and the body is through mnemonic marking. Intriguingly, nonstate collectives seem most often to mark individual bodies as a sign of inclusion, whereas states most often mark bodies precisely to exclude them. Thus in "traditional" practices such as circumcision, an individual comes to regard herself or himself as part of a particular subset of a particular human group, and the same individual can refer to those marks as indicating a personal history shaped by that very group belonging. In the case of torture or terrorism, the bodily practice marks both the boundary between violator and victim and, less obviously, the link that binds them in their reciprocal imaginings (Taussig 1984; see also Scarry 1985). When the marks of torture on the bodies of its victims are displayed—for example, by international human rights organizations—what was intended to terrorize the memory of the individual victim is transformed into a sign by which "the world" is made to remember the wrongs done that victim.

Are we dealing here with the politics of memory or the construction of identity? Insofar as consciousness, the ground of "identity," is constituted by the sum of all the impressions and imaginings retained in the brain, my hypothesis would be that identity and memory are virtually the same concept. But even if this hypothesis is correct, we need to be extremely careful about metaphorical transpositions from the individual to any collective. Here again we must bear in mind that memory is at once physical, intersubjective, and technical. It is worth restating the commonsense notion that the "place" of memory on the most material level remains the individual brain—not to reify the body once again, but rather to warn against any idea of memory as superorganic, and to recall as well that in *our* world, the notion of the individual cannot be transcended merely with a word. As Yosef Yerushalmi warns, "just as 'the life of a people' is a biological metaphor, so too 'the memory of a people' is a psychological metaphor" (1988: 12). Both "collective memory" and "collective identity" are rather the effects of intersubjective practices of signification, neither given nor fixed but constantly re-created within the framework of marginally contestable rules for discourse (Butler 1990: 145). Their rallying power within contemporary theory rests upon their close analogy to the ideal integrity ascribed to the memory and identity of the individual. One of the most striking aspects of liberatory movements within modern Western societies, in fact, is precisely the attempt to construct and deploy unitary group memories and identities for all those whom the movements claim as their own (women, Jews, African-Americans, Native Americans, and so on).

Maurice Halbwachs's work *The Collective Memory* ([1950] 1980), written before World War II, was an early attempt to give some social definition to this peculiar phantasm, which logically cannot have any substance but which seems nevertheless to work as a powerful force on our actions and imaginations. Essentially Halbwachs asserted that collective memories are reminiscences of the past that link given sets of people (a nuclear family, a class of schoolmates, the population of a village), for whom the shared identity remains significant at a later time when the memory is invoked. That is, collective memory is neither a fantasy about the common ancestors of a group of people defining themselves as a collective in the present nor the common but totally dissociated memories of a number of people who once formed a social grouping. "Collective memory," for Halbwachs, is the way a group of people maintain a shared identity through the course of their lifetimes. Halbwachs's exploration had the advantage of socializing the concept of memory without giving carte blanche to national self-representations as the expressed sum of each individual's personal associations. On the other hand, Halbwachs failed to historicize memory; not surprisingly, virtually all of his examples are of the sort that could be found in France in the early twentieth century, and a rather stereotyped, native-born, middle-class France at that. His analysis fails to include any awareness that the very notion of "collective memory" must have a significant history.

Thus if we content ourselves with Halbwachs we remain within the confines of collective memory imagined as some sort of objective entity. The "collective"—usually, as discussed above, thought of in terms of nation—is understood as a superorganic representative of all the individual consciousnesses that it comprises. This reified notion of collective identity or collective memory is inseparable from the stubborn idea of the nation as a "body." Without accepting this trope of nationalist rhetoric, we still do well to attend to the links among memory, embodiment, and nationhood. Feminist theory in particular insists on this kind of "thinking through the body" (Gallop 1988), articulating the links between consciousness, language, and ideology on one hand, and the body on the other. There are thus two distinct paths to this issue of the link between the body and the nation: the organic metaphor of nationalist ideology, and the insight that nationalist ideologies really do recruit bodies.

Some scholars might see this concern with the unmediated relation between the body and the nation as evidence of an unreliable or even dangerous literary turn, and suggest that rather than jumping directly to the analogy between embodied memories and national memories, it might be more prudent to trace through the historiography of the links between nationalism and sexuality (Mosse 1985; Theweleit 1987, 1989). Yet such studies, necessary as they are, should leave us aware that the idea of the ethnic nation (if not the reality of the nation-state) is grounded in the concept of a genealogically defined *people.* Thus it is altogether appropriate to study the links between the notions of nation and body (see Segal 1988, especially 308). The word "nation" itself derives from the Latin *nasci,* which has to do with birth. Thus the resistance to such critique may indicate the degree to which social theory is complicit in a rationalized, pluralistic, liberal notion of the state as a disembodied, "de-generated" assemblage of individuals. In this notion of civil society, the state is represented as simultaneously "free[ing] the social from the political intrusion of the past" (Cohn and Dirks 1988: 225) and keeping its "hands" off the body.[23] This representation is accomplished by techniques that "conspire to make the tentacles of state power (and related forms of state knowledge) appear to be discrete, disinterested, and diffuse" (Cohn and Dirks 1988: 227), notable among which is liberal political science. The modern state may then be said to employ two paradoxical yet complementary means of legitimation. The first is a rhetoric of "kinship" or "community," an assumption of common interests rooted in the putative "memory" of common origins (but in fact at least as often rooted in the shared forgetting of a common violence; see Renan [1882] 1990). The second is as guarantor of the individual's rationality and freedom from the shackles and demons of the past.[24]

The nation, then, works "through the body" in several ways. It generates loyalty analogous to that owed to parents. It rallies allegiance to its sovereign power through dramatizing the threat to its integrity from alien "bodies," to preserve its organic identity: "for the nation to be *itself*—for it to be strong, dominant, for it to save itself and resist its enemies—it must be racially and/or culturally pure" (Balibar 1990: 284; emphasis in original). Like a "body," the nation must grow or decay; and hence expansionary adventures are made to seem vital necessities. Like organisms, popularly and scientifically understood until quite recently to be controlled by a master logic, the nation must be hierarchically organized in order to maintain systemic functioning (Haraway 1991). Furthermore, if nations are bodies, then they inevitably grow from childhood to maturity. Hence the paternalistic domination of certain "Other" nations (e.g., Native Americans, Koreans, Palestinians) can be rationalized by rhetorically casting them as being in their "infancy," not ready for self-determination. Other ethnic groups that fail to fit schemata of universal progress can be seen as actually dead, walking fossils, such as the Jews for Hegel or Toynbee.

To summarize, focusing on "embodied memories" helps us think about space, time, and the politics of memory in at least two major ways. First, it reveals some of the hidden ways in which state ideologies appeal to organic experience and commonsense dimensionality to legitimize themselves. Those who elaborate and maintain such ideologies pretend, quite often with great success, to dictate both the contents of appropriate "memory" and the proper spatial borders of the collective. Second, it reminds us that our articulations of "space" and "time" are rooted in an organic world in which these dimensions are *not* (pace Kant!) separated out a priori.

We will lose these insights if we slide from "the body" to a reinstatement of the sovereign individual, if only because all concepts, including that of the sovereign individual, are intersubjective. Memory cannot be strictly individual, inasmuch as it is symbolic and hence intersubjective. Nor can it be literally collective, since it is not superorganic but embodied. The conundrum disappears as soon as we remember that what we are trying to understand is not really a relation between body and group via culture. What we are faced with—what we are living—is the constitution of both group "membership" and individual "identity" out of a dynamically chosen selection of memories, and the constant reshaping, reinvention, and reinforcement of those memories as members contest and create the boundaries and links among themselves.

Beginning Again: Remembering Walter Benjamin

For me, the idea of "the politics of memory" has two identifiable sources. The first is my own quest for a foundational fiction of Jewish identity, combined with my equally deep ethic of universal human identification. The second is my reading of Walter Benjamin, especially his "Theses on the Philosophy of History" (1969). Benjamin attempted to articulate memory as a resource for political action. In effect, he asserted that the past was a material resource—in Marxist terms, perhaps, "the means of imagination"—control of which was a key aspect of class struggle.[25]

Benjamin's influence has become so prevalent that it might be worthwhile to recall both his limitations and the stunning daring of his dicta in the context of his times. Benjamin did not explicitly spatialize memory, nor did he directly address the state, although scholars such as Michael Taussig have begun to push Benjamin's insights in both of those directions (Taussig 1987, 1990, 1992). On the other hand, his ideas were in a profound sense extraordinarily "radical" for a Marxist in the 1930s, when the dominant trend was still to stress the emancipatory claims of the international working class—cosmopolitanism, though Stalin had made it a dirty word. Benjamin's politics of "anamnestic solidarity" (Lenhardt 1975) was grounded in time; cosmopolitanism was grounded in the spatial morality of the world-city.

Are these necessarily two opposed principles, or perhaps two opposed aesthetics? Is it possible to conceive of a "coalition" or "dialogue" between the claims of dead ancestors and the claims of distant contemporaries? Doubtless Hegel's progressive realization of the world spirit is a chimera, for there is no world spirit, just as there is no collective memory. But it would be perilous to ignore Benjamin's lesson that one of the ways that life is maintained is through a constant effort to retain the image of the past — to rescue the dead and oppressed ancestors by giving their lives new meaning. Much as genetic information is a "narrative," memory resists the disintegration of consciousness. And the most powerful memory for this purpose is that of one's own "generations" — those from whom one stems "body and soul" — or those who can be metaphorically described as one's ancestors. Hence only a politics grounded in the honest effort to integrate the embodied memories of our distant contemporaries has any hope of adequacy in a world in which "the self-organization of the living" (Atlan 1985), the only exception to the general law of entropy, is in danger of extinction.

Notes

This essay was produced for a series of workshops sponsored by the Social Science Research Council and the John D. and Catherine T. MacArthur Foundation Program in International Peace and Security. My thanks go to my fellow participants Nadia Abu El-Haj, Adam Ashforth, Richard Ashley, Charles Hale, Carina Perelli, Charles Tilly, and Lisa Yoneyama, as well as to Robert Paine for reading a first draft and to Nicole Benoît-Lapierre for providing me with the French materials. Thanks are also due the Center for Studies of Social Change at the New School for Social Research, for housing me while I worked on this and other projects and for circulating an earlier draft as one of the center's working papers.

1. The politics of memory was also the theme of the 1991 Canadian Historical Society meeting.

2. Thus a recent introduction to the topic of social memory (Fentress and Wickham 1992) notes that individual and social memory actually represent quite different concepts, and contents itself with admitting that it is exclusively concerned with the latter. The overwhelming emphasis in this volume is on social memory as well, but much more remains to be said on the necessary relationship between the two concepts.

3. See also the pioneering study by Henri Lefebvre (to whom the postmodern geographers discussed below are deeply indebted), who writes that "abstract space ... is hard to distinguish from the space postulated by the philosophers, from Descartes to Hegel, in their fusion of the intelligible (*res extensa*) with the political—their fusion, that is to say, of knowledge with power. The outcome has been an authoritarian and brutal spatial practice, whether Haussmann's or the later, codified versions of the Bauhaus or Le Corbusier..." (Lefebvre 1991: 308).

4. The irritating quotation marks around the word "real" here are not intended to deny reality, but merely as a reminder that "Euclidean space is an imaginary space" (Durand 1992: 15).

5. Newer models aiming to delegitimize that project in retrospect may share the diffusionist and progressivist framework. Thus Homi Bhabha, in his usual allusive fashion, has suggested a critique of progressivism in the work of both Foucault and Anderson. Bhabha points out that both of these thinkers fail to deal effectively with the link between racism and Eurocentric imperialism, because Foucault saw racism "in the form of a historical retroversion," whereas "Anderson places the dreams of racism 'outside history' altogether" (1992: 83). By contrast, Bhabha writes, "the discourse of race that I am trying to develop displays the *problem of the ambivalent temporality of modernity* that is often overlooked in the more 'spatial' traditions of some aspects of postmodern theory" (1991: 196; emphasis in original).

6. Henri Atlan suggests that our tendency to conceive of time spatially is very hard to overcome, yet contingently linked to our mechanical science: "In fact it is always very difficult for us to represent time otherwise than through the intermediary of movements in space, probably because of the influence of mechanical time, which is that of stars and clocks; and one means of detaching ourselves from this representation of spatial time may be to become conscious of the role of our [formal—J.B.] knowledge in our perception of time" (1985: 125; my translation).

7. Louis Marin characterizes the general strategy described here as one that "consists in thinking *relatio* prior to its *relata,* producing them or their matrix, a construction that constitutes a powerful tool for the critical analysis of the so-called originary or primitive contradition of a given society in its structure and history. Needless to say, that is one of the basic axioms of structural analysis" (1993: 402). The reminder that this is a structural principle is in fact quite to the point, partly because younger scholars like myself may wish to see their work as free of any debt to structuralism, but also because *post*structural work helps us to see the irony in Marin's unwitting reinsertion of the dichotomy (his failure to think the *relatio*) between structure and history here.

8. Kearney's point is neatly complemented by Derek Gregory's claim that "*high* modernism—by which I mean those shifts in cultural and intellectual registers which were installed after the *Second* World War—is a much more plausible candidate for Soja's thesis about the subordination of space in social thought" (Gregory 1993: 304, footnote 6). But the very neatness of this presumed bifurcation between a "spatial" prewar orientation and a "temporal" postwar bias should give us pause: what authorizes the temporal bias of the distinction between "pre" and "post"?

9. A note on the politics of my own metaphor here: One might respond that the very phrase "see the world" is reflective of the kind of imperial fixation being criticized here, much as Fabian's book criticizes the predominance of ocularity. Although this criticism should be borne in mind, scholars have also begun reminding us that vision can play a positive critical role as well. "See," for incommensurate examples, Buck-Morss 1989 and the last chapter of my forthcoming book *Palestine and Jewish History.*

10. Thus Geertz is wrong when he confidently asserts that "another country is quite definitely *not* 'the past'" (Geertz 1990: 323; his emphasis). Although we do not use this expression, the idea behind it is common enough.

11. In an essay on the lessons of Foucault, John Rajchman has phrased this demand as "the question of a philosophical solidarity or community not modeled on mutual identification with an ideal or essence, or an agreement as to procedure, but which would be brought together by what is problematic, unacceptable, intolerable in what we say and do to one another, and with the possibilities of saying and doing otherwise" (1989: 97).

12. A reader of an earlier draft found the use of the word "pretend" in this quotation surprising. Mosès's article was translated, presumably from the French, where *prétendre* would usually be better translated as "assert." But my reader's further question — "Isn't 'the past' always a reading back from the present?" — does not give Mosès's formulation its full due. What Mosès refers to as modern trust in temporal irreversibility is more amply described by Mary Carruthers: "It seems to be typical of modern (Renaissance) consciousness to give the past, like other scientific subjects, objective status apart from present human memories. As a result, perhaps, a Renaissance scholar worried that the past had been 'distorted' through the mediation of the present, and sought to recover or resuscitate the dead past itself" (1990: 193). To assert that the past can be *modified* by the present — and not simply that the representation of the past can be distorted — is of course deeply troubling to a consciousness that believes in the "reality" of the past and the irreversibility of history. And this belief characterizes even most social theorists most of the time, except perhaps when we really have our thinking caps on and are constantly reminding ourselves that the past is always a reading from the present — or, in the example Reinhart Koselleck gives, that although "the events of 1933 have occurred once and for all ... the experiences which are based upon them can change over time" (1985: 274–75). The apparent contradiction that Koselleck's formulation neatly addresses is that if there really is no "past," the tension of temporality breaks down: there can be no present within which a past is constructed and to which it can be contrasted.

13. For a thorough and insightful account of the politics of history in postwar West Germany, see Maier (1988).

14. Though states do in fact more or less jealously guard their airspace, such surveillance is generally invisible to the civilian voyager.

15. Several writers have addressed this increasing "reach" of the state, not just around the globe, but into aspects of life that were once relatively autonomous (e.g., Kirby 1991, citing Giddens 1985). The Weberian thesis about the relations among industrialization, bureaucratization, and "rationalization" are taken up exhaustively in the second volume of Habermas's *Theory of Communicative Action* (1987: vol. 2, chap. 8). I hope it is clear that, despite my unavoidable use of dichotomous, analytic language, I do not mean to pose as firm and consistent a distinction between "technology" and "memory" as, for instance, Habermas employs between "system" and "lifeworld." Habermas seems inconsistent in his use of the term "lifeworld": sometimes it seems to mean the private sphere, sometimes consciousness. The general notion of the lifeworld he occasionally conveys, as an informal sphere of local or private freedom in traditional, prebureaucratic society, is in any case curious for this resolute champion of modernity. Nor do I assume that the processes first described by Weber are as universal as Habermas seems to think they are (on this point see also Appiah 1991). In my own discussion of changing conceptions of time and space here, I certainly do not mean to imply a progressive movement away from "authentic" or "immediate" experience (as Koselleck implies, there is no "immediate experience"; see note 12 of this chapter) toward co-optation into "inauthentic" systems.

16. Thus Dipesh Chakrabarty points out that things in the present are "from the past" only because we conventionally designate them as such: "Constructing 'evidence,' I want to argue, is a project of preservation, of making 'monuments' of certain objects that are actually contemporaneous with ourselves. For them to acquire the status of 'historical evidence,' however, we have to be able to deny them their contemporaneity by assigning them to a specified period in a calendrical past, an act by which we split the 'present' into the 'modern' and the 'traditional' or the 'historical,' and thereby declare ourselves to be modern. This denial of the contemporaneity of certain objects is what constitutes the historical sense of

anachronism. Without it there is no evidence, and without evidence, there is no 'history.' History is therefore a practice of 'monumentalising' objects — from documents to sculptures — of simultaneously acknowledging and denying their existence in our 'own' time" (1992a: 63). Australians are only some of the indigenous people who have taken control of their own images (Ginsburg 1991).

17. The Canadian historian and theorist Harold Innis anticipated these insights in important ways (Innis 1951, [1950] 1972; Paine 1992).

18. In a recent essay insisting that "critical" scholars overlook the basic power of transnational corporations at the risk of their own complicity with that power, Masao Miyoshi claims both that states have lost their pragmatic, service-affording functions, *and* that among what are, in effect, the deluded masses, the myth of organic nationhood is still effective: "The nation-state, in this sense, no longer works; it is thoroughly appropriated by transnational corporations. Thus for some, it is a sheer annoyance, but for a vast majority it serves as a nostalgic and sentimental myth that offers an illusion of a classless organic community of which everyone is an equal member. Such an illusion of national community stubbornly persists" (Miyoshi 1993: 744). This renewed emphasis on political economy clearly does suggest another "important thing to look at," but Miyoshi seems remarkably careless in his characterization of the presumed "vast majority." The essays in this book aim precisely at a more careful understanding of the place and time of the nation in the politics of identity, so that criticism can move beyond repeated and self-righteous calls for criticism to deal with "real" power.

19. Physical anthropology played an unusual role here as well, as Camille Martinet describes: "Apartheid could have died before it was officially born. Died of ridicule. It happened in 1934. That year, while the future Republic of South Africa was still under British control, thirty-three skeletons were discovered at Mapungubwe, a site on the southern bank of the Limpopo which there is every reason to believe dates from a period between the twelfth and the sixteenth centuries. Are these thirty-three skeletons prima facie evidence that black peoples did indeed arrive in these lands before the arrival of any white colonist? No, because Pretoria sent an anthropologist to the site. And the good man concluded, as those who sent him wished, that 'no Negro impurity soils the racial purity of the chief buried at Mapungubwe'" (Martinet 1987: 125; my translation).

An analogous concomitant of the Israeli-Palestinian conflict has been a weighty effort to document a claim that most of the Palestinian Arabs arrived *after* massive Zionist colonization had stimulated the local economy (Peters 1984). The book was largely dismissed as spurious in Israel, but received massive attention in the United States (see Finkelstein 1988).

20. Yi-Fu Tuan (1979: 206) generalizes this need for boundaries as a universal requirement of "cultures," with what seems to me now to be an unwarranted reification of the concept of "culture."

21. An example of this is the translation of Habermas's *Strukturwandel der Öffentlichkeit* as *The Structural Transformation of the Public Sphere* (1989).

22. Thus, complementing the link between memory and conception, our cultures also work on the body in addressing the problem, the *coupure,* of death (see Battaglia 1992; Boyarin and Boyarin 1994).

23. This slogan is used by defenders of abortion rights, while opponents of legal abortion explicitly assert the state's responsibility for protecting the fetus as a legal "person" — not the state's right to control a woman's body.

24. It is no surprise, then, that, faced with mounting awareness of the inherent contradictions of the European notion of civil society, a leading liberal political philosopher has recently attempted to bridge this paradox with a narrative of the genesis of civil society, or

that, in response, an Indian critic has emphasized the European particularism of this narrative without suggesting that it can be ignored in the search for an alternative (Taylor 1990; Chatterjee 1990).

25. Benjamin argued famously against historicism ([1939] 1969). His opposition may be somewhat clarified by a distinction de Certeau draws between the approaches to the past of psychoanalysis and historiography—a distinction that would place Benjamin, intriguingly enough, on the side of Freud: "Psychoanalysis and historiography thus have two different ways of distributing the *space of memory*. They conceive of the relation between the past and present differently. Psychoanalysis recognizes the past *in* the present; historiography places them one *beside* the other. Psychoanalysis treats the relation as one of imbrication (one in the place of the other), of repetition (one reproduces the other in another form), of the equivocal and of the *quiproquo* (What 'takes the place' of what? Everywhere, there are games of masking, reversal, and ambiguity). Historiography conceives the relation as one of succession (one after the other), correlation (greater or lesser proximities), cause and effect (one follows from the other), and disjunction (either one or the other, but not both at the same time)" (1986: 4).

Bibliography

Alonso, Ana Maria. 1988. "The Effects of Truth: Re-Presentation of the Past and the Imagining of Community." *Journal of Historical Sociology* 1 (1): 33–57.

Anderson, Benedict. 1983 (2d ed., 1991). *Imagined Communities: Reflections on the Spread of Nationalism.* London: Verso.

Appiah, Kwame Anthony. 1991. "Is the Post- in Postmodernism the Post- in Postcolonial?" *Critical Inquiry* 17 (Winter): 336–57.

Ashforth, Adam. 1990. *The Politics of Official Discourse in Southern Africa.* New York: Oxford University Press.

Ashley, Richard. 1989. "Living on Border Lines: Man, Poststructuralism, and War." In *International/Intertextual Relations: Postmodern Readings of World Politics,* ed. James Der Derian and Michael J. Shapiro. Lexington, Mass.: D. C. Heath and Company (Lexington Books) 259–321.

Atlan, Henri. 1985. "Temps biologique et auto-organisation." *Communications* 41: 23–31.

———. 1987. "Mémoire du corps et école de pensée." *Revue de l'Université de Bruxelles* 1–2: 179–94.

Atran, Scott. 1990. *Cognitive Foundations of Natural History: Towards an Anthropology of Science.* Cambridge: Cambridge University Press.

Baier, Lothar. 1988. "Les bénéfices de la mauvaise conscience." *Le Genre humain* 68: 211–25.

Balibar, Etienne. 1990. "Paradoxes of Universality." In *Anatomy of Racism,* ed. David Theo Goldberg. Minneapolis: University of Minnesota Press. 283–94.

Baranczak, Stanislaw. 1992. "Memory: Lost, Retrieved, Abused, Defended." *Ideas from the National Humanities Center* 1 (1): 3–14.

Battaglia, Debbora. 1992. "The Body in the Gift: Memory and Forgetting in Sabarl Mortuary Exchange." *American Ethnologist* 19 (1): 13–18.

Bender, John, and David E. Wellbery, eds. 1991. *Chronotypes: The Construction of Time.* Stanford, Calif.: Stanford University Press.

Benjamin, Walter. 1969. *Illuminations.* Trans. Harry Zohn. Ed. Hannah Arendt. New York: Schocken Books.

Benvenisti, Meron. 1986. *Conflicts and Contradictions*. New York: Villard Books.

Bhabha, Homi. 1991. "'Race,' Time, and the Revision of Modernity." *Oxford Literary Review* 13 (1–2): 193–219.

———. 1992. "Race and the Humanities: The 'Ends' of Modernity?" *Public Culture* 4 (Spring): 81–85.

Bommes, Michael, and Patrick Wright. 1982. "'Charms of Residence': The Public and the Past." In *Making Histories,* ed. Richard Johnson et al. Minneapolis: University of Minnesota Press. 253–301.

Boyarin, Jonathan. 1992. *Storm from Paradise: The Politics of Jewish Memory*. Minneapolis: University of Minnesota Press.

———. Forthcoming. *Palestine and Jewish History*. Berkeley and Los Angeles: University of California Press.

Boyarin, Jonathan, and Daniel Boyarin. 1994. "Self-Exposure as Theory: The Double Mark of the Male Jew." In *Rhetorics of Self-making,* ed. Debbora Battaglia. Berkeley and Los Angeles: University of California Press.

Brennan, Timothy. 1990. "The National Longing for Form." In *Nation and Narration,* ed. Homi K. Bhabha. New York: Routledge. 44–70.

Brow, James. 1990. "Notes on Community, Hegemony, and the Uses of the Past." *Anthropological Quarterly* 63 (1): 1–6.

Buck-Morss, Susan. 1989. *The Dialectics of Seeing: Walter Benjamin and the Arcades Project*. Cambridge: MIT Press.

Bury, J. B. 1932. *The Idea of Progress: An Inquiry into Its Origins and Growth*. New York: Macmillan.

Butler, Judith. 1990. *Gender Trouble: Feminism and the Subversion of Identity*. New York: Routledge.

Carruthers, Mary J. 1990. *The Book of Memory: A Study of Memory in Medieval Culture*. New York: Cambridge University Press.

Carter, Paul. 1989. *The Road to Botany Bay*. Chicago: University of Chicago Press.

Casey, Edward. 1987. *Remembering: A Phenomenological Study*. Bloomington: Indiana University Press.

Chakrabarty, Dipesh. 1992a. "The Death of History? Historical Consciousness and the Culture of Late Capitalism." *Public Culture* 4 (Spring): 47–65.

———. 1992b. "Postcoloniality and the Artifice of History: Who Speaks for 'Indian' Pasts?" *Representations* 37 (Winter): 1–26.

Chatterjee, Partha. 1986. *Nationalist Thought and the Colonial World: A Derivative Discourse?* London: Zed Books, for the United Nations University.

———. 1990. "A Response to Taylor's 'Modes of Civil Society.'" *Public Culture* 3 (1): 119–34.

Church, Jonathan T. 1990. "Confabulations of Community: The Hamefarins and Political Discourse on Shetland." *Anthropological Quarterly* 63 (1): 31–42.

Cohn, Bernard S., and Nicholas B. Dirks. 1988. "Beyond the Fringe: The Nation State, Colonialism, and the Technologies of Power." *Journal of Historical Sociology* 1 (2): 224–29.

Comay, Rebecca. 1990. "Redeeming Revenge: Nietzsche, Benjamin, Heidegger, and the Politics of Memory." In *Nietzsche as Postmodernist,* ed. Clayton Koelb. Albany: State University of New York Press. 21–38.

Connolly, William E. 1991. *Identity/Difference: Democratic Negotiations of Political Paradox*. Ithaca, N.Y.: Cornell University Press.

Conrad, Joseph. [Circa 1924] 1970. "Geography and Some Explorers." In *Last Essays*. Freeport, N.Y.: Books for Libraries Press. 1–21.

de Certeau, Michel. 1984. *The Practice of Everyday Life*. Berkeley and Los Angeles: University of California Press.

———. 1986. *Heterologies: Discourse on the Other*. Trans. Brian Massumi. Minneapolis: University of Minnesota Press.

Duncan, James, and David Ley, eds. 1993. *Place/Culture/Representation*. London and New York: Routledge.

Durand, Gilbert. 1992. *Les Structures anthropologiques de l'imaginaire*. Paris: Dunod.

Elkana, Yehuda. 1988. *Anthropologie der Erkenntnis: Die Entwicklung des Wissens als episches Theater einer listigen Vernunft*. Trans. V. Achlama. Frankfurt: Suhrkamp.

Ermarth, Elizabeth Deeds. 1992. *Sequel to History: Postmodernism and the Crisis of Representational Time*. Princeton, N.J.: Princeton University Press.

Fabian, Johannes. 1983. *Time and the Other*. New York: Columbia University Press.

Fentress, James, and Chris Wickham. 1992. *Social Memory*. Oxford (England) and Cambridge, Mass.: Blackwell Publishers.

Ferguson, James, and Akhil Gupta, eds. 1992. Special issue: *Space, Identity, and the Politics of Difference*. *Cultural Anthropology* 7 (1).

Finkelstein, Norman. 1988. "Disinformation and the Palestine Question: The Not-So-Strange Case of Joan Peters' *From Time Immemorial*." In *Blaming the Victim: Spurious Scholarship and the Palestine Question*, ed. Edward W. Said and Christoper Hitchins. New York: Verso. 33–69.

Foucault, Michel. 1980. "Questions on Geography." In *Power/Knowledge*, ed. Colin Gordon. New York: Pantheon Books. 63–77.

Fox, Richard, ed. 1990. *Nationalist Ideologies and the Production of National Cultures*. American Ethnological Society Monograph Series no. 2. Washington, D.C.

Friedland, Roger, and Deirdre Boden, eds. 1994. *NowHere: Space, Time and Identity*. Berkeley and Los Angeles: University of California Press.

Funkenstein, Amos. 1989. "Collective Memory and Historical Consciousness." *History and Memory* 1 (1): 5–26.

Gallop, Jane. 1988. *Thinking through the Body*. New York: Columbia University Press.

Geertz, Clifford. 1973. "Person, Time, and Conduct in Bali." In *The Interpretation of Cultures*. New York: Basic Books. 360–411.

———. 1990. "History and Anthropology." *New Literary History* 21 (2): 321–35.

Giddens, Anthony. 1985. *The Nation-State and Violence: A Contemporary Critique of Historical Materialism*. Vol. 2. Berkeley and Los Angeles: University of California Press.

Ginsburg, Faye. 1991. "Indigenous Media: Faustian Contract or Global Village?" *Cultural Anthropology* 6 (1): 92–112.

González-Echevarría, Roberto. 1987. "The Law of the Letter: Garcilaso's *Commentaries* and the Origins of the Latin American Narrative." *Yale Journal of Criticism* 1 (1): 107–32.

Gould, Stephen Jay. 1987. *Time's Arrow, Time's Cycle: Myth and Metaphor in the Discovery of Geological Time*. Cambridge: Harvard University Press.

Gregory, Derek. 1993. "The Historical Geography of Modernity." In *Place/Culture/Representation*, ed. James Duncan and David Ley. London and New York: Routledge. 272–313.

Habermas, Jürgen. 1987. *The Theory of Communicative Action. Vol. 2, Lifeworld and System: A Critique of Functionalist Reason*. Boston: Beacon Press.

———. 1989. *The Structural Transformation of the Public Sphere*. Cambridge: MIT Press.

Halbwachs, Maurice. [1950] 1980. *The Collective Memory*. New York: Harper and Row.

Haraway, Donna J. 1991. *Simians, Cyborgs, and Women*. New York: Routledge.

Harvey, David. 1989. *The Condition of Postmodernity*. Oxford (England) and Cambridge, Mass.: Blackwell, Inc.

Hawking, Stephen. 1988. *A Brief History of Time: From the Big Bang to Black Holes.* New York: Bantam Books.

Helms, Mary W. 1988. *Ulysses' Sail.* Princeton, N.J.: Princeton University Press.

Herzl, Theodor. 1973. *Zionist Writings: Essays and Addresses.* Vol. 1. New York: Herzl Press.

Hobsbawm, Eric, and Terence Ranger, eds. 1983. *The Invention of Tradition.* Cambridge: Cambridge University Press.

Holquist, Michael. 1989. "From Body-talk to Biography: The Chronobiological Bases of Narrative." *Yale Journal of Criticism* 3 (1): 1–35.

Hudson, Brian. [1977] 1985. "The New Geography and the New Imperialism: 1870–1918." *Antipode* 17 (2): 35–41.

Innis, Harold A. 1951. *The Bias of Communication.* Toronto: University of Toronto Press.

———. [1950] 1972. *Empire and Communications.* Revised by Mary Q. Innis. Toronto: University of Toronto Press.

Jackson, Michael. 1989. *Paths toward a Clearing: Radical Empiricism and Ethnographic Inquiry.* Bloomington: Indiana University Press.

Jankélévitch, Vladimir. 1974. *L'Irréversible et la nostalgie.* Paris: Flammarion.

Kant, Immanuel. [1781] 1964. "The Relational Theory of Space and Time." In *Problems of Space and Time,* ed. J. J. C. Smart. New York: Macmillan. 104–23.

Kapferer, Bruce. 1988. *Legends of People, Myths of State: Violence, Intolerance, and Political Culture in Sri Lanka and Australia.* Washington, D.C.: Smithsonian Institution Press.

Kearney, Michael. 1991. "Borders and Boundaries of State and Self at the End of Empire." *Journal of Historical Sociology* 4 (March): 52–72.

Kemp, Anthony. 1991. *The Estrangement of the Past: A Study in the Origins of Modern Historical Consciousness.* New York: Oxford University Press.

Kern, Stephen. 1983. *The Culture of Time and Space, 1880–1918.* Cambridge: Harvard University Press.

Kirby, Andrew. 1991. "The Great Desert of the American Mind: Concepts of Space and Time and Their Historiographic Implications." In *The Estate of Social Knowledge,* ed. JoAnne Brown and David K. van Keuren. Baltimore: Johns Hopkins University Press. 22–44.

Knapp, Jeffrey. 1992. *An Empire Nowhere: England, America, and Literature from "Utopia" to "The Tempest."* Berkeley and Los Angeles: University of California Press.

Koselleck, Reinhart. 1985. *Futures Past: On the Semantics of Historical Time.* Cambridge: Harvard University Press.

Lefebvre, Henri. 1991. *The Production of Space.* Cambridge, Mass.: Basil Blackwell, Inc.

Leibniz, Gottfried. [1716] 1964. "The Relational Theory of Space and Time." In *Problems of Space and Time,* ed. J. J. C. Smart. New York: Macmillan. 89–98.

Lenhardt, Christian. 1975. "Anamnestic Solidarity." *Telos* 25: 133–54.

Lestienne, Rémy. 1985. "L'Espace perdu et le temps retrouvé." *Communications* 41: 5–26.

Leveau, Rémy, and Gilles Kipel, eds. 1988. *Les musulmans dans la société française.* Paris: Presses de la Fondation nationale des sciences politiques.

Lloyd, David. 1989. "Kant's Examples." *Representations* 28: 34–54.

Lowenthal, David. 1984. *The Past Is a Foreign Country.* New York: Cambridge University Press.

McNeill, William B. 1986. *Polyethnicity and National Unity in World History.* Toronto: University of Toronto Press.

Maier, Charles S. 1988. *The Unmasterable Past: History, Holocaust, and German National Identity.* Cambridge: Harvard University Press.

Malin, James C. 1944. "Space and History: Reflections on the Closed-Space Doctrines of

Turner and Mackinder and the Challenge of Those Ideas in the Air Age." *Agricultural History* 18 (April): 65–74.

Malkki, Liisa. 1990. "Context and Consciousness: Local Conditions for the Production of Historical and National Thought among Hutu Refugees in Tanzania." In *Nationalist Ideologies and the Production of National Cultures*. American Ethnological Society Monograph Series no. 2. Washington, D.C. 32–62.

Marin, Louis. 1993. "Frontiers of Utopia: Past and Present." *Critical Inquiry* 19 (3): 397–420.

Martinet, Camille. 1987. "Les archéologues sud-africains lavent plus blanc!" *Autrement* 88 (March): 125–29.

May, J. A. 1970. *Kant's Concept of Geography and Its Relation to Recent Geographic Thought*. Toronto: University of Toronto Press, for the University of Toronto Department of Geography.

Mitchell, W. J. T. 1990. "The Violence of Public Art: *Do the Right Thing*." *Critical Inquiry* 16 (4): 881–99.

Miyoshi, Masao. 1993. "A Borderless World? From Colonialism to Transnationalism and the Decline of the Nation-State." *Critical Inquiry* 19 (4): 726–51.

Morin, Edgar. 1985. "Présentation." *Communications*, no. 41: 3–4.

Morris, Meaghan. 1990. "Metamorphoses at Sydney Tower." *New Formations*, no. 11 (Summer).

Mosès, Stéphane. 1989. "The Theological-Political Model of History in the Thought of Walter Benjamin." *History and Memory* 1 (2): 5–34.

Mosse, George. 1985. *Nationalism and Sexuality*. Madison: University of Wisconsin Press.

Nadel-Klein, Jane. 1991. "Reweaving the Fringe: Localism, Tradition, and Representation in British Ethnography." *American Ethnologist* 18 (3): 500–517.

Newton, Isaac. [1682] 1964. "Absolute Space and Time." In *Problems of Space and Time*, ed. J. J. C. Smart. New York: Macmillan. 81–88.

Nora, Pierre. 1989. "Between Memory and History: *Les Lieux de mémoire*." *Representations* 26:7–25.

Ong, Walter J. [1958] 1983. *Ramus, Method, and the Decay of Dialogue: From the Art of Discourse to the Art of Reason*. Cambridge: Harvard University Press.

Paine, Robert. 1992. "Time-Space Scenarios and the Innisian Theory: A View from Anthropology." *Time and Society* 1 (1): 51–63.

Perelli, Carina. 1991. "Settling Accounts with Blood Memory: The Case of Argentina." Paper presented at workshop, Space, Time, and the Politics of Memory, Portsmouth, New Hampshire, May 19–21.

Peters, Joan. 1984. *From Time Immemorial*. New York: Harper and Row.   *A fraud*

Pred, Allan. 1990. *Making Histories and Constructing Human Geographies: Essays on the Local Transformation of Practice, Power Relations, and Consciousness*. Boulder, Colo.: Westview Press.

Price, Richard. 1983. *First-Time: The Historical Memory of an Afro-American People*. Baltimore: Johns Hopkins University Press.

Rajchman, John. 1989. "Crisis." *Representations* 28: 90–98.

Rappaport, Joanne. 1990. *The Politics of Memory*. New York: Cambridge University Press.

Reichenbach, Hans. 1991. *The Direction of Time*. 2d ed., ed. Maria Reichenbach. Berkeley and Los Angeles: University of California Press.

Renan, Ernest. [1882] 1990. "What Is a Nation?" In *Nation and Narration*, ed. Homi K. Bhabha, New York: Routledge. 8–22.

Riffaterre, Michael. 1988. Response to Edward Said. Remarks at the School of Criticism and Theory, Dartmouth College.

Rosaldo, Renato. 1989. *Culture and Truth*. Boston: Beacon Press.

Sahlins, Peter. 1989. *Boundaries: The Making of France and Spain in the Pyrenees*. Berkeley and Los Angeles: University of California Press.

Said, Edward. 1989a. "Representing the Colonized: Anthropology's Interlocutors." *Critical Inquiry* 15 (2): 205–25.

———. 1989b. "Yeats and Decolonization." In *Remaking History*, ed. Barbara Kruger and Phil Mariani, Seattle: Bay Press. 3–29.

Scarry, Elaine. 1985. *The Body in Pain*. New York: Oxford University Press.

Schivelbusch, Wolfgang. 1986. *The Railroad Journey: The Industrialization of Time and Space in the Nineteenth Century*. Berkeley and Los Angeles: University of California Press.

Segal, Daniel A. 1988. "Nationalism, Comparatively Speaking." *Journal of Historical Sociology* 1 (3): 301–21.

Soja, Edward W. 1989. *Postmodern Geographies: The Reassertion of Space in Critical Social Theory*. London: Verso.

Spence, Jonathan D. 1984. *The Memory Palace of Matteo Ricci*. New York: Viking Penguin.

Spivak, Gayatri Chakravorti. 1989. Who Claims Alterity? In *Remaking History*, ed. Barbara Kruger and Phil Mariani. Seattle: Bay Press. 269–92.

Stock, Brian. 1990. *Listening for the Text: On the Uses of the Past*. Baltimore: Johns Hopkins University Press.

Taussig, Michael. 1984. "Culture of Terror, Space of Death: Roger Casement's Putumayo Report and the Explanation of Torture." *Comparative Studies in Society and History* 26: 467–97.

———. 1987. *Shamanism, Colonialism, and the Wild Man: A Study in Terror and Healing*. Chicago: University of Chicago Press.

———. 1990. "Violence and Resistance in the Americas: The Legacy of Conquest." *Journal of Historical Sociology* 3 (3): 209–25.

———. 1992. *The Nervous System*. New York: Routledge.

Taylor, Charles. 1990. "Modes of Civil Society." *Public Culture* 3 (Fall): 95–118.

Theweleit, Klaus. 1987. *Male Fantasies*. Vol. 1, *Women, Floods, Bodies, History*. Minneapolis: University of Minnesota Press.

———. 1989. *Male Fantasies*. Vol. 2, *Male Bodies: Psychoanalyzing the White Terror*. Minneapolis: University of Minnesota Press.

Tilly, Charles. 1990. *Coercion, Capital, and European States, A. D. 990–1990*. New York: Basil Blackwell.

Toulmin, Stephen. 1992. *Cosmopolis: The Hidden Agenda of Modernity*. Chicago: University of Chicago Press.

Trumpener, Katie. 1992. "The Time of the Gypsies: A 'People without History' in the Narratives of the West." *Critical Inquiry* 18 (4): 843–84.

Tuan, Yi-Fu. 1974. *Topophilia*. Englewood Cliffs, N.J.: Prentice-Hall.

———. 1979. *Landscapes of Fear*. New York: Pantheon Books.

Vidal-Nacquet, Pierre. 1982. "Herodote et l'Atlantide: Entre les grecs et les juifs — Réflexions sur l'historiographie du siècle des Lumières. *Quaderni di Storia* 16: 5–74.

Walker, R. B. J. 1989. "*The Prince* and 'the Pauper': Tradition, Modernity and Practice in the Theory of International Relations." In *International/Intertextual Relations: Postmodern Readings of World Politics,* ed. James Der Derian and Michael J. Shapiro. Lexington, Mass.: D. C. Heath and Company (Lexington Books). 25–48.

Wallerstein, Immanuel. 1974. *The Modern World System*. New York: Academic Press.

Wilcox, Donald J. 1987. *The Measure of Time: Pre-Newtonian Chronologies and the Rhetoric of Relative Time*. Chicago: University of Chicago Press.

Yates, Frances. 1966. *The Art of Memory*. Chicago: University of Chicago Press.

Yerushalmi, Yosef Haim. 1982. *Zakhor: Jewish History and Jewish Memory*. Seattle: University of Washington Press.

———. 1988. "Réflexions sur l'oubli." In Yerushalmi, Yosef Haïm et al., *Usages de l'oubli*. Paris: Editions du Seuil. 7–21.

Yerushalmi, Yosef Haïm, et al. 1988. *Usages de l'oubli*. Paris: Editions du Seuil.

Yoneyama, Lisa. 1991. "Postmodern Dysmnesia: Hiroshima Narratives and the Politics of Urban Renewal." Paper presented at workshop, Space, Time, and the Politics of Memory, Portsmouth, New Hampshire, May 19–21.

Young, James. 1992. "The Counter-Monument: Memory against Itself in Germany Today." *Critical Inquiry* 18 (2): 267–96.

2

Memoria de Sangre
Fear, Hope, and Disenchantment in Argentina

Carina Perelli

PERHAPS ARGENTINA COULD best be described as a "has been" country, where nostalgia flourishes. Argentines tend to use the often mytholo-
gized past as a source of strength to face the future. Still smarting from the
decline of their country and unable to come to terms with the fact that
Argentina doesn't count any more in the roster of the nations, they obtain
a measure of comfort and an increased sense of self-esteem from belonging to a country that was in the near past different from — *sous-entendu,*
better than — the rest of the Latin and North American nations, a country
that could even, in its time, teach some lessons to the European states.

Since the past is such a central political commodity in the has-been
countries,[1] the politics of memory tend to be a crucial factor of social stability. A narrative of the past, with central premises and a general outline
shared by the different groups of society, is a powerful unifying force in
any country. In the has-been countries, this narrative is even more significant, as so much of people's sense of self-worth and identity depends on
what is perceived as the countries' grand heritage and historical tradition.

The possibility of developing such a narrative in Argentina has been
seriously undermined by the political events of the past three decades. The
violent resolution of political conflicts has not only generated a polarized
memoria de sangre (blood memory) among — and circumscribed to — direct

participants of the contest, but has also left common people suffering from the consequences of the culture of fear that prevailed under military rule.

We call *memoria de sangre* the memory that arises from an experience of fear, hardship, pain, and loss so extreme as to turn it into *the* salient fact of the past. *Memoria de sangre* is such a pivotal experience that it becomes the standard of evaluation against which every single situation — past, present, and future — will be judged. It becomes the sole criterion of friend and enemy. In the chiaroscuro of memory, *memoria de sangre* is a polestar. By its very presence, it determines what is remembered and what must be forgotten.

We prefer to use the concept in its Spanish version as in this language the term has more polysemies than in English and conveys some ambivalence as to its meaning. As *memoria de la sangre vertida* or memory of the blood spilled during the confrontation, it relates the issue to the remembrance of those who were killed or severely wounded and introduces the whole issue of the cult of the dead. It can also be interpreted as *memoria de mi/nuestra sangre,* a memory so powerful that it has become as much an essential part of ourselves as the blood that runs in our veins. As *memoria de mi/nuestra sangre vertida,* it is the memory of the spilled blood of our people: the blood as boundary that divides us from them. Therefore, *memoria de sangre* can also be taken as a memory that is at the origin of blood feuds. In any of its possible interpretations, it implies an experience that breaks the perceived continuum of one's life in two. With *memoria de sangre* there is always this notion of before and after, this idea of a life order disrupted by the situation and reconstructed after it. This feeling of fracture is immediately apparent in any of the participants' tales or memoirs. By its very nature, *memoria de sangre* seriously hinders any possibility of elaborating a common narrative of the period.

The enormity of the experience has made it very difficult to settle accounts with the recent past. The difficulties inherent in this situation have been magnified by the vicissitudes of transition compounded with the very strategies devised to cope with the problem of an unbearable and dissonant past. The attempt to come to terms with the *memoria de sangre* (blood memory) of the *guerra sucia* (dirty war) through exemplary legal proceedings against both *guerrilleros* and the members of the military juntas has backfired.

The politics of memory chosen, that is, the impartial inquiry to determine what, exactly, had happened during those years and in the subsequent trial of those perceived as holding the ultimate responsibility for the atrocities committed during the dirty war, failed on several counts. The strategy selected failed politically, as it did not quell the power of the groups targeted (mainly the armed forces, as the guerrilla movements had lost much of their appeal after the experience of the dirty war), nor did it reestablish or consolidate a sense of the supremacy of law—and therefore of the *estado de derecho*[2]—in a democratic state. It also failed socially and culturally, as it did not enable people to work out their own experiences of paralyzing terror, repressed guilt, and projection.

Coping with Violence and Fear

Even though the political history of the Argentine Republic in the twentieth century is one of violence, what sets apart the period we are about to consider is the fact that, for the first time, violence and fear became generalized and involved society as a whole. From 1974 onward, the very notion of innocent bystanders disappeared from the scene: everybody was at least potentially at risk of being caught in the grinding machine of destruction. Previous conflicts and their consequences had been limited to those participating directly in the confrontation; the era of violence and fear inaugurated with the dissensions inside the Peronist movement and especially with the death of Juan Domingo Perón on 1 July 1974 deeply affected all levels of society.

From 1968 on, several guerrilla movements began to operate in Argentina. Among those, the two most politically powerful and most virulent were the Ejército Revolucionario del Pueblo (People's Revolutionary Army), better known as ERP, a Guevarist group; and Montoneros, a Peronist leftist group.[3] Revolutionary activism had arisen among disgruntled working-class and middle-class sectors whose expectations were seriously hurt by the economic crisis. This activism was particularly noticeable among students, unionized workers, and liberal sectors of the Catholic clergy, imbued with the principles of the Second Vatican Council.[4]

The transition first to the democratically elected government of President Héctor Cámpora in 1973 and then to the government known by the formula "Perón/Perón"[5] in October of the same year did not quell the revolutionary movement.[6] Perón's administration soon had to resort to repression. However, while Perón lived, he was able to keep the situation from further deteriorating and maintain it in a state of unstable equilibrium both by his style of leadership and by the many symbolic elements crystallized in his person.

At the death of Perón,[7] his wife, Isabel Perón, took power. She soon established an ultraconservative government program to exterminate subversion. During her administration, several civilian paramilitary groups were created to literally eradicate what was conceived as the actions of subversive movements.

The levels of violence increased as leftist guerrilla groups responded with violence to the action of the paramilitary groups, to the official repression directed against intellectuals and students, and to the economic chaos brought about by the economic policies of the government. Inflation skyrocketed; labor expressed its discontent through general strikes and massive demonstrations. For common citizens, who had to deal with the rapid decline of their earning power, with the closing of many enterprises and the ensuing layoffs, and with the escalation of violence, life in Argentina became both distressful and puzzling. Changes in heroes and utopias, in languages and mores, encompassed a more profound mutation of society. "Business as usual" could not continue under these new circumstances; the rules of the game for Argentine social relations had been turned upside down.

At the beginning of 1976, in a bloodless coup, the military ousted Isabel Perón from power. A military junta composed of the commanders of the three armed services and headed by Gen. Jorge Rafael Videla, commander in chief of the army, took control of the country. The *guerra sucia* against subversion thus began.[8] It was not waged exclusively against *guerrilleros* caught arms in hand. Those who belonged to "suspect" categories were also prime targets of the campaign against subversion.[9]

Argentines were forced to reinvent language to describe the new atrocious reality. Thus, the term *chupar* (to suck) and the words associated with it—*chupado/chupada* (sucked) and *chupadero* (place where people suck or where one gets sucked)—refer both to the methods of disappearance of the victims of the dirty war and to the consequences of such an action. The words evoke two associations. On the one hand, *chupar* comes from the expression "Es como si se lo hubiera chupado la tierra," which means literally "It is as if he/she had been sucked up by the earth." The expression means that the disappearance has been total and immediate: the person has left no traces. It was normally used by people at the "receiving end" of the process of disappearance, who felt helpless facing such a procedure. However, military officers of the period also used the concept of *chupar,* connecting it with the image of a vacuum cleaner: they had made a person disappear with the finality and swiftness of a homemaker cleaning house by sucking the dust and dirt into the vacuum cleaner.

By the same token, Argentines had to learn new verb forms and conjugations. *Desaparecer* (to disappear) had always implied a voluntary action of the subject. Violating grammar as much as sanity, in the new culture of fear the verb's subject became an object. No longer did a person disappear by an act of volition (*desapareció*): he or she was made to disappear (*lo/la desaparecieron*). *Capucha* (hood) no longer referred to a headdress to protect oneself from the elements; it became a part of the ritual of terror in the operations of *chupado* and in the interrogatories of the suspects. The new use of *boleta* (ticket) superimposed a new layer of sinister meaning on the existent ones: combined with the verb "to be" (*ser boleta*), it meant being condemned to death.

This campaign of death and terror was senseless in appearance only. Actually, it was rooted in an Argentine adaptation of the French *doctrine de guerre révolutionnaire.*[10] According to this doctrine, subversive warfare is a war to conquer the soul of the population; it uses armed confrontations but does not rely exclusively on them. The armed forces thus had two tasks: to identify, isolate, and eliminate subversives, and to prevent the infection from spreading inside society.

In Argentina, they chose to induce a state of terror in the people to deter them from heeding the siren song of subversive propaganda. Thus, in 1977, Gen. Ibérico Saint Jean, then governor of the province of Buenos Aires, publicly said: "First, we will kill all subversives, then all their collaborators, ... then those who sympathize with them, ... immediately afterwards those who remain indifferent, and, finally, we will kill all those who are lukewarm in this matter"(Vázquez 1985: 73; my translation).

The dire consequences of becoming a suspect or of being even unknowingly guilty of associating with suspects shaped a culture of fear peculiar to the Argentine people.[11] At the time, people became not only mute but also deaf and blind. They learned "not to see" what was happening in their immediate surroundings and, when forced by circumstances to acknowledge that something was happening, they assumed that it was not their business to know.[12] This culture of fear was conducive to an extreme individualization and privatization of human beings. People tried to isolate themselves from their social environment and emotional attachments in order to attain that state of detachment necessary to ignore the shouts for help and the cries of despair of their neighbors as they were abducted, as well as the episodes of violence that always took place when an operation of *chupado* was occurring.

Not all silence was induced by fear, however. Important sectors of Argentine public life shared the goals of the antisubversive campaign: leaders of the Catholic church[13] and of the unions; some members of the political class and of the press. They saw the dirty war as an unsavory but necessary procedure to cleanse Argentine society from the cancer of subversion, so that a new political order could be built that would reflect the "natural order."

Argentines at the time attained a state of perverse ataraxia. The operations of *chupado* were by no means furtive but followed a well-established procedure. Security personnel in civilian clothes arrived at a house in a car with no plates — the notorious Ford Falcon, as this model was spacious enough for several kidnapped people to be thrown on its floor. The abductors took their prisoners but also looted the house, terrorized the remaining relatives, and destroyed what they couldn't or wouldn't take with them. Even if these operations were conducted mostly at night, because the darkness was considered an extra psychological asset, many were carried out in broad daylight, sometimes under the very eyes of policemen detached to guard embassies or banks.[14]

It was precisely the police who first fell victim to this sort of perverse ataraxia, for police officers had strict orders to ignore any report regarding operations of *chupado* and *desaparecimiento de personas* (the act of sucking and making people disappear). They could not intervene if a *desaparecimiento* took place in front of their own eyes; they could not respond to a house call if an operation of *chupado* was taking place there. In the same vein, employees of the judiciary would not accept habeas corpus for a *desaparecido,* as many felt it too compromising to do so.

The victims were torn out of their homes or workplaces blindfolded and manacled, amid shouts and obscenities. That was the last image people had of the victims of repression before they disappeared into one of the "black holes" of the universe of terror. From then on, they would become, in the words of Jacobo Timerman, "prisoner[s] without a name, cell[s] without a number"[15] in one of the 340 clandestine detention centers, the majority of them never to resurface. The use of torture was routine in those centers; the dehumanization of prisoners through torture, rape, and humiliation, systematic.[16]

For their family and friends, for their neighbors and colleagues, the dehumanization of the victims would entail more subtle and perverse means. From the moment the *desaparecidos* were sucked into one of the black holes, they became an unchangeable reminiscence stuck in time, a presence made of physical absence. Prisoners of their own images in the photographs, of their own beliefs at the time of their *desaparecimiento,* they became icons to be venerated, legends to be lived up to.

The particular brand of Argentine culture of fear entailed the rupture of connectedness and its most immediate consequence: social fragmentation. Survival—or so people were led to think by the apparatus of terror put in place by the state—depended on people's ability to refrain from acting according to what in normal times would be considered their best inclinations. It entailed being able to abstain from reacting to one's environment; to curb the impulse to provide assistance and comfort to one's neighbors, coworkers, or fellow students; to forgo caring and sharing for the sake of staying alive.

The culture of fear thus transformed the ingrained urban tendency not to meddle in other people's affairs into an almost obsessive detachment from the unsavory aspects of reality. Fear induced a state of learned helplessness, a passive submission to and acceptance of the seemingly senseless and unending terror.

To force the population to reach this condition was the ultimate goal of the state-controlled and managed terror apparatus in Argentina.[17] It not only reduced citizens to obedience but also utterly destroyed the possibility of emergence of a horizontal voice[18] by abolishing the essence of the dialogical principle. By shattering the bridges of connectedness and empathy, this culture of fear reduced society to a set of separate individuals living their atomized lives under the supervision of all-powerful authorities.

Only some of the relatives of the *desaparecidos,* basically the mothers and grandmothers[19] who had seen their sons, daughters, and grandchildren disappear without trace, escaped this process of detachment. Slowly and painfully, they began to get organized to make inquiries regarding their loved ones, to share information, and to protest in regular Thursday vigils—wearing diapers on their heads to symbolize the character of mothers and wearing photographs of their *desaparecidos* over their hearts[20]—at the Plaza de Mayo (May Square).[21] Other human rights organizations appeared, especially toward the end of the Proceso or during the early phases of democratization.[22] These groups are important in that they testify to the resilience and courage of individuals in extreme situations. In political terms, their action was very limited and had no noticeable impact on the population; however, it influenced the process of transition indirectly, as their constant advocacy in international forums put a strain on the relations of the military government with Western countries.

The armed forces did not remain unscathed by the process they had initiated.[23] The officer corps as a whole was at the very least tainted by its complicity with the unmilitary conduct of the dirty war. However, only a small sector of the officers conducted the highly decentralized and irregular dirty war against subversion. Many of them were only lieutenants or captains, but, as in all other places where dirty wars have taken place, members of the *grupos de tareas* (task groups) sometimes had broader powers of life and death than a normal senior military officer. The gap between the forces who were prepared to wage conventional war and those whose mission was the fight against subversion, between senior officers in their posts of command and junior officers on the ground, was to prove a major cleavage during transition and a significant frontier of military memory. Nonetheless, nobody seemed, at the time, to realize what wreckage the dirty war and its aftermath worked on the principles of discipline, obedience, and hierarchy inside the military institution.

By 1978 the regime considered it had won the war against subversion. The time was ripe to implement the first steps toward a future democratization of the country. Amid factional infighting, the military began a slow process of timid political openings and elite accommodation.[24] This process took new impetus under the more moderate government of General Viola, who succeeded General Videla as president of the junta in March 1981. General Viola's presidency, however, was short-lived: in December of the same year, he was ousted in a coup staged by the army commander, Gen. Leopoldo Galtieri, and backed by the army hard-liners who considered any transition dangerous and who resented Viola's overtures toward civilian political groups.

The Galtieri coup not only slowed the process of political liberalization but also broke down the very legality the armed forces had tried to impose since 1976. The malaise and divisiveness of the military institution was made public at a time when Argentina's economic crisis and social decay made it impossible for people to continue practicing their particular form of perverse ataraxia. Amid growing popular discontent, labor demonstrations, and political protests, the armed forces were obliged to rethink their options.

In the end, a plan to invade the Malvinas/Falkland Islands — originally drawn to rally support for Galtieri's aspirations to the presidential candidacy in the 1984 elections — was revamped. The South Atlantic War thus began, mostly as a way of diverting Argentine public opinion from the political and economic crises and of rallying all sectors under the banner of a national claim of sovereignty over the long-lost territories.

International reaction to the occupation of the islands by the Argentine troops was swift. The Argentine armed forces were compelled to surrender to the British, and Galtieri finally acknowledged defeat on 15 June 1982.

After the Malvinas/Falklands disaster, Galtieri and his junta were forced to resign.[25] The government of retired general Reynaldo Bignone could do little to quell popular discontent and to set the pace of an orderly transition. Restrictions on parties were lifted and elections announced. In April 1983 the military junta produced its "Final Document of the Military Junta on the War against Subversion and Terrorism" ([Argentina, Junta Militar] 1983), denying responsibility for any "excesses" committed during the dirty war, praising the armed forces, and vindicating their fight against the enemy. In September the government passed the so-called Law of National Pacification,[26] an attempt to give amnesty to all those involved in the repressive apparatus.

Coping with Guilt and Freedom

One of the main issues of the campaign of Alfonsín, in the months that preceded his election as president of the Argentine nation, was the systematic condemnation of the human rights abuses committed by the military in the de facto regime.

After Alfonsín was inaugurated as president, one of his major concerns was to bring to trial those deemed responsible for the Argentine social and political violence.[27] Alfonsín saw those trials as more than an opportunity to "do justice" in the broad sense of the term. He wanted those trials to be as exemplary as possible, in order to prevent episodes of violence and authoritarianism from recurring. Therefore, the armed forces had to be preserved as an essential state institution while being "tamed" and purged of those rabid antidemocratic elements who actively supported the war against subversion and the methods employed during the dirty war.[28] For this strategy to succeed, it was essential that only the members of the juntas and certain notorious senior practitioners of the dirty war be prosecuted,[29] and also, that the trials be conducted by the military, thus allowing the institution to "cleanse its own house."

In order to bring to trial those considered responsible for the sad state of affairs of the previous years, some preliminary measures were necessary. These included repealing the Law of National Pacification passed by the military[30]; issuing orders to prosecute the members of the juntas[31] and some notorious repressors, such as Gen. Ramón J. Camps and Gen. Carlos Suárez Masson[32]; and ordering the prosecution of former guerrilla leaders, such as Mario Firmenich, Fernando Vaca Narvaja, Enrique Gorriarán Merlo, and Roberto Perdía.[33] These persons were clearly identified as responsible for the Argentine tragedy by what was later to be known as the Doctrine of the Two Demons.[34] The "doctrine" tried to provide an answer to what Alfonsín saw as two grave political dilemmas: first, how to hold military officers accountable for the atrocities committed during the dirty war while still saving the armed forces as an institution; and second, how to condemn the role of revolutionary armed organizations without adding to the suffering of many of the surviving members who had endured loss of family, torture, and disappearance. In other words, the doctrine tried to provide an adequate frame to reprocess memory without increasing the chasms that separated Argentine society. This doctrine was completed and made instrumental by the so-called Doctrine of the Three Levels.[35]

Before one could even think about holding someone accountable for what had happened, however, it was necessary to know what had taken place in Argentina during those years. In December 1983 Alfonsín appointed the Comisión Nacional de Investigación de Desaparición de Personas [National Commission for Investigating the Disappearance of Persons], better known as CONADEP.[36] In September 1984 CONADEP produced a report containing some fifty thousand pages of hard evidence: the disappearance of 8,961 individuals was documented and 340 clandestine prisons identified.[37] The report also identified 1,300 members of the security apparatus — belonging either to the police force or to the armed services — undeniably tied to the repression of the dirty war.

The military accused were first tried by their peers,[38] amid the protests of the human rights organizations, who opposed the trials in special courts, under "favorable" conditions for the accused. However, the sentence passed by the Supreme Council of the Armed Forces in September 1984 declared the officers at the "first level" only indirectly responsible for any abuses committed by their subordinates, as the council had been unable to find anything objectionable in the decrees and orders given by the military leaders. Furthermore, the verdict affirmed that there was nothing objectionable in defending the country against its enemies.

This pronouncement of the Supreme Council of the Armed Forces utterly destroyed any attempts made by Alfonsín to dissociate the military institution as such from the events of the past. On the contrary, it backfired, as both the armed forces and the human rights groups—for obviously opposed reasons—were determined to state the issue of *memoria de sangre* in institutional terms. On the one hand, the military considered the most unsavory aspects of the dirty war an unwelcome albeit sometimes necessary consequence of the major crusade against subversion, a crusade that had saved Argentine society and the Western way of life from a fate considered by many officers as "worse than death." On the other, the human rights organizations[39] wanted the armed institution to be held accountable for what was evaluated as an intentional reign of terror created from above and responding to a design of the military corporation: they considered that there had been no excesses, as all acts had been part of a premeditated plan to control society. Eventually, in accordance with Argentine law,[40] the resistance of the military courts to the plan set by the government enabled civilian justice to act: the members of the former military juntas[41] were thus judged by the Federal Court of Appeals in Buenos Aires. Even though the trials, begun in April 1985, were open to the public, the members of the former juntas refused to grace the court with their presence except when absolutely necessary.[42]

The trial awakened extraordinary interest in Argentine society. An ad-hoc periodical, *Diario del juicio* (Journal of the trial), containing edited transcripts of trial testimony, averaged two hundred thousand street sales per week. All the media gave ample coverage to an event that was discussed in squares and cafes, by poor and rich alike. Through this discussion, a public space was reappropriated, a voice rediscovered, a relationship more transcendent than a passing acquaintance recovered. A public space for catharsis was opened for a short while. It seemed as though common people would be able at last to come to terms with their own experiences of fear, silence, and death.

The indictment of the juntas focused on discrete crimes against individual victims,[43] giving the trial a poignancy difficult to describe, as the survivors took the stage one by one to describe their sufferings at the hands of their captors. It was, as Mark Osiel puts it, "an avalanche of gruesome stories of excruciating human suffering" (1986: 156). However, the collective dimension of repression tended to be lost in this bleak recitation of individual pain and despair. There was no place in this narrative for the common people who had not been imprisoned, disappeared, and tortured. There was no designated time to mourn the loss of a certain dimension of collective innocence. There was no site where common people could come to grips with the idea that they had also been victims of the system of terror. The trial failed to provide an outlet for the feelings of personal inadequacy, anger, and frustration repressed during the years of extreme individualization, under the culture of fear. On the contrary, the testimony of so much individual suffering tended to enhance the individual guilt and rage for not having acted according to moral principle. These feelings quickly translated into a sense of moral outrage, resulting in the irate condemnation of the armed forces as a whole.

The members of the juntas were found guilty on diverse counts and sentenced to prison terms that ranged from life for Videla and Adm. Emilio Massera to three years and nine months for Brig. Gen. Orlando Ramón Agosti.[44] The condemned had to serve their terms in the Magdalena military prison. When Videla arrived, the military director of the prison was awaiting him, surrounded by officers: all of them rendered military honors to the prisoner.

In 1986, the results of the first criminal and civil suits against individual members of the armed forces began to be seen. The tribunals gave prison sentences to several military officers as well as to security personnel and members of the paramilitary groups. Others were in similar peril. It seemed as if nothing would detain the flood of adverse judgments and of what were perceived as "unjust reprisals" by certain sectors of the army.

This judicial tide was accompanied by a parallel movement of publicly recalling the past. Something akin to a divesting of memory began to occur among certain sectors whose voices had long been suppressed. All sorts of memoirs by survivors were published at the time, as well as accounts and interpretations of the past from several political and intellectual groups.[45] Both movements were happening at the time when the Alfonsín government was cutting down the defense budget and initiating reforms in the armed forces.[46]

At the end of 1986, two episodes, involving the navy, signaled that all was not well in the best of possible worlds. The first bombshell was the inclusion of the name of Capt. Alfredo Astiz in a list of officers to be promoted. Captain Astiz had long been associated with the darkest side of repression. His arrest was requested by both the French and the Swedish governments, as he had kidnapped and "disappeared" citizens of those countries. He had been identified by human rights groups as an undercover agent who had infiltrated several groups of human rights activists and had later conducted the operation of *chupado* of their members. As a soldier during the Malvinas War, however, he had surrendered his post at the South Georgia Islands without a fight. Therefore, his intended promotion was judged by many to be as much an act of provocation as a test case for the relative strengths of both the government and the armed forces. The result was a precarious stalemate that would end, a year later, in a victory of the navy over the government.[47] At the time, however, it was perceived by the citizenry as a partial conquest of the civilian camp. It was also seen as an important step in the struggle to recover the control on the official interpretation of the past.

The second confrontation between armed forces and government was objectively won by the government. When, in the course of a suit regarding the *desaparecidos* of the Escuela de Mecánica de la Armada (Mechanical School of the Navy), better known as ESMA, the retired admirals who were former directors of ESMA refused to be subjected to arraignment, the high command of the navy supported their position. The government then issued an ultimatum: the high command would withdraw this declaration or have its supplies of water, gas, food, and electricity cut in all barracks and garrisons. The president also threatened to call for a massive popular demonstration in front of the barracks.[48] The navy surrendered.

As a result of this confrontation, however, the government passed the Ley de Punto Final (Law of Fullstop):[49] this law fixed a deadline[50] for filing suits against the security and military personnel in cases related to human rights violations. Nonetheless, the human rights organizations had compiled such a mass of evidence on what had happened during the dirty war that they were able to file a huge number of suits before the deadline passed. The horrors disclosed by the testimony of the victims during the trial of the juntas had also aroused enormous revulsion. In many places, tempers flared with this new resolution. The federal courts of seven provinces[51] canceled their usual January recess to continue with the prosecutions and indicted over three hundred senior officers.[52]

At the beginning of 1987 a state of deep unrest prevailed inside the armed services as the judicial calendar marked the approaching date when army officers would have to either comply with the indictments of the civil and criminal courts or declare themselves in rebellion. The year also saw increasing calls from the human rights organizations for the reappearance of the *desaparecidos*. The fact that some of the long-lost children were found at the time did not pacify an already heavily laden emotional and political climate.

On Wednesday of Holy Week, 15 April 1987, Maj. Ernesto Barreiro, a mediocre army officer accused of human rights violations, fled from justice. Alfonsín immediately expelled him from the army. The incident should have been closed then and there except that Barreiro took refuge in a regiment in Córdoba. At the same time, a group of officers, later to be known as the *Carapintadas* (Painted Faces),[53] led by Lt. Col. Aldo Rico, abandoned their post and advanced toward the capital city. Once in Buenos Aires, they occupied the garrison of Campo de Mayo near Buenos Aires and put forth a politicomilitary proclamation. What they themselves called Operación Dignidad (Operation Dignity) had begun.[54]

Operación Dignidad is important as the first articulate expression of the armed forces on the subject of memory that did not come only from those directly implicated in human rights violations, who were at risk of being prosecuted for their past deeds, or from those in the higher echelons of command. It expressed the feelings of officers in midcareer, disappointed with the way the transition process had been conducted with regard to the armed forces and the politics of forgetting and remembering.[55] The text of the proclamation, widely distributed in a very professionally made videocassette, is extremely interesting, as it tries to articulate the process of identity formation and relations with society through the evolution of the members of a generation of professional soldiers. Thus it highlights the historical events that shaped their identity: the war against leftist guerrillas in the province of Tucumán and the war against subversion while they were still junior officers; the Malvinas War; the transition period and the trials of the juntas; their rejection by a society of loose morals under a democratic regime. Even though it is a political document, the angst behind this first crystallization of military feelings sounds true. This authenticity was later to be lost, as the group behind Operación Dignidad professionalized itself as a political group in the public arena. The Carapintadas, headed by Rico, stressed that their action was not an attempt to overthrow the government: it was merely an armed protest, a demonstration backed by tanks and guns.

Alfonsín hesitated between several courses of action. This hesitation, which would cost him dearly, was immediately conspicuous: marathon cabinet sessions were followed by no action whatsoever. Still worse, instead of following the plan that had so successfully cowed the navy the previous year, the government ordered the armed forces to quell the rebellion. It soon became apparent that the military institution was deeply divided on the question and that this cleavage followed lines of generation and therefore of rank.[56] This division paralyzed the armed forces, as many officers refused to obey the orders to repress the rebels. Others only went through the motions of following the commands of their chiefs.

The citizenry was quick to respond: the population took to the streets. For several days,[57] people demonstrated in the Plaza de Mayo and around the barracks of the Campo de Mayo. For the common people, this episode had tremendous meaning, as it broke down the pattern of learned helplessness they had developed during the years of military rule. People felt empowered and elated: for the first time in many years, they believed their action had been decisive in a political outcome.

Finally, Alfonsín parleyed with the rebels. Upon returning from their cantonment, the president announced that the insurgents were ready to surrender without conditions and that this had been a great victory for the people and for democracy. He ended his discourse at the Plaza de Mayo by asking the people to return to their homes and wishing them a happy Easter.

The rebels effectively surrendered. However, the victorious mood of the military insurgents while relinquishing their arms should have alerted the population that some sort of agreement had been reached.

The most immediate consequences of the rebellion were felt inside the military structure. Several senior officers, among them the chief of staff of the army,[58] were assigned to other posts or retired. Rico and his clique were accused of serious breaches of the military code of discipline.

However, the stalemate inside the army made it impossible for them to be either straightforwardly expelled from the military organization or pardoned.[59] On a practical level, Aldo Rico, while still in prison, became a celebrity.[60]

The most serious consequence of this first military revolt was still to come. In the month after it the Alfonsín government passed the Ley de Obediencia Debida (Law of Due Obedience).[61] In essence, this law stated that, as the military institution is a hierarchical organization based on the principle of due obedience to one's superiors, no officer could be accused of having committed acts that under normal situations would be considered crimes if he had done so under the due obedience principle.[62] In fact, the law provided a way out for an important number of junior and middle-rank officers arraigned for human rights violations.

The impact of this law upon society was enormous. The population felt betrayed. The law seemed undeniable evidence of the existence of a secret pact between Alfonsín and the Carapintadas. His exultant "Happy Easter" seemed a mockery in the light of the new circumstances. Moreover, the politics of memory had been, until then, the only area in which the Radical government had shown a measure of success. After the euphoria of thinking that they were "putting the military in their proper place," Argentines received the new law as a blow. They felt dispirited and disenchanted. A typical Río de la Plata discourse whose central theme is "There is no alternative" resurfaced. The Law of Due Obedience can be considered as the beginning of the end of hope.

A second unwanted consequence of the law was that the human rights organizations — especially, but not only, those with a large component of relatives of the *desaparecidos* — entered a phase of new belligerence both in their discourse and in their practice. For the first time, they had to face the possibility that those who had tortured, kidnapped, and killed people by the thousands would escape punishment. This led many groups to assume an antagonistic discourse against the government and to enter more and more into the partisan arena. This fact was increasingly used by the government to discredit their stands and by the military to accuse them of being the instruments of the very subversion the armed forces had fought in the dirty war.

In January 1988, after a secret negotiation between the chief of staff of the army, Gen. Dante Caridi, and the rebel leader Aldo Rico, the latter was allowed to return home under house arrest.[63] Whatever the provisions of this pact, Rico fled from his place of detention to head a very extended insurrection, known as the Rebellion of Montecaseros. Even though Rico was primarily concerned with his own prospects both as a military officer and as a rising political and media star, the rebellion rapidly extended to units and officers stationed throughout the country. The conciliatory steps taken by the government had not satisfied an organization increasingly divided internally and confronting a society that shunned it.

However, the popular response to the Montecaseros rebellion constitutes a good indicator of how such measures as the Law of Due Obedience had harmed the credibility of the government and affected the attitude of the population toward the politics of memory. Faced with the uprising, the entire Argentine political class expressed its solidarity with the government. However, there was no public call to demonstrate against the rebels. No one dared run the risk of losing face by calling the people to the streets only to see the streets deserted. Therefore, the Montecaseros rebellion was only a military operation, on the one hand, and an affair of professional politicians, on the other. The military operation ended with the defeat of Rico's troops, the swift sentencing of Aldo Rico and his partisans by a military court, and their imprisonment in the Magdalena prison.

On the political level, an agreement was reached among political parties: it was felt that a change of approach was needed to close the chasm created by *memoria de sangre*. Instead of delving into the past, the idea was to look into the future by creating the legal and institutional arrangements that would prevent an episode such as the dirty war from occurring. The instrument selected for such a task was the Ley de Defensa (Law of Defense). The Law of Defense dealt with the missions and uses of the armed forces in a democratic regime. Among other things, it created a new series of crimes: those against democracy. It also forbade the use of the armed forces and of military intelligence in internal conflicts, including the internal control of the population.

While this law was being discussed, throughout 1988, a new trial for human rights violations momentarily stirred the attention of a population that had covered itself with a mantle of indifference: the extradition from the United States of former general Carlos Suárez Masson, one of the best known "butchers" of the dirty war. However, his trial did not spark any response inside the military institution, as Suárez Masson had voluntarily withdrawn from the army when he fled the country during the transition process, saying that he did not want to be the scapegoat for the years of military rule. Even though the Suárez Masson trial did not shake the indifference of the general public, the heinousness of the crimes for which he was prosecuted and his amoral personal character helped further radicalize the discourse of the human rights groups.

In December 1988 a new military insurrection took place, the Rebellion of Villa Martelli, headed by an almost mythical right-wing personage, Col. Mohammed Ali Seineldín.[64] When the government denied him a promotion to general and as retirement time approached, Seineldín returned to the country from Panama and headed what he hoped would be a successful march toward Buenos Aires. His banners were the usual vindication of the past, coupled for the first time with a vindication of the members of the juntas still imprisoned at Magdalena. However, he also demanded a new and more orderly social order, inspired by ultramontane Catholic doctrine.

As in the past, Alfonsín ordered the armed forces to repress the mutiny. Again, as in the first Rico insurrection, the army was slow to respond to his command. The malaise among military officers was notorious: they had been ordered to fight against a myth. After the halfhearted semblance of a battle, a truce was reached. Seineldín surrendered, stating that he did not want to see the blood of brother officers shed because of him.

Even though the garrison of Villa Martelli is in the middle of a populous working-class neighborhood and the mutiny received tremendous media coverage, a population dissatisfied with the general performance of the Radical government and with its successive surrenders to military pressure followed the episode on television with a kind of indifferent lassitude. Only the more militant elements of society took to the streets and demonstrated against the rebels. However, the virulence of these demonstrations made observers fear the reappearance of violence in Argentina's public arena. The end of the mutiny did not disappoint the skeptics: Colonel Seineldín entered the same kind of limbo that Rico had known during his first insurrection.

A month later, on 23 January 1989, the mantle of disabused indifference of the population at large was torn apart by another armed rebellion. This time, the rebels came from unexpected quarters: a grassroots-cum-human-rights organization. The group, called Todos Por la Patria (Everybody for the Motherland) and better known as TPP, was composed of former ERP members, progressive clergy, and Trostkyite elements, as well as many youths whose political awakening had coincided with the meanders of the politics of memory in Argentina.

Nobody has been able to determine what triggered this group to act as it did. In January 1989 they took the garrison of La Tablada, killing several draftees and noncommissioned officers in the process. This time, the population was galvanized: all eyes were riveted to the television, as the Argentines saw the incredible spectacle of rebels and police exchanging fire while the armed forces refused to enter the conflict, as their intervention was specifically forbidden by the recently enacted Law of Defense.

It took only a few hours of inaction for the military institution to reconquer all it had lost with the politics of memory during the transition. Alfonsín signed a decree so modifying the Law of Defense as to transform it completely. All the prohibitions regarding the intervention of the armed forces in internal conflicts were lifted. The army intervened with a vengeance: it was one of the most ferocious operations of recent times, made even more so by a press coverage that relished the most morbid details it could find. Thirty-nine persons were killed and sixty-two injured.

But the worst was still to come, as the villains of the day before became the popular heroes of the day at hand. Their intervention was acclaimed, their decisive attitude hailed. Very few voices dared ask why the same vigor and decisiveness had not been employed in curbing previous military insurrections. The human rights organizations had lost any possibility of a plausible voice in this concert of praises for the valiant soldiers who once again had saved the nation. The political class had lost its last battle in the war over memory. On 25 January 1989 President Alfonsín announced the creation of the Consejo Nacional de Seguridad (CONASE) or National Security Council, whose mission was to advise the president in matters of "antisubversive action."

Faced with the possibility of a resurgence of armed leftist groups, the population did what they had usually done since 1930 in Argentina: they expected the military to come to the rescue, as an all-powerful deus ex machina. All the strategies designed to assure that there would be a Never More had failed.

In May 1989 Dr. Carlos Menem was elected as the new president of the Argentines. Amid the measures of his platform, one referred to the politics of memory: amnesty for those who had participated in the dirty war. The amnesty was finally granted in 1990. It applied not only to the former members of the juntas and the leader of the Montoneros, Mario Firmenich, but also to such notorious butchers as Ramón Camps, Suárez Masson, and Comisario General Miguel Osvaldo Etchecolaz. In his first public declarations after his release, Gen. Jorge Rafael Videla affirmed that, for him, the combat had not ended. The war against subversion should be vindicated, he declared, and its rightness recognized. After so many years and so much suffering, the circle closed onto itself.

Coping with Disenchantment: A Tentative Conclusion

Where did the Argentines go astray? What was wrong and what was right with the ways in which they tried to implement their politics of memory? Has something been gained by the whole process? Can something be learned from it?

Argentines chose as scapegoats for all the evils of the past both the guerrillas and the armed forces, but especially the armed forces, instead of entering the long, soul-draining, and painful revision of a past full of violence. In a sense, for very different reasons, politicians, human rights organizations, and the armed forces provided a Nuremberg trial of sorts[65] without denazification.

Nobody dared propose a deviolentization of Argentine life. This would have meant shedding layers upon layers of pretexts, justifications, and bad faith to confront the realities of a weak political system, of interest groups battling each other with all the means at hand, of fragile institutions, and of a military organization so politicized as to become a substitute party system of its own. It would have added up to discussing what Argentina is today, where it wants to go, and by what means, as opposed to dreaming of what Argentina has been. It would have entailed discussing the very notion of limits for acceptable behavior in a society and a culture that glorifies transgression.

Nobody, either, attempted to address the concerns of ordinary "little people" and show that the other side of the coin of violence is fear, the kind of paralyzing fear that does not leave room for decent feelings and concerns to flourish and become actions. Nobody ventured just to say that it is all right to be afraid and refrain from acting when one lives in the middle of a maelstrom of violence. Nobody stated that it is normal to develop behaviors aimed at ignoring dreadful aspects of reality when the texture of that reality is interrupted by black holes into which people get sucked, never to reappear again.

While trying to implement the chosen strategy, politicians and human rights organizations alike forgot that the Nuremberg trials could take place only in an occupied country and with a vanquished army. Therefore, they were unprepared for the consequences when the armed forces refused to play the game.

The rational construction on which Alfonsín based his whole strategy implied that the military organization would have "cleansed itself" and thus redeemed itself in the eyes of society through what would have amounted to such a breach of esprit de corps as to be considered treason against brothers-at-arms. Worse still, the Alfonsín strategy played down the centrality in the military worldview of the tenets of the war against subversion and the importance of this victorious war in their representations of the world, especially after the Malvinas/Falklands fiasco. Finally, the Alfonsín plan did not overcome the fact that no organization willingly commits suicide: as the number of officers indicted for human rights abuses augmented, as the trials multiplied, the situation went beyond what the institution could tolerate. From then on, it was only a matter of time before a reaction occurred.

As for the human rights organizations, their attitude towards the armed forces was one of outright condemnation. For them, as the slogan chorused in demonstrations clearly stated, there were no excesses: the abuses committed had been part of a grand strategy of the armed forces, and the organization and its members were fully responsible for what had happened. For this, and for all the suffering they had caused, the human rights groups wanted retribution: the cause of justice would be served only when the last officer who had participated in the dirty war through commission or omission had been jailed and when the last detail of the last disappearance had been made fully known. In this universe, populated by absences, issues tended to get defined in black and white. The military had been judged and found wanting: many of the human rights activists considered the armed forces little more than a criminal organization responsible for genocide. As for the military, they considered the human rights organizations little more than a new head of the hydra of subversion set to destroy Western civilization and its defenders.

In these conditions, there was not much space left for dialogue, negotiation, or reconciliation among the actors involved. At the end of the process, there is a military institution almost destroyed by internal divisions but strong enough to defend itself from any external (societal) enemy. There is a disabused and skeptical society that nevertheless hails any savior when it sees its comfort or its way of life threatened. There are organizations of good and courageous people who began defending common human rights and values until they were forced into partisan politics and radical discourse by a no-win strategy. There are, finally, thousands of victims whose deaths and disappearances have been in vain.

Notes

This essay is a revised and expanded version of "Settling Accounts with Blood Memory: The Case of Argentina" (Perelli 1992). The author wishes to thank the Social Science Research Council and John D. and Catherine T. MacArthur Program in International Peace and Security, which made possible the workshops on "Space, Time, and the Politics of Memory" in Santa Barbara, California, in 1990 and in Portsmouth, New Hampshire, in 1991.

1. Another very important member of this group is Argentina's neighbor state Uruguay.

2. Literally, the state of law (*Rechtstaat, état de droit*). In the Anglo-Saxon common-law tradition, the "rule of law."

3. For a study of the Montoneros see Gillespie (1982). There exists no similar study for ERP.

4. The consequences of the Second Vatican Council (1962–65) were extremely important among all Catholic communities, but it had an enormous social and particularly political impact in heavily Catholic Latin America. The Second Vatican Council was followed by the Latin American Bishops' Conference in Medellín, Colombia, in 1968. Both events were fundamental in shaping the consciousness of liberal Catholic sectors in the region.

5. Before the 1973 elections the government of General Lanusse established eligibility requirements for all presidential candidates. One of them was a residence requirement, with which Juan Domingo Perón, then living in Spain, refused to comply. In his stead, Perón appointed as presidential candidate Dr. Héctor Cámpora. Cámpora won 49.5 percent of the votes in the 1973 election but his tenure was short. In July of the same year, amid increasing violence and lacking the support of his leader, Cámpora resigned. Perón and his vice-president cum wife, María Estela Martínez de Perón, better known as Isabel Perón, were inaugurated in October 1973.

6. The chasm between mainstream Peronism and leftist Peronist youth movements became evident when Perón condemned the latter publicly in the Plaza de Mayo on 1 May (Labor Day) 1974.

7. On 1 July 1974.

8. The most intensive phase of this war against the "internal enemies" was carried out between 1976 and 1979.

9. These categories were considered more prone to antinational or disruptive activities or feelings. The lists of *desaparecidos* collected by Comisión Nacional de Investigación de

Desaparición de Personas (CONADEP) include leftist union members, students, politicians, and members of professional groups such as lawyers, clergy, bankers, psychiatrists, scientists, artists, and teachers. Often, the fact of being a relative or an associate of a *desaparecido* or inquiring about somebody who had been *chupado* (sucked) constituted grounds enough to become a *desaparecido*.

10. For a more detailed analysis of the influence of the French *doctrine de guerre révolutionnaire* on the approach to the problem of subversion taken by both Argentine and Uruguayan armed forces see Perelli (1991).

11. For an excellent approach to the subject of the culture of fear in Argentina see Corradi 1982. On the phenomenon of social fragmentation and loss of connectedness, see O'Donnell (1986a; 1986b).

12. This phenomenon was masterfully analyzed by Guillermo O'Donnell in a short piece, *¿Y a mi qué me importa? (And What Do I Care about That?)* (1985). O'Donnell chose for his title a colloquial expression of the Río de la Plata much used at the time in Argentina. It is pronounced stressing the *I,* in order to emphasize that other people's troubles are not my own.

13. For an impassioned analysis of the role of the Catholic church during those years, see Mignone (1988). Dr. Mignone, a fervent Catholic, lost his daughter Mónica in 1975, when she was kidnapped from their home by a group of armed men.

14. For more details on this subject, see CONADEP (1984).

15. Jacobo Timerman, a journalist, was one of the lucky ones: he lived to tale the tale in *Prisoner without a Name, Cell without a Number* (1981).

16. The report *Nunca más* collected by CONADEP contains detailed descriptions, obtained from the testimony of survivors, of what happened in each of the clandestine centers. See also Familiares de Desaparecidos y Detenidos por Razones Políticas (1984), vols. 7–9. A complete description of the characteristics of the repression can be found in Cámara Nacional de Apelaciones en lo Criminal y Correccional de la Capital (1987, vol. 1, chapters 11–16).

17. Juan Corradi provides an excellent analysis of this (1982: 62ff.).

18. For the concept of voice, see O'Donnell (1985; 1986a).

19. Some spouses also intervened in those movements. However, in the processes of *chupado,* spouses often suffered identical fates.

20. Appropriately enough, the organizations born of these spontaneous movements were called Madres de Plaza de Mayo (the Plaza de Mayo Mothers) and Abuelas de Plaza de Mayo (the Plaza de Mayo Grandmothers). Many paid dearly for their activism: a significant proportion of the founding Madres and Abuelas disappeared.

21. The Plaza de Mayo (May Square), at the heart of Buenos Aires, is flanked by the presidential palace, the Casa Rosada (Pink House); the Roman Catholic cathedral; and the Ministry of Social Welfare. Consequently, the Plaza de Mayo is a focal point for rallying in Argentine political life.

22. There are three broad categories of human rights organizations:
   1. Those directly linked to persons affected by repression: Madres de Plaza de Mayo (the Plaza de Mayo Mothers); Familiares de Detenidos y Desaparecidos por Razones Políticas (Relatives of Detainees and People Made to Disappear for Political Reasons), Abuelas de Plaza de Mayo (the Plaza de Mayo Grandmothers).
   2. Those that try to provide assistance to survivors, usually linked to church groups: Servicio de Paz y Justicia (Service of Peace and Justice), better known as SERPAJ; Movimiento Ecuménico por los Derechos Humanos (Ecumenical Movement for Human Rights); and others.

3. Those designed to provide legal services to the victims or collect information: Asamblea Permanente de los Derechos Humanos (Permanent Assembly for Human Rights); Centro de Estudios Legales y Sociales (Center for Legal and Social Studies), better known as CELS; Liga Argentina por los Derechos del Hombre (Argentine League for Human Rights).

Most of these organizations came to prominence during the democratization period. On the human rights movement in Argentina, see Brysk (1990).

23. For a more complete analysis of the changes brought about in the sense of self and identity of the military by the political intervention of the armed forces, see Perelli (1989).

24. There were at least six military proposals for political transition. An analysis of them can be found in González Bombal (1991), San Martino de Dromi (1988), and Vázquez (1985).

25. On 17 June 1989.

26. Law 22.924.

27. For a good study on the different positions and strategies on the issue of human rights and accountability in Argentina with respect to the trials, see Osiel (1986). As regards the position of the human rights organizations, see Mignone, Estlund, and Issacharoff (1984). For a treatment of the question from a scholarly perspective, see Acuña and Smulovitz (1991).

28. Alfonsín and his team of advisors considered that only one third of the members of the armed forces fitted this description.

29. As opposed to the officer corps as a whole, for instance. A different strategy at the time would have been to declare the officer corps at the time a criminal organization.

30. The newly elected Congress repealed the law on 14 February 1984 through Law 23.040.

31. Decree 158/83.

32. Decree 3090/84.

33. Decree 157/83.

34. This "doctrine" stated that Argentina had suffered from the combined evils of two demons: the revolutionary guerrillas and the armed forces set to combat them. Both were a manifestation of a dangerous authoritarian mentality that had taken the rest of society as a hostage. Together they had set Argentine political life aflame and pushed the country into a turmoil of violence, death, and suffering. Society had been a victim of these two forces. It was only just that both should be judged for their past actions: this would provide the truth and justice needed to enter an era of peace and reconciliation.

35. According to the Doctrine of the Three Levels, not all members of the armed forces shared equal responsibility for the iniquities of the dirty war. In the first level, there were those totally responsible—and therefore, those that had to be considered completely accountable—for what had happened: they were those who had issued the orders and drawn the plans to carry out the systematic repression of whoever was considered a foe. Thus, the first level was occupied by the members of the former military juntas since 1976. In the second level were those who had committed acts considered so atrocious and aberrant as to go against the very core of humanity. Those too had to be held accountable for their acts. As to the third level, composed of the rest of the officer corps, they were not considered responsible for what had happened, as their acts fell under the principle of due obedience to one's superior inside a military organization.

36. CONADEP had no power to subpoena. This executive commission was preferred by the government to a more powerful bicameral legislative commission, favored by the human rights organizations, as a way to hold the investigation to the limits of the government's grander strategy on the politics of memory. However, the conscientious work of CONADEP had a greater impact on society than the government expected.

37. The commission also explicitly stated that it suspected many more disappearances to have occurred, although it had been unable to find hard proof of them.

38. There were two separate trials: one, related to the conduct of the dirty war, which we will treat in the present study; the other, referring to the conduct of the Malvinas/-Falklands War, which began in 1985 and never ended. We will not enter in the terrain of the politics of memory the Malvinas war entailed inside the military institution, as this would mean writing a short history of the military unrest, malaise, and insurrections from 1985 onward.

39. All of them also filed civil and criminal suits against members of the security apparatus in the case of *desaparecidos.*

40. Law 23.049 of Reform of the Military Code confers initial jurisdiction for the prosecution of military personnel on the Supreme Council of the Armed Forces. But it also establishes an automatic instance of appeal in civilian courts.

41. With the exception of the last one, led by General Bignone. The last military junta was spared, as the government considered that this junta had directed the transition to democracy and thus had made possible the return to civilian rule. However, human rights organizations filed a civil case against General Bignone and he was indicted and arrested: two communist conscripted soldiers had disappeared while serving in the military college under his command in 1986.

42. The attitudes of the different members of the juntas toward the court varied. In one extreme, Gen. Rafael Videla did not recognize the court's jurisdiction nor its impartiality; he assumed that the federal tribunal was a political arena set by his former political opponents to condemn his political decisions as president. On the other, Adm. Emilio Massera used the court as a political forum to voice his political opinions; according to him, it was precisely because the dirty war had been won and Western civilization saved by the military that any court of justice was possible.

43. The human rights organizations had strongly objected to this procedure, on the grounds that the indictment of "genocide" would have been much more appropriate to describe — and thus to make sense of — the state-managed mechanisms of terror put into place in order to control the population better.

44. As to the second "demon" of Argentine politics, the revolutionary armed groups, the most notorious episode of their being held accountable for what happened was the extradition from Brazil and later trial and condemnation of the leader of the Montoneros, Mario Firmenich. He began serving his sentence at the Devoto Prison in Buenos Aires.

45. Among those, one of the most widely known was the award-winning film *La historia oficial,* starring Norma Aleandro.

46. These included the forced retirement of twenty-five army generals, twelve admirals, and twelve air force brigadier generals; the alteration of the command structure; and a new and more important role for the Ministry of Defense.

47. The promotion of Astiz was suspended for a year, the idea being to suspend his promotion twice, a measure that would have forced the officer to retire. Later events forced the civilian government to revise its original position and to concede the promotion.

48. The possibility of assembling an unarmed militia was not far from the minds of the government and the senior military officers.

49. The law was passed on 23 December 1986.

50. Sixty days after the promulgation of the law, on 23 February 1987.

51. Córdoba, Bahía Blanca, Tucumán, Mendoza, Rosario, La Plata, and Comodoro Rivadavia.

52. For a detailed account of this period see Verbistky (1987) and González Solá (1990).

53. They used black camouflage paint on their faces and wore commando fatigues, thus using their symbols of their trade as elite soldiers of the Malvinas/Falklands War.

54. For an account of Operación Dignidad see Grecco and González (1990) and Chumbita (1990). For an analysis of this and the rebellions that followed see Fraga (1989).

55. Basically the proclamation of Operación Dignidad addressed the question of military professionals who felt they had won a war against a covert and dangerous enemy (subversion) only to be rejected by a society that jailed their leaders and scorned their ideals. It put on the table the whole question of military identity torn by the politics of memory. It also addressed the problem of the internal malaise of the army, an organization in which the senior officers were beginning to be perceived as accomplices of a government that had enabled activists to criticize and at least attempt to destroy the armed forces through their continual attacks to its "moral strength." It is thus not surprising that the Operación Dignidad movement called for an end to what was seen as the systematic persecution of military officers and demanded that the attacks against the armed forces cease immediately. It also maintained that the members of the military juntas had not been properly tried: they had been accused of the wrong deeds. The charges brought against them should not have been those of murder and crimes against humanity. They should have been charged with sheer incompetence for having shed unnecessary blood and permitting excesses during the war against subversion. They should also have been tried on the same grounds as those accused of mishandling the Malvinas War. On both counts, the "natural" tribunal for such a trial should have been the military courts.

56. Two new terms were coined to describe the situation: there were the *generales de escritorio* (desk generals) and the *combatientes* (combatants), the majority of whom were popularly known as *malvineros* for their participation in the Malvinas/Falklands War.

57. The rebellion, begun on Thursday, ended on Easter Sunday.

58. Gen. Héctor Ríos Ereñú.

59. During the year that followed the uprising, this group of military officers entered a sort of limbo: nobody knew exactly whether they were still part of the army or had been cast out of it.

60. He openly received so many visitors in his quarters—members of the armed forces, trade union leaders, and politicians alike—that the high command had to regulate his visiting rights.

61. The bill was proposed to the Congress by the executive on 13 May 1987 and passed on 4 June.

62. Moreover, the law inverted the weight of the proof. Before it was enacted, a suit could be filed against an officer accusing him of human rights violations and what the prosecution had to prove was that the person indicted had effectively committed the crimes of which he was accused. Under the Law of Due Obedience, the prosecution had this burden plus the obligation of showing that the person had not committed those crimes in a situation broadly characterized as due obedience.

63. According to certain versions, Rico would have agreed, in exchange for this concession, to withdraw from the army before starting a political career.

64. Despite his name, Seineldín is an "integralist" Catholic, of Syrian parentage. He is also both a fanatic and a charismatic leader, very well thought of among junior officers who took him as a role model. Before the rebellion he had been one of Gen. Manuel Noriega's chief advisers in Panama, training Noriega's special guard. Seineldín had always had very high career aspirations: he wanted to become a general, convinced that he was the best-suited candidate for that rank.

65. There were many formal differences between the Nuremberg trials—or the Tokyo trials, for that matter—and the trial of the juntas in Argentina, the main one being, perhaps, the fact that formally nobody tried to condemn the Argentine armed forces as a criminal organization. However, as we hope to have shown, the dynamics of the situation transformed the trial into a condemnation of the armed forces as a whole, as an institution. It is at this level that we are establishing the parallel.

Bibliography

Acuña, Carlos H., and Catalina Smulovitz. 1991. *¿Ni olvido ni perdón? Derechos humanos y tensiones cívico-militares en la transición argentina.* Buenos Aires: CEDES.

[Argentina, Junta Militar.] 1983. "Final Document of the Military Junta on the War against Subversion and Terrorism." *El Bimestre político y económico,* March–April: 86–100.

Bryst, Allison. 1990. "The Political Impact of the Argentine Human Rights Movement: Social Movement, Transition, and Redemocratization." Ph.D. diss., Stanford University.

Cámara Nacional de Apelaciones en lo Criminal y Correccional de la Capital. 1987. *Texto completo de la sentencia.* Buenos Aires: Imprenta del Congreso de la Nación.

Chumbita, Hugo. 1990. *Los Carapintadas: Historia de un malentendido argentino.* Buenos Aires: Editorial Planeta.

CONADEP (Comisión Nacional de Investigación de Desaparición de Personas). 1984. *Nunca más.* Buenos Aires: EUDEBA.

Corradi, Juan. 1982. "The Monster of Destruction: Terror in Argentina." *Telos* no. 54 (Winter): 61–66.

Familiares de Desaparecidos y Detenidos por Razones Políticas. 1984. *Testimonios sobre la represión y la tortura.* Buenos Aires.

Fraga, Rosendo. 1989. *La cuestión militar, 1986–1989.* Buenos Aires: Editorial Centro de Estudios para la Nueva Mayoría.

Gillespie, Richard. 1982. *Soldiers of Perón: Argentina's Montoneros.* Oxford: Oxford University Press.

González Bombal, Inés. 1991. *El diálogo político: La transición que no fue.* Buenos Aires: CEDES (no. 61).

González Solá, Joaquín. 1990. *Asalto a la ilusión.* Buenos Aires: Editorial Planeta.

Grecco, Jorge, and Gustavo González. 1990. *Felices Pascuas.* Buenos Aires: Editoral Planeta.

Mignone, Emilio. 1988. *Witness to the Truth: The Complicity of Church and Dictatorship in Argentina, 1976–1983.* Maryknoll, N.Y.: Orbis Books.

———, Cynthia Estlund, and Samuel Issacharoff. 1984. "Dictatorship on Trial: Prosecution of Human Rights Violations in Argentina." *Yale Journal of International Law* 10 (Fall): 118–50.

O'Donnell, Guillermo. 1985. *¿Y a mi qué me importa?* Buenos Aires: CEDES.

———. 1986a. "On the Fruitful Convergences of Hirschman's *Exit, Voice, and Loyalty.*" In *Development, Democracy, and the Art of Trespassing,* ed. A. Foxley, G. O'Donnell, and M. McPherson. Notre Dame, Ind.: University of Notre Dame Press.

———. 1986b. "Shifting Involvements: Reflections from the Recent Argentina Experience." In *Development, Democracy, and the Art of Trespassing,* ed. A. Foxley, G. O'Donnell, and M. McPherson. Notre Dame, Ind.: University of Notre Dame Press.

Osiel, Mark. 1986. "The Making of Human Rights Policy in Argentina: The Impact of Ideas and Interests on a Legal Conflict." *Journal of Latin American Studies* 18: 135–80.

Perelli, Carina. 1989. "The Legacies of the Processes of Transition to Democracy in Argentina and Uruguay." In *The Military and Democracy: The Future of Civil-Military Relations in Latin America,* ed. Louis Goodman, Johanna Mendelson, and Juan Rial. Lexington, Mass.: D. C. Heath and Company (Lexington Books). 39–54.

———. 1991. "The Influence of the French *Doctrine de Guerre Révolutionnaire* on the Political Thinking of the Argentine and Uruguayan Armed Forces." Montevideo: Peitho Working Papers.

———. 1992. "Settling Accounts with Blood Memory: The Case of Argentina." *Social Research* 59: 415–51.

San Martino de Dromi, María Laura. 1988. *Historia política argentina, 1955–1988.* Buenos Aires: Editorial Astrea.

Timerman, Jacobo. 1981. *Prisoner without a Name, Cell without a Number.* Trans. Toby Talbot. New York: Alfred A. Knopf.

Vázquez, Enrique. 1985. *Proceso de reorganización nacional—La última: Origen, apogeo y caída de la dictadura militar.* Buenos Aires: EUDEBA.

Verbistky, Horacio. 1987. *Civiles y militares: Memoria secreta de la transición.* Buenos Aires: Editorial Contrapunto.

3

"Wan Tasbaya Dukiara"
Contested Notions of Land Rights in
Miskitu History

Charles R. Hale

For more than nine thousand years, the Miskito, Sumo and Rama Nations have watched the rising sun, fished the turtle, and nurtured the young and respected the elder. . . . At the root of [these] enduring cultures is wan tasbaia, *our land.*

(Menzies 1985)[1]

The idea, then, is that merely to be Indian entails an inalienable and self-evident supranational right, which stands apart from history and social development. It is a type of divine grace, apart from human conditions and struggles, and by extension at odds with efforts at national liberation. These [Miskitu] leaders' proposal is little more than an infantile religious vision of the final judgment, in which they have a front-row seat.

(Jorge Jenkins, Sandinista intellectual, 1986)

AFTER A SHORT TIME living in the Miskitu Indian community of Sandy Bay Sirpi, it became clear to me that people there assigned great importance to "the land." When I first arrived in 1985 the area had been engulfed in war for three years. Nicaraguan troops stationed in Sandy Bay since 1983 had clashed repeatedly with combatants from MISURASATA,[2] the Indian organization in arms against the government. In April 1985 MISURASATA and the Nicaraguan government agreed to "cease offensive activities," thereby giving Sandy Bay a respite from the war, allowing

the government to resume services to the community, and generally raising hopes for a peaceful settlement to the conflict. Government leaders
also had recently announced their commitment to recognize Miskitu (and
other Atlantic Coast peoples') rights to autonomy, which further contributed to the atmosphere of reconciliation. Yet MISURASATA combatants—whom community members called "bush people"—remained
nearby and well armed. In my efforts to understand why the conflict arose
and how a lasting resolution might be achieved, I repeatedly asked community members, "What are the bush people fighting for?" They frequently responded, "Wan tasbaya dukiara"—for our land.

A great deal hinged on what they meant by this response.
MISURASATA leaders had been promoting the position that Miskitu,
Sumu, and Rama Indian peoples were "nations" with aboriginal rights to
an immense territory within Nicaragua's Atlantic Coast region. The
Nicaraguan government, in contrast, maintained that the republic consisted of one nation-state with sovereignty over the entire national territory. Consequently, the government-backed autonomy proposal guaranteed Indians rights only to "the communal lands, waters, and forests that
have traditionally belonged to the communities." These conflicting definitions of land rights rested on two equally irreconcilable historical narratives.
MISURASATA leaders claimed that Indian nations had existed from time
immemorial and that Indian peoples had maintained enduring spiritual and
economic ties to their land; they fiercely resisted repeated attempts by outsiders to usurp their title to it. The Sandinista narrative revolved around
an integral Nicaraguan nation, equally timeless and linked to the same territorial boundaries that define the contemporary nation-state. According
to this latter account, Indians had played an important role in nation
building only until the late nineteenth century, when the initiative had
passed to mestizo (Spanish-speaking) peasants and workers. Indian culture
became part of the nation's rich heritage from the past, whereas the future
was portrayed as resolutely mestizo.[3]

Not surprisingly, negotiations between the two parties did not prosper.
When they met in May 1985, hoping to turn the preliminary cease-fire into
a lasting settlement, they did not move beyond first principles. MISURASATA
wanted a firm recognition of Indian rights to self-determination as a prior
step to a permanent cease-fire, but the government insisted that a cease-
fire (an implicit recognition of Nicaraguan national sovereignty) come
first. Negotiations broke down; MISURASATA denounced the Sandi-

nista-backed autonomy proposal as a "pseudoproject of administrative re-organization" and went back on a war footing. The story of the subsequent political process need not concern us here, except to note that the return to peace continued nonetheless, and that civilian Miskitu townspeople played an important role in preventing the resumption of armed conflict. This divergence between Miskitu townspeople and MISURASATA leaders — despite the general stance of support and solidarity by the former for the latter — adds another angle to the initial question. How did Sandy Bay people's notions of history in general, and of land rights in particular, differ from those of their own leaders? How did these differences come about and what is their contemporary significance?

To address these issues, this essay encompasses two distinct lines of inquiry, one focused on historical explanation and the other on the politics of memory. First, I examine Miskitu people's consciousness during four historical moments beginning in 1894, when the Nicaraguan state formally annexed the coastal region where Miskitu people lived. Next, I reexamine each moment, seeking to understand how Miskitu townspeople and MISURASATA leaders represent these same events today.[4] The analysis therefore proceeds through the juxtaposition of three voices: what Miskitu people in Sandy Bay remember; the MISURASATA rendition of these same events; and my own historical reflections, based mainly on documents from the period. I omit reference to the Sandinista narrative until the conclusion, where I reflect briefly on the broader issues of theory and politics that the analysis raises.

Throughout the essay I take the "MISURASATA position" to include the statements of both MISURASATA leaders and the group of analysts/activists aligned with that cause.[5] This step is justified because members of the latter group, though not formally part of the organization, deeply influenced how the conflict would be perceived in Nicaragua and internationally; also, and most importantly, they helped to shape the content of the MISURASATA position itself. I also should note that for two reasons I do not include voices from MISURA, the other antigovernment Miskitu organization, which had closer ties to the U.S. government, received more funding and fielded more combatants than MISURASATA. In Sandy Bay, unlike areas farther north, most townspeople identified with MISURASATA; moreover, it would have been much more difficult to identify a discrete "Indian discourse" among MISURA leaders, since they tended to portray their struggle in terms similar to those of the Spanish-speaking Contra and the Reagan administration. This omission must be clarified from the outset, to avoid reinforcing a common pattern of the 1980s, whereby international observers came to understand the Miskitu struggle through the sanitized discourse of MISURASATA leaders, which obscure some of the movement's more troubling contradictions.

Sandy Bay townspeople's voices come from a large corpus of taped interviews meant to elicit their memories of the past. For the most part I conducted these interviews in Miskitu, alone with the speaker, asking general questions and encouraging lengthy, free-flow answers. Townspeople did, of course, vary in their interpretation of many details of the narrative, especially those related to internal matters within the community (such as interfamily rivalries). However, I found a striking degree of uniformity on the major points that involved the relations of the community (and indeed of all Miskitu people) with outsiders, both Anglo-Americans and Spanish speakers. These points, in turn, make up the heart of the four moments of history that I analyze below.

The "Reincorporation" of 1894

In the seventeenth century British colonists established economic relations with Miskitu Indians and created a political institution of indirect rule known as the Mosquito Kingdom. Although successive Miskitu kings between 1687 and 1894 appear to have come from a single line (Olien 1983), by 1840 the ethnopolitical character of the "Mosquito government" had changed. "Creoles" — Creole-English-speaking people of African descent — had gained a dominant position within the coastal ethnic hierarchy and in the Mosquito government as well. The government seat moved south to the predominantly Creole town of Bluefields, and the Treaty of Managua between Great Britain and Nicaragua, signed in 1860, pared down the territory under Mosquito government rule, excluding more than half of the total Miskitu population (see Figure 1). This treaty also marked the beginning of the Nicaraguan government's efforts to acquire sovereignty over the coastal region. These efforts culminated in 1894.

In February 1894 a contingent of Nicaraguan troops under the command of Gen. Rigoberto Cabezas occupied Bluefields and declared a state of siege throughout the Atlantic Coast. Lured by a potential bonanza of

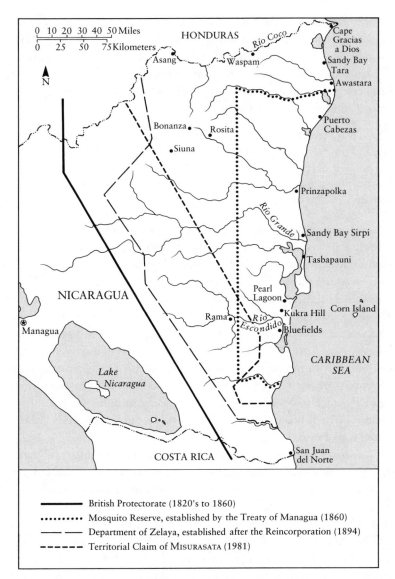

Figure 1. Territorial demarcations in the history of the Atlantic Coast region of Nicaragua. The solid line represents the British protectorate (1820s to 1860); the dotted line, the Mosquito Reserve, established by the Treaty of Managua (1860); the light dashed line, the Department of Zelaya, established after the "Reincorporation" (1894); and the heavy dashed line, the territorial claim of MISURASATA. Reprinted from Hale (1994) with permission of the publisher.

tariff revenues, and spurred on by tacit consent from the United States, Nicaraguan President José Santos Zelaya ordered Cabezas to "occupy Blue-fields militarily: dispose the Mosquito chief and leave the consequences to me" (William Sorsby, personal communication). The original pretext for sending troops—a border clash with Honduras—soon gave way to a more definitive and inflammatory rationale:

> The Treaty [of Managua] has lost its juridical validity, since it was created for the protection of Mosquito Indians ... who have withdrawn deep into the jungle ... while the reserve government has become a contemptible fiction under the control of black usurpers [*negros usurpadores*].[6]

Resistance to the occupation on the part of Atlantic Coast people at first took a form befitting British subjects: petitions to the Crown. Although local British authorities had strict instructions not to become embroiled in local affairs, they did press for the withdrawal of Nicaraguan troops, which occurred in early May.[7] Opponents of the annexation then grew more courageous and tensions mounted. On July 5 violence broke out between Creole residents and the few soldiers that had remained as Cabezas's police force. This quickly escalated into a rebellion, which spread from Bluefields to the nearby port of Bluff, and then to Corn Island and Prinzapolka, where Creoles violently deposed Nicaraguan authorities, vowed allegiance to Mosquito Chief Clarence, and called for a return to the status of British protectorate.[8] Temporarily outmaneuvered, Cabezas retreated to the town of Rama on 11 July.

Nicaraguan authorities returned with five hundred soldiers on 3 August, with explicit consent and military backing from the United States, and reestablished control of Bluefields. Over the next few months Zelaya's government embarked with fervor on the task of national integration. He renamed the vast Atlantic Coast region as the "Department of Zelaya" (see Figure 1), made Cabezas the first governor, sent Mosquito Chief Clarence into exile, and formed a municipal government in Bluefields composed of residents (mainly foreigners) amenable to annexation. The crucial step, however, was to achieve the Miskitu Indians' "voluntary incorporation" into the Nicaraguan nation-state, thereby relieving Britain of all prior treaty obligations. Cabezas arranged for this culminating act during September and October, summoning Miskitu headmen from throughout the Atlantic

Coast. On 20 November about eighty Miskitu delegates concluded a three-day convention in Bluefields by signing a "Decree of Reincorporation."

This "Mosquito Convention" is the critical event of the first historical moment. Under what conditions did the Miskitu delegates attend the convention and sign the decree? What exactly did they perceive themselves to be giving up?

Documentary Evidence. Although the annexation did involve coercion and violence in Bluefields, I found no evidence of clashes between Miskitu people and Nicaraguan troops. To summon delegates to the convention, Nicaraguan officials traveled to Miskitu communities in the company of Andrew Hendy, a Miskitu leader from the north. At these meetings, the Nicaraguans laced their rhetoric with promises:

> The [Indians] were to have their own laws and customs and be free
> from taxes; the Government would provide school and church for
> them; their new chief should rule as in olden time from Black
> River (Truxillo) down to Greytown; all of the headmen of villages
> would get a good salary paid every six months.[9]

A British consular official reported that "all sorts of threats and bribery" accompanied these promises, and claimed that most village headmen refused to make the trip, with the result that only twelve of the eighty delegates were legitimate.[10] Yet a large number of Miskitu townspeople went to the convention on their own volition, and the event took place without major disruption. Miskitu communities remained tranquil during 1894, while great turmoil prevailed in Bluefields and other centers of the Creole population.[11]

Accounts of Miskitu alienation from the Mosquito government, like that cited above, are in general highly suspect. Nicaraguan authorities' attempts to convince the Miskitu that they were "slaves" at the hands of the "black usurpers" contained blatantly racist and self-interested hyperbole. At the same time, it is beyond question that Creoles controlled the Mosquito government, and certainly plausible that Miskitu townspeople felt marginalized. For example, this observation by a North American visitor made in 1892, well before the annexation began, though deprecatory toward Indians, was probably less guided by the desire to justify a particular outcome:

The Indian ... cannot comprehend [the machinery of government]
and he hates [it] because he feels the pressure of its iron heel when
he disobeys its regulations. Instead of seeking to control [the
government] by constitutional means, [the Indian] speculates as to
methods for outwitting it, or for crushing it. The negroes, on the
contrary, respond with enthusiasm to the call for conventions ...
and so, when the sense of the meeting is taken, it is found to be
wholly African.... The strife at times reaches a high tension.
(Dekalb 1893: 275)

As for Miskitu delegates' attitudes toward the land question, we have
very little to go on. Before the annexation Miskitu townspeople practiced
subsistence agriculture, hunting, and fishing on lands and in coastal waters
for which they held no legal titles.[12] The petitions of protest against the
annexation, which Miskitu headmen signed, spoke of "this country" in
general terms, emphasizing a form of political rule more than territorial
rights:

God ... has given this country, called the Mosquito country, to us.
So our fathers have been living here from time immemorial. We
have not known any other nation, neither made friend with any
other save the English. They only came to us caring for and
protecting us, and it was out of their hands likewise received we our
King.... Do, we beseech you ... rescue our country out of the
mire.[13]

Most complaints about the annexation focused on the abusive presence of
Nicaraguan troops, fears of increased taxation, and the firm perception of
Nicaraguans as a people "who have not the slightest interest, sympathy, or
good feeling for the inhabitants of the Mosquito Reservation."[14]

The Mosquito Convention therefore presents an interpretive dilemma.
On the one hand, if the delegates vehemently opposed annexation, then
their apparently consensual signing of the Reincorporation Decree and
the relative absence of frontal resistance would be difficult to explain. On
the other hand, if the delegates' actions did involve an element of consent,
then there would be cause to question the vehemence of their opposition
and the severity of the threat to their perceived land rights. The importance of this dilemma becomes evident in light of contemporary memories of the convention.

Contemporary Perspectives.   Mauro Salazar,[15] a man of about eighty, is known in Sandy Bay as the one who remembers most about "king times." He begins by explaining something about the Miskitu king:

> At first there was no king. When Columbia [*sic*] reached Cape Gracias [*a Dios*], only Miskitu and Sumu lived there, no Blacks, no Spaniards.[16] Later on, when the Miskitu crowned a king, England found out. Then there were two: here the Miskitu king, there the English king. Our king ruled this whole area from Roman Bar to San Juan. He lived in Bluefields, had guns and everything. His suit and cap, gifts of the English, glowed like hot coals.

He then accounts for the kingdom's demise:

> Two Spaniards, Ruben Darios and Zelaya, plotted to take over the coast. They came from Leon to Bluefields through the bush. Upon arriving they called the king: ... "You Miskitu are too poor. We want to help you. You do not know how to read, you are ignorant; we'll give you schools, help your poor and widowed, give you all kinds of things. Just give us a chance [to rule] for fifty years, and then we'll return it to you." The king said: "I can't do that; England has not given permission." They kept talking; the Spaniards kept telling lies and took out two bottles of rum. The king drank a little with them. When he went to sleep, they stayed behind, writing a document. In the morning when the king awoke, they said, "You see, you made the deal, you signed when you were drunk." The king claimed he hadn't done it, they argued, and finally the king gave in: "All right, I'll give you fifty years, but when the time is up you have to keep your promise and give the land back."

The fifty years passed a long time ago, Salazar hastens to add, and the "Spaniards" haven't given back the land or fulfilled the promises.

A MISURASATA document written in September 1981 explains the episode in this way:

> In 1894, under the liberal government of J. S. Zelaya, the central town of Bluefields was occupied militarily, the Miskitu authorities were deposed, and this illegal act was announced nationally as the "Reincorporation of the Mosquitia." A convention was held on 4 December of that same year, with communal headmen that soldiers

brought to Bluefields and entertained [*agasajados*] there for a number of days with great quantities of liquor. The Indian headmen were then forced to sign the misnamed "Pledge of Adhesion" of the Moskitia to Nicaragua, and renaming the Moskitia, almost as a bad joke, the Department of Zelaya, in honor of the liberal president. (MISURASATA 1981b; my translation)

The chronology of Miskitu history written by Bernard Nietschmann a few years later basically concurs, though placing more emphasis on resistance and omitting reference to drunkenness.[17]

Nicaraguan military invades Indian territory to "reincorporate" the Miskito, Sumo and Rama and their homelands into the Republic of Nicaragua. Miskitos organize military defense forces, but British-supplied arms are discovered and confiscated. Indian leaders forced to agree to the "reincorporation." (Nietschmann 1985: 10)

Salazar's memory of the event diverges markedly from the MISURASATA rendition on a crucial point. Although both portray the Miskitu as having lost a large amount of territory, the Miskitu king maintains, for Salazar, a certain dignity and righteousness. He refuses the Spaniards' rum and does not unwittingly sign anything. Moreover, Salazar makes no reference to organized Miskitu resistance and does not attribute the king's signing of the decree to brute force. Although cajoled by the Spaniards, the king ultimately signs in return for Nicaraguan promises to help his people. This emphasis on the consensual nature of the accord is especially striking in view of Salazar's ardent support for MISURASATA and the antigovernment mobilization of the post-1979 period.

Salazar's account tends to reinforce my view that historical accounts of the convention have too fully embraced the conclusion that the Nicaraguans achieved consent through brute force and trickery. Miskitu village headmen evidently mistrusted the Nicaraguans, and had much to fear from the annexation. Yet they had countervailing sentiments as well: a sense of exclusion from the Creole-dominated Mosquito government, which surely increased their receptivity to Nicaraguan promises. Perhaps Cabezas's tactics created a prior selection process, whereby only those delegates more receptive to the annexation ended up attending. Then the two explanations would be at least partially reconciled. Even this argument would seem implausible, however, if the delegates understood themselves to be signing away territorial rights to land and resources. I suspect that such

rights simply were not a salient issue in 1894, so long as the resources necessary for Miskitu subsistence activities were not threatened. Miskitu delegates to the convention, I suggest, endorsed the decree in return for Nicaraguan promises, giving away land in excess of what they used, for which
they had no need, and political control of the Mosquito government, which
they perceived already to have lost.

What, then, of Salazar's memory that the king signed away rights to
the land? If my historical argument is correct, this part of his narrative
came about more recently. As explained below, MISURASATA's post-
1981 territorial demands generated great popular support among Miskitu
community members. Since the post-1981 mobilization revolved around
territorial rights, Salazar could have revised his memory to make territory
(in addition to autonomous political rule) central to what the Miskitu king
had given away.[18] On the basis of evidence available, it would be a mistake
to assume that rights to control over territory in the contemporary sense
formed part of Miskitu people's consciousness in 1894.

The Achievement of Community Land Titles (1911–15)

If some Miskitu did indeed decide to test Nicaraguan promises in 1894, it
took only a short time for widespread disillusionment to set in. Nicaraguan government officials fulfilled none of their commitments; burdened
the Indians heavily with taxes and an abusive military presence; and, perhaps most importantly, posed serious threats to Indians' subsistence plots.
Petty government officials, whose salaries came from Managua irregularly
if at all, plundered Indian lands as a means to secure their own livelihood.
The procedure by which Indians could acquire legal titles involved a petition to these same abusive government officials, tipping them off as to
lands that were prime for usurpation. British authorities in Bluefields received visits "almost daily" from delegations of Indians and Creoles, who
presented complaints and petitioned for the Crown's assistance.[19]

Hoping to withdraw definitively from prior treaty obligations and to
end this deluge of petitions, Britain negotiated the Harrison-Altamirano
Treaty with Nicaragua. Ratified in 1906, the treaty affirmed full Nicaraguan sovereignty over the Atlantic Coast and reaffirmed the procedure for
the legal recognition of Creole and Indian lands. However, since abuses

continued (indeed increased) after 1906 and virtually no titles were granted, the treaty only dragged Britain further into the controversy.[20] The British consul in Bluefields urged a more active role for his government, on the premise that "the Indians harbour the deepest distrust of all Nicaraguans, and for the present could not be persuaded to deal directly with any [Nicaraguan] lawyer.[21] The Foreign Office consented reluctantly in 1914, and sent veteran diplomat H. O. Chalkley to revive and coordinate efforts of the Land Titles Commission (Comisión tituladora).

With Chalkley publicly in charge, Indians responded to the commission with a groundswell of enthusiasm, in contrast to the previous eight years. Miskitu from communities throughout the Atlantic Coast sent delegations to Bluefields to meet with Chalkley. On his request, headmen carried out detailed censuses and collected contributions from each adult community member to defray the cost of lawyers' and surveyors' fees. The Miskitu assigned great importance to Chalkley's involvement, interpreting it as a sign that Britain finally had decided to intervene on their behalf, perhaps even to reinstate the Mosquito government under British protection. When Chalkley tried to correct these misconceptions, community members responded with "unconcealed disappointment and some incredulity."[22] By early 1916, the commission had surveyed and granted some thirty collective titles, which guaranteed community lands for all Indians who lived inside the boundaries of the old Mosquito Reserve.[23] Everything outside these demarcations became known as "national lands" and fell under the exclusive jurisdiction of the state.

Here lies the crux of this second historical moment. How did Miskitu people view the community land–titling process? Did it constitute, in their perceptions, a violation of "territorial sovereignty"? An undesirable but necessary compromise? A proper validation of their rights? The question is especially relevant given the tiny amount of land included in the community titles—eight *manzanas* per family of four—and the commission's explicit designation of all territory outside these community plots as "national lands."[24]

Documentary Evidence from Sandy Bay.   Soon after Chalkley arrived, Sandy Bay headman Benito Rodriguez traveled to Bluefields to discuss his claim on behalf of 144 families from Sandy Bay and three other Río Grande District communities. At first they claimed "lands at thirty different places, mostly *vega*," which added up to less total land than the treaty allotted.[25] Chalkley opposed the individual claims, arguing that it "would be much simpler if [everyone] could apply for one or two large areas ... in order to avoid a large number of small surveys." Advised of this concern, and of the further condition that the claim not run into "conflict with others who have already obtained titles to lands [in] the vicinity," Rodriguez and representatives of the three neighboring communities resubmitted a collective claim.[26] They asked for "2,000 hectares ... between Mairin Laya and Plantingni creeks ... bordered on all four sides by national lands," and 2,000 hectares grazing land (see Figure 2).[27] By May of the next year Sandy Bay's title — for a total of 4,000 hectares — was recorded in the Bluefields Civil Registry.

Contemporary Perspectives. Sandy Bay Miskitu vividly remember these events and substantiate their memories with reference to documents presently in their possession. Says Simon Gonzales:

> The English king said to the Miskitu king, "You know what? We'll take over your land. I'll give you money, or anything you want for it." The Miskitu king said no. He wanted nothing other than the land, and a formal title to back up his claim. This title, the [Miskitu] king said, would be a source of strength for his people. When England heard this, she agreed, handing over the title with signature and all. Each community received one.

Manuel Rodriguez describes the same event from the perspective of community history:[28]

> [Then] the treaty was calling all the community [to] come in to Bluefields, come make a title. Benito Rodriguez him is the first man come Sandy Bay, [so he] collect some eggs, and people them give him some chicken, like that, and come walk from Sandy Bay to Tasbapauni, and then from Tasbapauni get dory and come to Bluefields ... and make out that title.

Successive village headmen took responsibility for guarding documents that emerged from this process, and especially the title itself, which people described to me as a map drawn on special paper, with a British seal, showing the precise boundaries of their community lands.[29] In efforts to assert his authority or to drive home a key point during community meetings, Headman Rodriguez often brandished these documents, reread parts of them, and recounted his grandfather's key role in achieving community

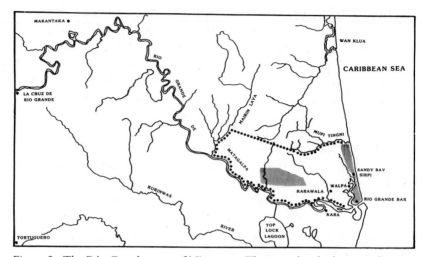

Figure 2. The Río Grande zone of Nicaragua. The cross-hatched areas indicate land included in the community land title granted to Sandy Bay Sirpi, Río Grande Bar, Walpa, and Insinkita in 1916. The total area is 4,000 hectares (40 square kilometers). The dotted line marks the domain of community land rights according to popular conceptions among the Sandy Bay Sirpi in 1985–87; it has an estimated total area of 307 square kilometers.

land rights. Although opinions of Rodriguez varied, townspeople assigned the utmost significance to the land title, to the rights it conferred, and to historic ties with Great Britain for which it provided tangible evidence.

MISURASATA offers a contrasting rendition of the land titles episode:

> The British Empire reached an agreement with the Nicaraguan government, called the Harrison-Altamirano treaty, which constituted a radical and violent disruption of the rights of territorial possession of the Indian peoples and communities. It reduced the land to eight *manzanas* per family, leaving [land rights] nothing more than an appendage of Anglo-Saxon and French-Roman law based in private property.... The concept of national land ... is incompatible with the millennarian territorial rights of the Indian peoples and communities. (Unpublished communiqué, 28 July 1981: 11)

According to Nietschmann, "Great Britain gave to Nicaragua something it didn't have—sovereignty over Indian nations" (1985: 10). His chronology states:

Late 1800s. British survey Indian and Creole lands and present
written title and cadastral map to each community.... *1905.*
Harrison Altamirano Treaty. Nicaragua promises to recognize
Indian and Creole land titles.

That Nietschmann got the date of the land survey wrong is unimpor-
tant.[30] The omission of reference to what Indians thought about these
community land titles, however, is crucial. For Sandy Bay people, the titles
are a highly charged symbol of community rights, and of a historic process that they remember and recount with the utmost enthusiasm. For
MISURASATA, in contrast, the Land Titles Commission spelled the demise of the legal-historical basis for territorial demands. Once Indian rights
were delimited to communities, their claims to the vast areas lying between these community lands lost their legal viability.

The historical evidence provided above adds a fascinating twist to this
disparity. It appears that before 1915 Sandy Bay Miskitu did not think in
terms of community-based land rights. This is the only way to explain why
Headman Rodriguez presented an initial claim for thirty *individual* plots
(probably corresponding to thirty kin-based work groups). When Sandy
Bay Miskitu mobilized to protect a preexisting notion of subsistence land
holdings, the cost-conscious British consul, by urging a single collective
claim, may actually have introduced the concept of community ownership. At the same time, conflicts with an oppressive central government
gave prominence to Miskitu demands for a return to the Mosquito kingdom. For this to occur, memories of Creole dominance must have faded,
allowing the kingdom to conjure up images of political autonomy, freedom from taxes, and the absence of abusive government officials—the most
pressing Miskitu demands. The content of these demands would subsequently change, but the return to a Miskitu-controlled government on
the Atlantic Coast would remain a potent and unifying source of political
imagery.

"Company Times," 1890–1940

Foreign lumber companies operated along the Río Grande during the
1890s, hiring local wage labor to cut enormous quantities of mahogany
and other valuable hardwoods. Banana production soon followed, reach-
ing the Río Grande by the first years after 1900. Over the next three

decades, United Fruit, Cuyamel Fruit, and at least three smaller foreign companies worked the Río Grande, with local offices at the river mouth town of Río Grande Bar, three miles south of Sandy Bay. At its height in the 1920s Cuyamel ran a cluster of enormous plantations near the upriver town of El Gallo, with some five thousand hectares in cultivation and three thousand salaried workers (Araya Pochet 1979: 30). With the onset of the Great Depression major enterprises pulled out of the Río Grande area, leaving the Kukra Development Company to continue operations on a reduced scale until 1940, when a hurricane destroyed its installations. Kukra never rebuilt after the hurricane, and Río Grande banana production abruptly ended.

How did Sandy Bay people respond to this company presence in their vicinity? Did they claim to have rights to the lands and resources that the companies exploited, or were their conceptions of land rights commensurate with the rather small plots of subsistence lands which the companies left in their hands?

Documentary Evidence.   During the banana boom, foreign capitalists had no trouble acquiring vast land concessions — at times in the millions of acres — despite the presence of Indian communities.[31] On the Río Grande, the banana enterprises followed a diversified production strategy: running large plantations with wage laborers and buying the fruit on contract from small-scale independent growers. Consequently, while the boom lasted the banks of the lower Río Grande were lined with small banana farms operated by townspeople from Sandy Bay and other nearby communities. Although Sandy Bay Miskitu already had these farms planted in 1915 when the land titles process began, the rich riverbank lands were not included in their community title.[32] It appears that the companies had already spoken for these lands, and gave Miskitu only temporary usufruct rights in return for a production commitment.[33] Scraps of evidence from episodes of land titling point to perceptions of this tension; in one case a village headman urged haste in getting the title approved, because "the companies are coming down upon us."[34] There also is at least one account of unrest and violent conflict between company owners and wage workers, although the latter appear to have been mainly Creole and mestizo rather than Miskitu.[35] In general, however, Miskitu reactions to the companies' presence seem to have been neutral to positive, and certainly did not include extensive frontal resistance.

Contemporary Perspectives. Sandy Bay people have good memories of "company times" when the *miriki nani* (North Americans) worked on the Atlantic Coast. David Lora provides a typical account:

> Things were good in the company times. People had money, lumber, everything, and everyone had work, every day. We never ran short of food; the store shelves were full of rice, beans, lard ... and we had money from all the work. Americans had good manners, respectful. They would talk to us, just like you and I right now, never cussing or speaking sharply. And if you worked well, they paid you well. Previously people had been ignorant; with no companies, who were they supposed to learn from? But with the companies, we began to learn all kinds of things (mechanics, driver, everything).... The Americans don't like the Spaniards, whom they call "Greasers." ... We all talk the same language, but the Americans don't speak Spanish.[36]

The MISURASATA interpretation of company presence on the Atlantic Coast is critical mainly of the "Spanish" central government:

> The depredation of our territories that began in 1905 continued throughout the Somoza period, as the government made concessions to the foreign companies for the exploitation of minerals and precious lumber. Although these resources lay inside the Indian lands, we did not even receive a percentage of the profits from the exploitation. (1981a: 12)

Nietschmann's chronology concurs:

> *1900s–1950s.* Nicaragua attempts to indirectly control and profit from Indian Nations by allowing foreign companies to extract Indian gold, timber and sea resources. (1985: 10)

Theodore MacDonald, another MISURASATA-aligned analyst, offers a somewhat different analysis. Acknowledging that Miskitu townspeople actually favored North American company presence, he accounts for these attitudes by arguing that the Miskitu had a "moral economy," which focused on the "security and economic independence" of subsistence agriculture (1988: 121), and led them to ask "What is left?" rather than "How much is taken?" (114).[37] Since the companies left their subsistence economy "largely intact," and caused "no major disruption of Indian life," Miskitu approved of company presence, and viewed the access to wage labor and consumer goods as an unmitigated benefit.

Differences between the MISURASATA rendition and grassroots Miskitu memories of this period are again crucial. With the exception of Mac-Donald, the MISURASATA portrayal emphasizes the companies' exploitative presence, and leaves the impression that Miskitu townspeople opposed it as such. Sandy Bay Miskitu, in contrast, have nothing but praise for both the companies, and for American presence in general. It is not hard to imagine why MISURASATA discourse omits these grassroots perceptions. The assertion that Miskitu people are a nation with a history of fierce resistance to threats on their sovereign national territory runs aground in light of ethnographic reports, before and after 1979, that Miskitu yearned for the companies' return, and viewed white North Americans in such positive terms.[38]

MacDonald's argument is significant in its effort to reconcile the MISURASATA epistemology with grassroots consciousness. If procompany sentiments actually grew out of a preexisting and thoroughly "Indian" cultural ethic, as MacDonald suggests, then the MISURASATA position avoids contradiction. However, this solution raises a new problem. If the Miskitus' "moral economy" focused solely on "subsistence lands," then they could not have espoused a consciousness of *territorial* rights. In an effort to elude this problem as well, MacDonald asserts both arguments at once. The definition of the Miskitu moral economy, he explains, also "transcends mere subsistence" to include "broad religious concepts of land" and "aboriginal claims to ... land and resources" (1988: 114). This brings us back to the original question: why that second feature of the "moral economy" did not bring the Miskitu into conflict with the companies, we are not told.

I suspect that townspeople's glowing contemporary memories of "company days" have a firm basis in their experiences at that time. The terms on which Sandy Bay Miskitu were drawn into banana production, while highly exploitive from the perspective of company profits, allowed them unprecedented access to cash and quickly established their addiction to imported consumer goods. While the boom lasted, they feasted on flour, oil, rice, beans, tobacco, and sugar, and supplemented these activities with subsistence production of cassava, coconuts, and sea turtles as needed.

This explanation could hold, however, only if MacDonald's second element of the Miskitu "moral economy" turns out to be a retrospective invention. Company presence did not evoke strong negative response, I suggest, because the companies worked on lands that Miskitu people did not have in use and did not consider as territory that they had the right or the need to control.[39]

Contemporary Roots of the MISURASATA Mobilization, 1940–81

The departure of the U.S. companies from the Atlantic Coast drove the region into severe economic depression. Small amounts of foreign capital continued to operate in forestry, mining, and agriculture, but for the most part Miskitu townspeople were forced to return to subsistence and petty commodity production. By the 1960s the Nicaraguan state began to make its presence felt in the region. With the help of international funds, especially plentiful because of the Alliance for Progress, the Somoza state invested in infrastructure, social works, and productive enterprises, which partially revived the ailing economy but also accentuated interethnic tensions. Miskitu people began to organize, first in agricultural cooperatives, then in an organization called ALPROMISU, to defend their rights as Indians. ALPROMISU took a cautious approach to the land demands, focusing attention on the Indian communities that did have formal titles, and remaining silent on the question of territorial autonomy.[40]

Soon after the Sandinistas came to power, ALPROMISU changed its name to MISURASATA and received full government recognition.[41] The organization quickly achieved an immense grassroots following among Miskitu throughout the coast, and MISURASATA leaders, buoyed by their ascendant political power, made escalating demands on the central government in the areas of cultural, political, and economic rights. By mid-1980, when relations between MISURASATA and the government were tense but still functional, land had become a key issue of contention. In a formal agreement signed in August 1980, the two sides coincided on one fundamental principle: Indians had inalienable rights to their traditional community lands.[42] Yet this agreement contained a fundamental ambiguity that eventually became the focus of controversy. If the community lands, once established, did not turn out to be contiguous, this left an area in between, known under the existing arrangement as national land, with an ill-defined and contested legal status.

Leaving the ambiguity unaddressed, both parties simply agreed that MISURASATA would present a proposal demarcating the boundaries of all Indian community lands on the coast, which would then provide the basis for negotiations toward their legal recognition. An extraordinary mobilization followed. MISURASATA leaders traveled throughout the coast, held meetings in every community, and explained that now, finally, Indians would achieve their full historic rights to the land. The leaders also convinced communities to part with their coveted land maps, to provide legal backing for the claim, and commissioned a study of the legal history of Indian land rights on the Atlantic Coast.[43] Plans to present the conclusions of these efforts in a large public gathering in Puerto Cabezas in February 1981 were never carried out. Just before that gathering, Sandinista security forces arrested MISURASATA leaders, and accused them of promoting "separatism." Although the leaders were soon released, subsequent Miskitu-government relations rapidly deteriorated. Within less than a year Miskitu townspeople by the hundreds, and nearly every MISURASATA leader, had turned to armed struggle.

Sandy Bay Perspectives.   In 1985–87, when I asked Sandy Bay townspeople to specify the boundaries of their community lands, they spoke enthusiastically about the land granted to them by the original 1916 title. Yet when they proceeded to specify that land, they described an area eight times larger than what had been legally stipulated (see Figure 2). No one seemed concerned about the discrepancy. Since 1916, as the community's population grew and the people put more land into use, the boundaries of their communal land rights grew accordingly. The title remained an important validating symbol of community identity and rights, although its actual legal content had long since been forgotten or actively ignored.

When asked about the land question in the context of the MISURASATA mobilization, the responses of the Sandy Bay townspeople focused on territorial rather than community rights. Those who were directly involved in the mobilization, like Simon Gonzales, knew the precise boundaries of that territory, and details of how MISURASATA arrived at the claim:

[MISURASATA leader] Steadman [Fagoth] and the others were waiting for the government to fulfill its promise. The government told them, "If you know where your land is, give us the measurements." Since we have no professional surveyor, Steadman asked a Salvadoran named Mauricio Polanco to help. After much work, they established the boundaries: from Santo Tomás to Yakal Pahani, near the mines; from San Juan to Cape Gracias, on the border with Honduras. Just as they finished, Polanco drowned. We all contributed to his memorial fund, but his mother said she wanted no money. She only wanted the Indians to have their freedom.

Gonzales goes on to explain what happened with the claim, expressing the views of many in Sandy Bay:

Then the Sandinistas came to sign the land document. But when they saw the measurements they were shocked: "In the Pacific we don't have anything, just a little cotton and coffee." All the riches are on the Coast, you know, gold, lobster, oil. The Sandinistas changed their minds because they didn't want to give up these riches.

When the Sandinistas "changed their minds," townspeople explain, all this "war trouble" began.

MISURASATA discourse on the land question underwent a radical change around the time of the February 1981 arrests. Leaders began to refer to Indian peoples as nations (*naciones*) rather than ethnic groups (*étnias*), claimed that the "right of Indian nations to the territory of its communities overrides the right of states," and, most importantly, firmly rejected the idea of *community* land rights in favor of a demarcated *territory* within which they would exercise their "aboriginal rights" to "self-determination." Their proposed territorial boundaries included every Indian community of the Atlantic Coast and encompassed an immense area totaling 45,407 square kilometers (see Figure 1).[44] The commissioned legal-historical study substantiated this claim by contesting the very concept of "national lands" and negating the validity of all treaties signed in the coast's history, for lack of Indian participation.[45]

Simultaneously, these leaders and analysts elaborated on other facets of Miskitu history. They emphasized a continuous history of resistance, in defense of *wan tasbaya,* by peoples who "have never lost sovereignty over their nations by means of any treaty of cession or by conquest." Within these "Indian nations," by one account, "there is a natural correspondence of society, culture, and politics," which makes them peace-loving, in contrast to non-Indian states, which have similarly "natural" tendencies toward expansion and usurpation of aboriginal lands (Nietschmann 1985: 10). The peoples of the Atlantic Coast, another document states, "live in harmony." Their "traditional territory is *Yapti Tasba* (Mother Earth), which was passed to them over millennia from their ancestors." The term *Yapti Tasba* connotes a cosmology, entailing "broad religious concepts of land" similar to those of other Indian peoples throughout the Americas, which has guided Miskitu political consciousness and action for at least a century (MacDonald 1988: 114, 122–23). Finally, these descriptions always extol the virtues of Miskitu Indian "subsistence life":

> We fish and hunt to eat, not to destroy. This is why we must secure our territory.... We do things in the normal, natural way, in small amounts, on a small scale.... For us, it is a constant and widely held value to consider the land and the natural elements as the most important thing.... Our villages have no electricity, no running water. None of them.... The Indian life ... is a hard one. But it is ours, and we love it. The subsistence life. The values of that life. We, as Indians, love it. (Wiggins 1981: 7–8)[46]

The escalating Miskitu-Sandinista conflict has been analyzed extensively elsewhere from a variety of perspectives, which need not be summarized here. I want to suggest merely that specific consideration of the land question brings another factor, largely unexamined, into focus. Having assembled community land maps and other legal documents from village headmen throughout the coast, MISURASATA leaders must have been shocked by the implications. In strictly legal terms they had rights only to community lands, a tiny portion of the Atlantic Coast's total territory, even less than the area they currently held by tradition and usufruct.[47] Unlike Native Americans of North America, whose negotiated treaty rights — though patently exploitive and unjust — had provided the basis for subsequent political struggles, the Miskitu had no legal-historical leg to stand on. This discovery surely influenced the leaders' decision to jettison the notion of community lands altogether and to opt for a new definition. If Miskitu people were a "nation" with national rights to a unified territory, then the whole question of community lands became irrelevant or, at most, a detail to be worked out once the territory was secured.

An Indian nationalist discourse already existed, with a sophisticated historical and theoretical grounding, a long experience of political struggle, and a strong constituency among liberal-left sectors in the United States and Western Europe. However, it needed to be adapted to the specificities of the Miskitu case. Beginning in 1981, MISURASATA analysts applied themselves to this task, "reinventing" Miskitu history and identity, making Miskitu territorial rights appear to emerge from time immemorial and from immutable features of Miskitu culture. At the grassroots level, Miskitu had no problem assimilating that redefinition of land rights. As Sandy Bay people often explain, "some of our leaders from the north became educated and found out the true extent of our rights." Before MISURASATA, they add, "we were blind, but now we understand." Indeed, Miskitu townspeople responded with an enthusiasm bordering on euphoria, upon hearing of vast claims that MISURASATA "discovered" now belonged to the Indians, which the government had "promised" to turn over.

Yet other details of the leaders' discourse never made an impact on the community level—eulogies to the subsistence way of life,[48] the repudiation of Western culture and technology, and the unambivalent identity of Miskitu "nationhood," to name a few. Even the notion of territorial land rights did not completely replace the previous one. Sandy Bay townspeople retained the idea that they "owned" whatever they used, and fused this with the newer (post-1915) idea that the land in use for subsistence and petty-commodity production belonged to the whole community. This hybrid notion of land rights—community based but much beyond what they legally owned—prevailed when the Sandinista Front for National Liberation (FSLN) came to power in 1979. In the course of the post-1979 mobilization, the MISURASATA leaders' notion of a "national territory" became yet another facet of local understandings of "land rights." Grassroots consciousness thus remained complex and polysemic, reflecting an accumulation of experiences over the previous century.

Conclusions

First and foremost, I hope to have shown that the meaning Miskitu people have attached to land rights since 1894 has undergone cumulative change.

Under the Mosquito government, they assigned importance to the land that kin-based work groups used in the course of subsistence activities. The notion of communal lands came into existence in the 1910s, when townspeople mobilized to defend these use rights, threatened by the abuse and usurpation of Nicaraguan government officials. This definition of "communal lands," though at first associated with the area stipulated by the community titles, gradually expanded to remain commensurate with the lands that community members used on a regular basis. The community-based notion of land rights persisted until MISURASATA's programmatic shift of 1981. Only then did Miskitu townspeople begin to make an explicit association between themselves as a people and the demand for territorial sovereignty.

Second, this analysis brings into relief the differences between leaders' discourse and grassroots consciousness within the antigovernment mobilization. These differences did not add up to incompatibilities; rather they are best understood, paradoxically, as contrasting tendencies toward heterogeneity and reductionism. Miskitu community members espoused a complex and multifaceted notion of land rights, in contrast to the MISURASATA leaders, who attempted to promote a single, internally coherent, and unified discourse to express and advance their struggle. By portraying Miskitu land rights as emerging from an original state, unchanged since time immemorial, these leaders' discourse obscured the historical conditions of its own emergence. It rested on a series of stark dichotomies that placed Indians inherently at odds with their adversary: aboriginal rights versus territorial sovereignty of the nation-state, a cosmology of harmony with nature versus the state's ideology of acquisitive development, and, ultimately, Indian versus Western culture. Miskitu community members fully and enthusiastically supported the mobilization, but stopped short of taking on the leaders' discourse exclusively as their own.

Many Sandinista-aligned analysts have attempted to link these two conclusions with a broader critique, which casts doubt on the validity of the MISURASATA political project (Jenkins 1986; Vilas 1989). The quotation from Jenkins that serves as the epigraph for this essay is indicative: the extensive claims of territory and nationhood are obviously fabricated and patently absurd, he implies, when juxtaposed to the (real, historically grounded) prerogatives of the Nicaraguan nation-state. Such a line of

argument, quite apart from its dubious political merits, is exceedingly vulnerable to counteranalysis. If Miskitu people came to fully endorse the
MISURASATA discourse as an accurate (if incomplete) version of their
history, identity, and rights, considerations regarding its social construction
would hardly seem to matter. As we have learned from Benedict Anderson (1983), all protonationalist and nationalist movements arise from the
discourse of an "imagined community," which relies on essentialized and
reconstructed notions of history.

Far from an act of delegitimation, my analysis affirms that the
MISURASATA discourse became a powerful catalyst and unifying banner
for mobilization, in large part because it represented Miskitu people's
hopes to ameliorate longstanding conditions of cultural oppression and
political economic inequity. From this it follows that the same broad conclusion applies to the Sandinista narrative as well: both were highly politicized social constructions of the past, effective in mobilizing a particular
constituency, but historically constituted in ways that placed them in
direct contradiction with one another.

At the same time, I hasten to disassociate this dual assertion from an
exclusive emphasis on social construction, which is apt to end up stuck in
the quagmire of cultural relativism. Such a stance would leave the Miskitu-
Sandinista conflict portrayed as little more than a battle of discourses; by
relativizing the oppression that afflicts subordinated people, it tends to un-
dermine their claims to vindication.[49] The challenge, then, is to arrive at a
theoretical position that, to use the formulation of Donna Haraway, can
"simultaneously [provide] an account of radical historical contingency for
all knowledge claims and knowing subjects ... *and* a no-nonsense commitment to faithful accounts of a 'real' world" (1988: 579; emphasis in
original). Haraway's effort to achieve this balance begins, significantly, with
a vigorous critique of cultural relativism; she calls instead for vision from
the standpoint of "subjugated" peoples, and a privileging of their forms of
knowledge. In this way, she can advance a (provisional) claim to objectivity,
based on these real political alignments, and more importantly, on the subjugated groups' real potential for generating transformative knowledge,
"potent for constructing worlds less organized by axes of domination"
(1988: 585–86).

Haraway's "new metaphor" of subjugated knowledge is not without
ambiguities, two of which become evident when applied to the Miskitu-

Sandinista conflict. First, in the conflict over land rights in Nicaragua, there was no single "subjugated standpoint" with which to align. MISURASATA leaders contested "oppression" by the Nicaraguan state, which clearly is a more powerful entity. Yet the Sandinistas were engaged in a struggle for self-determination against a U.S.-created surrogate army, a herculean effort to assert their own "subjugated standpoint," to challenge the powerful logic of U.S. imperialism. To complicate matters further, MISURASATA leaders were deeply dependent on U.S. funds and material for their own struggle.[50] Second, as Haraway acknowledges, alignment with the "subjugated standpoint" must not be romanticized or uncritical but, rather, must be subjected to "critical reexamination, decoding, deconstruction, and interpretation" (1988: 584). Yet it is difficult to conceive of how this critical endeavor proceeds without a noncontingent analytical grounding, without some basis to distinguish "transformative" knowledge from that which merits critique. These ambiguities notwithstanding, Haraway's provisional solution may well be the best available, short of a reintroduction of an objectivist analytical premise that runs against the entire thrust of this volume's inquiry into the politics of memory.

Another crucial feature of Haraway's "new metaphor" is that it directs our attention back to the terrain of practical politics. To follow that mandate, I want to conclude by pointing very briefly to how this analysis speaks to events since the Sandinista electoral loss of 1990. Both my specific emphasis on differences between leaders and base, and broader observation regarding the constant change in meanings attached to the land, have been dramatically borne out in the present era. Who would have imagined, for example, that Brooklyn Rivera, the MISURASATA leader who most vehemently promoted the idea of Miskitu people as a "nation" with "sovereign rights to a territory," would be working in the cabinet of a central government explicitly opposed to the principles of autonomy? At the community level, Miskitu people appear to be torn between loyalty for Rivera and locally defined interests that dictate support for autonomy and opposition to all those—Rivera included—who stand in its way. Thus in the period since the elections, perhaps more markedly than ever before, grassroots Miskitu consciousness has remained polysemic, combining conclusions drawn from a "successful" struggle for autonomy in the Sandinista era with a partial endorsement of much less militant ideas about ethnic rights, which have gained currency since the Sandinista defeat.

This multiple stance toward the land, indeed toward the entire question of indigenous rights, presents autonomy with an enormous challenge. If Miskitu people's ethnic militancy, so evident during the previous era, continues to dissipate, this promising experiment in self-government could easily fail.[51] The consolidation, indeed the survival, of their autonomy today awaits the emergence of a political organization and discourse that draw on existing elements in the grassroots Miskitu consciousness and combine them with newly developed notions of support for democratically elected and multiethnic autonomous government. It depends on a discourse that could capture Miskitu people's political imagination with the same mobilizing force as did MISURASATA leaders when, for a brief moment, the collective struggles and aspirations of an entire people were expressed in a single phrase: "wan tasbaya dukiara."

Notes

I am grateful for comments on previous drafts of this article from Orin Starn, Jean Jackson, Martin Diskin, Galio Gurdian, Carlos Castro, Charles A. Hale, Richard N. Adams, Edmund T. Gordon, and the members of two workshops on "Space, Time, and the Politics of Memory" sponsored by the Social Science Research Council and the John D. and Catherine T. MacArthur Foundation. Support for research and writing came from the National Science Foundation, the H. F. Guggenheim Foundation, and the SSRC-MacArthur Program in International Peace and Security.

1. The quotation is from the preface to an anonymous chronology collected by Menzies (1985: 1–10). The same chronology is reported by Bernard Nietschmann (1985: 10).

2. MISURASATA is an acronym that stands for "MIskitu, SUmu, RAma, and Sandinista Asla TAkanka (working together)." At that time, it was one of two major Miskitu organizations in arms against the government. The second organization, MISURA, had its base of operations farther to the north.

3. For a more extended version of this argument, see Hale (1994, chap. 4). While the Sandinista narrative changed somewhat with the advent of autonomy, the original premises proved to be highly resilient.

4. As the analysis moves closer to the present, these two lines of inquiry begin to merge. Since the antigovernment mobilization was ongoing and still inconclusive in 1986, when people (leaders and community members) talked about the movement they also defined and changed it. There could be no clear distinction between what happened in this fourth moment and how people represented these events.

5. One of the noteworthy features of this conflict is that the distinction between "objective analyst" and "political activist," dubious in any case, became blurred beyond recognition. White academics such as Bernard Nietschmann and Theodore MacDonald became deeply engaged in the conflict as advisors to MISURASATA and wrote articles both of an "academic" and an explicitly partisan nature. Native American intellectual-activists such as

John Mohawk (1982), James Anaya, Ward Churchill, and Russell Means also played important roles in support of MISURASATA.

6. Cited in Cuadra Chamorro (1944: 11–13) from a statement by Carlos Alberto Lacayo, an official of the Zelaya government, made shortly after the occupation of Bluefields.

7. Britain's principal concern was to make a graceful exit from existing treaty obligations to the Mosquito government (Bayard to Gresham, 22 December 1894, in papers relating to the affairs of Bluefields, published in *Congressional Record* 1895 (53rd Cong., 3d sess., 5 January 1895).

8. Braida to Uhl, 18 July 1894; O'Neil to Herbert, 9 July 1894, 25 July 1894; in *Congressional Record* 1895. *Diario nacional* 1895: 6 January 1895, no. 57: 2.

9. A white Moravian missionary described the promises after a visit to the "country stations." Although he qualifies them as "nonsense," he surely was biased by another element in the Nicaraguans' rhetoric: their qualification of church offerings paid by the Indians, and the pious Moravian code of moral conduct, as "oppression." (*Periodical Accounts* 2:468).

10. Harrison to the earl of Kimberly (16 March 1895, 20 April 1895), both reprinted in Wunderich and Rossbach 1990 (411–24).

11. Although Moravian missionaries initially described Indians as "exceedingly angry" (*Periodical Accounts* 2:322), they reversed this conclusion later on. In September 1894, the Moravian superintendent visited all ten mission stations and reported "that in comparison with Bluefields and Magdala (Pearl Lagoon), [the Miskitu Indians] had scarcely felt the effects of the Nicaraguan occupation of their territory" (2:468). The station diary from the community of Yulu (Moravian Archives, Bethlehem, Pennsylvania) records daily happenings of the community during 1894 in great detail. Although it refers to the "frightful news ... of the taking of Bluefields by the Spaniards," there is no mention of Miskitu resistance or even intent to resist.

12. Their lack of titles was observed explicitly by the British involved in the land titles episode, described in the next section. The Mosquito government granted titles to foreigners and some Creoles but not to Indians (Chalkley [Bluefields] to Young [Guatemala], 17 November 1915, in Crowdell Papers).

13. Headmen to British Commander Stuart, 31 July 1894 (Wunderich and Rossbach 1990: 386).

14. Robert Henry Clarence to Queen Victoria, 8 March 1894 (Wunderich and Rossbach 1990: 367–69).

15. All community members have been given pseudonyms.

16. In the remainder of this essay I use the term "Spaniards" when attempting to evoke the way Miskitu talked or thought about Spanish-speaking Nicaraguans.

17. Although the drunkenness argument is typical of many accounts of the convention, one can understand why Nietschmann omitted it from his chronology. For examples of accounts in which it is included, see one "pro-British" observer, cited in Wunderich and Rossbach (1985: 43), and a Creole/Miskitu petition: Indians and Creoles of the Moskito Reserve to U.S. Secretary of State Charles Evans Hughes (7 March 1924; State 1910–29, roll 94).

18. Bernard Nietschmann traveled the Atlantic Coast in the early 1970s, asking people about their memories of the nineteenth century, and reports in at least one case that the "collective historical perspective [of people Kuamwatla, a Miskitu community near Sandy Bay] seemed to go back no further than the 1920s and 1930s when foreign missionaries and businesses began to expand into the area. [We] were seeking a point in their history which had long been erased by a new ideology and economics" (1979: 53). This supports my assertion that people had less vivid and less politicized memories of the kingship before the

MISURASATA mobilization, and that the image of the king giving away a vast portion of territory is a recent addition to their collective memory.

19. These complaints, hand-written in Creole English, form part of the Crowdell Papers, located in the Bluefields archives of CIDCA, the Center for Research and Documentation on the Atlantic Coast.

20. Creoles from Bluefields and Pearl Lagoon did present some claims, mainly for urban lots, during this period. For purposes of brevity, the discussion of the land question that follows refers exclusively to Indians.

21. Chalkley (Bluefields) to Cardens (Guatemala), 27 May 1911 (Crowdell Papers).

22. Young (Guatemala) to Grey (Foreign Office), 17 March 1915 (Crowdell Papers). A similar sentiment is recorded in Oliver Thomas to H. O. Chalkley, 22 October 1915 (Crowdell Papers).

23. See Figure 1. Indians outside those boundaries had no recourse to the commission, and went without land titles until the 1960s.

24. One *manzana* is equal to 0.7 hectares or 1.7 acres. The 1905 treaty stipulates eight *manzanas* per family of four and two *manzanas* for each additional family member. The land measurements and final allotment, however, are recorded in hectares. When the British took over the titling process, they probably substituted the measurement with which they were most familiar.

25. Undated memorandum to the Foreign Office from the Land Titles Commission (Crowdell Papers). *Vega* is a Spanish term, which I assume refers to the strip of land just inside the beach.

26. Chalkley to Hooker, 25 October 1915; Hooker to Chalkley, 29 October 1915 (Crowdell Papers).

27. Benito Rodriguez et al. to Chalkley, 8 November 1915 (Crowdell Papers).

28. All interviews except this one were taped in Miskitu. In this one Rodriguez spoke in Creole English, of which he has a much better command than most Sandy Bay inhabitants. Transcription of Creole English is a complicated and politically charged problem. For the sake of clarity, I have chosen to use Standard English orthography. However, it should be noted that this method obscures the significant differences in pronunciation between Creole and Standard English.

29. I never saw the map because, as will be explained below, in 1980 the communities turned them over to MISURASATA. However, all the other documents are still in Rodriguez's possession.

30. Given Simon Gonzales's account cited above, Nietschmann's mistake is understandable. Gonzales explains the land title process as if it happened in the nineteenth century, when the Miskitu king still ruled and Britain still had limited sovereignty over the Coast.

31. For example, the Great Southern Cattle and Land Company issued a bond for production on the Río Grande in 1908, having been granted 2,755,000 acres "from the Atlantic Ocean running westward on both shores of the Río Grande" (Oakman to Symington, 4 November 1908; CIDCA-Managua Archives). In at least one case, the expansion of banana production led to the wholesale relocation of an Indian community. Inhabitants of Tumarin, who formerly lived at the site of the El Gallo plantation, were forced to move about 40 kilometers upriver. See *Periodical Accounts* 1918: 10 (no. 114): 239.

32. Rodriguez to Lawder, 2 July 1915 (Crowdell Papers).

33. Indirect support for this contention comes from the exchange between Chalkley and Hooker (see note 26). When Hooker reports that he helped Sandy Bay people choose a plot

avoiding the property already claimed by others, I infer that his reference was to company-owned lands.

34. Elias to Hon. W. N. Lawder, 18 January 1915 (Crowdell Papers).

35. Interview with Lino Lopez by D. Brautigam-Beer, published in *Nicarauac* no. 8: 180–84 (1982).

36. Of twenty-six Sandy Bay community members with whom I spoke at length about this issue, only five gave responses that included a critique of U.S. presence.

37. MacDonald draws theoretical inspiration for this analysis from the work of James C. Scott (1976).

38. For pre-1979 observations to this effect, see, for example, Helms (1971: 224); for post-1979 observations, see Hale (1994).

39. Another, more complex issue is whether and in what ways the presence of North American institutions, especially missionaries, actually helped to constitute this "fit" between Miskitu Indian consciousness and company production. I have addressed this problem at greater length (Hale 1994: chap. 2).

40. ALPROMISU stands for Alliance for the Progress of Miskitu and Sumu Indians. My information on ALPROMISU's stance on land rights comes from Richter (1986), Herta Downs (interview with the author, Limón, Costa Rica, 1987), and especially Rojas (1976: 49–51).

41. Since numerous detailed chronologies and analyses of political events during this period have been published elsewhere, there is no need to offer yet another review here. See, for example, Nietschmann (1989), Diskin et al. (1986), Jenkins (1986), and Mohawk and Davis (1982). For an extensive annotated bibliography, see Bourgois and Hale (1989).

42. MISURASATA (1980) also confirms this community-based notion of land rights in its General Regulations, issued in April 1980.

43. Both the mobilization and the study were funded by Cultural Survival, an Indian rights advocacy organization based in Cambridge, Massachusetts.

44. *Propuesta de la tenencia de la tierra de las comunidades indigenas y criollas de la Costa Atlántica* (unpublished MISURASATA communiqué, 28 July 1981, Managua). For an appreciation of the previous demands and terminology, see MISURASATA (1980).

45. See *El litigio* (unpublished manuscript, CIDCA-Managua archives).

46. Wiggins is Miskitu and a former leader of MISURASATA, who since 1981 has lived in Washington, D.C., and worked for the Indian Law Resource Center. Though somewhat more prosaic, this portrayal of Miskitu subsistence life coincides with that of MacDonald (1988).

47. A calculation of Indian community lands based exclusively on legally registered community land titles comes to 120,590 hectares, or 1,206 square kilometers. MISURASATA's 1981 claim, in contrast, amounted to 45,000 square kilometers.

48. I found Miskitu people's contemporary attitudes to directly contradict these eulogies. Sandy Bay people (and especially the youth) constantly complained about the drudgery of agricultural work, and expressed nothing but admiration (mixed with some envy) for those who could avoid it by hiring wage labor, or getting a steady "payday." For further confirmation of this point during the period before 1979, see Weiss (1977: 172). The only subsistence production activity about which Sandy Bay Miskitu are uniformly enthusiastic was turtle fishing.

49. This argument has been made cogently by Renato Rosaldo (1990), in specific reference to "social constructionist" approaches to ethnicity theory. He names the problem I refer to as "the postmodern problem of weightlessness." David Harvey (1989: 117) makes a very similar point.

50. Another complication comes with the observation that the MISURASATA discourse is contested by Sumu Indians, who also want land and autonomy but fear a continuation of Miskitu dominance.

51. I develop this analysis further in a separate article (Hale 1991).

Bibliography

Anderson, Benedict. 1983. *Imagined Communities: Reflections on the Origin and Spread of Nationalism.* London: Verso.

Araya Pochet, Carlos. 1979. "El enclave bananero en Nicaragua." Unpublished manuscript.

Bourgois, P., and C. R. Hale. 1989. "The Atlantic Coast of Nicaragua." In *Sandinista Nicaragua,* ed. N. Snarr. Ann Arbor, Mich.: Pierian Press.

Congressional Record. 1895. Fifty-third Congress. 3d session.

Crowdell Papers. Bluefields archives of CIDCA (Center for Research and Documentation on the Atlantic Coast).

Cuadra Chamorro, Pedro. 1944. *La reincorporacion de la Mosquitia.* Managua.

Dekalb, Courtenay. 1893. "Nicaragua: Studies on the Mosquito Shore." *Journal of the American Geographical Society* 25: 236–88.

Diario nacional (Nicaragua). 1895. Managua: Biblioteca Nacional.

Diskin, Martin, et al. 1986. "Peace and Autonomy on the Atlantic Coast of Nicaragua: A Report of the LASA Task Force on Human Rights and Academic Freedom." Pittsburgh: Latin American Studies Association.

Hale, Charles R. 1991. "Miskitu: Revolution in the Revolution." *NACLA* 25 (3): 24–28.

———. 1994. *Resistance and Contradiction: Miskitu Indians and the Nicaraguan State, 1894–1987.* Stanford, Calif.: Stanford University Press.

Haraway, Donna. 1988. "Situated Knowledges: The Science Question in Feminism and the Privilege of Partial Perspective." *Feminist Studies* 14 (3): 575–99.

Harvey, David. 1989. *The Condition of Postmodernity.* London: Blackwell.

Helms, Mary. 1971. *Asang: Adaptation to Culture Contact in a Miskito Community.* Gainesville: University of Florida Press.

Jenkins Moliere, Jorge. 1986. *El desafio indígena en Nicaragua: El caso de los Miskitos.* Mexico City: Editorial Katun.

MacDonald, Theodore. 1988. "Moral Economy of the Miskito Indians." In *Ethnicities and Nations,* ed. Remo Guidieri, Francesco Pellizzi, and Stanley J. Tambiah. Austin: University of Texas Press. 107–53.

Menzies, Elenore, ed. 1985. *Indian War and Peace in Nicaragua.* Snoqualmie, Wash.: Center for World Indigenous Studies.

MISURASATA (Miskitu, Sumu, Rama, Sandinista Asla Takanka). 1980. *Lineamientos generales: La unidad indígena de las tres etnias del Atlántico de Nicaragua.* Managua.

———. 1981a. Press communiqué, 27 July 1981.

———. 1981b. "Informe de la problemática indígena con la revolucion sandinista en Nicaragua." Unpublished memorandum.

Mohawk, John. 1982. "The Possibilities of Uniting Indians and the Left for Social Change in Nicaragua." *Cultural Survival Quarterly* 6 (1): 9–11.

Mohawk, John, and Shelton Davis. 1982. "Revolutionary Contradictions: Miskitu and Sandinistas in Nicaragua." *Akwesasne Notes* 14 (3, Spring): 7–10.

Nietschmann, Bernard. 1979. *Caribbean Edge: The Coming of Modern Times to Isolated People and Wildlife.* New York: The Bobbs-Merrill Company.

———. 1985. "Invasion and Defense of Indian Nations." *Akwesasne Notes* (late summer): 10.

———. 1989. *The Unknown War: The Miskitu Nation, Nicaragua, and the United States.* Boston: University Press of America.

Ohland, Klaudine, and Robin Schneider, eds. 1983. *National Revolution and Indigenous Identity: The Conflict between Sandinistas and Miskito Indians of Nicaragua's Atlantic Coast.* Copenhagen: IWGIA.

Olien, Michael. 1983. "The Miskito Kings and the Line of Succession." *Journal of Anthropological Research* 39 (2): 198–241.

Periodical Accounts (Moravian mission reports from Nicaragua).

Popular Memory Group. 1982. "Popular Memory: Theory, Politics, Method." In *Making Histories: Studies in History-Writing and Politics,* ed. Richard Johnson et al. Minneapolis: University of Minnesota Press. 205–52.

Richter, Ernesto. 1986. "El movimiento indígena en la Costa Atlántica de Nicaragua en la decada del 70 y su contexto." Unpublished mimeograph (July).

Rojas, Aramando. 1976. *Origin histórico y situación jurídica de las comunidades indígenas miskitas.* Monografia, Facultad de Ciencias Jurídicas y Sociales de la UNAN. León, Nicaragua.

Rosaldo, R. 1990. "Others of Invention." *Voice Literary Supplement* (February): 27–29.

Scott, James C. 1976. *The Moral Economy of the Peasant.* New Haven: Yale University Press.

State, U.S. Department of. 1910–29. Records of the Department of State relating to the internal affairs of Nicaragua.

Vilas, Carlos M. 1989. *State, Class, and Ethnicity in Nicaragua: Capitalist Modernization and Revolutionary Change on the Atlantic Coast.* Boulder, Colo.: Lynne Rienner.

Weiss, Brian. 1977. "Economía del Torgua: En cada venta una perdida." In *Memorias de Arecife Tortuga,* ed. B. Nietschmann. Managua: Banco Central.

Wiggins, Armstrong. 1981. "Colonialism and Revolution — Nicaraguan Sandinism and the Liberation of the Miskito, Sumu, and Rama Peoples: An Interview with Armstrong Wiggins." *Akwesasne Notes* 8 (4): 4–15.

Wunderich, Volker, and Lioba Rossbach. 1985. "Derechos indígenas y estado nacional en Nicaragua: La convención Mosquita de 1894." *Encuentro* 24 (5): 29–54.

4

Taming the Memoryscape
Hiroshima's Urban Renewal

Lisa Yoneyama

Please rest in peace, for we shall not repeat the mistake.
(Cenotaph inscription in the Peace Memorial Park, Hiroshima)[1]

O deceased,
do not rest in peace. . . .
You must perturb and awaken
the avaricious living souls.
The first evil
may have been a mistake
but the second is a treachery.
Faithfulness to the dead
we shall not forget.
(Kurihara Sadako 1989)[2]

A PROPOSAL BY an inquiry commission in 1988 put forth a vision of Hiroshima, originally outlined in 1970, as an "International Peace and Cultural City."[3] The city proposes to establish a municipal environment that fully anticipates features of the "coming new age": internationalization, further development of high technology (*hai teku*), of high-level information systems (*kôdo jôhôka*), the overall aging of society, and "diversification of individuals' values." The making of a "*messe* (trade show and market)

99

and convention city," or *messe konbenshon shitî*, was confirmed as the most adequate objective for future development. In order to achieve this goal the city called for an urgent "internationalization" (*kokusaika*) of the city and its people, further technological advancement (*gijutsu kakushin*), and enhancement of its capability to dispatch information of "higher quality" (Hiroshima-shi 1983).

This rearticulation of national as well as regional images is underlined by a general agreement, despite an obscurity about the content, that the country has been witnessing and welcomes such thoroughly pervasive trends of the new age often characterized as postindustrial or postmodern. The use of dazzling images of the new age, embellished with such fancy concepts as "internationalization," "high technology," "high-level information society," or the idea of trade shows and conventions—almost every sign thinkable for a late capitalist society—is common enough in recent urban planning. These images serve as tantalizing and sweeping concepts that are both descriptive and prescriptive, providing the urban planners with everything from the necessary causes, motives, and future goals to the means with which to achieve what is to come.

Hiroshima is no exception. Not unlike other major metropolises—such as Osaka, Fukuoka, Kobe, Nagoya, or Tokyo, places that were utterly devastated by air raids during the war—Hiroshima experienced a "miraculous" recovery from the atomic ashes. But Hiroshima differs significantly from other Japanese cities in one respect. As the world's first nuclear war site and a mecca for peace pilgrimages, its planning must somehow embrace the notion of "world peace."

Easy though it may sound, the call for peace could be too much for Hiroshima to handle, for the concept has too often been linked to the city's atom bomb experience. The widely chanted peace slogan "No more Hiroshimas," too, entraps city planners in the dilemma. It indeed endows the city with internationally unassailable moral authority. For the world, however, "Hiroshima" is also a name that will be remembered only as an antithesis. The city must rest on a self-negating premise. But if other places have the luxury to produce souvenir goods bearing such slogans as "I love New York" or "I love Kyoto," why must this city refrain from exploiting the phrase "I love Hiroshima"?

Urban planners have attempted to solve the dilemma in several ways. One city official, one of the central promoters of Hiroshima's 1989 prefectural exposition, told me that he did not necessarily wish to appeal to the familiar notion of Hiroshima as a sacred site for peace in advertising the Expo. "Peace is too often associated with the atomic bomb," he claimed,

> but the Expo should not offer an uptight [*katai*] image — it must be a festive occasion, a *matsuri*. I would rather like people to think about peace at the Peace Memorial Park [located near the hypocenter]; and at the Expo, people should genuinely enjoy themselves.... We cannot forever rely on the Atom Bomb Dome [the preserved ruins of the former Industrial Promotion Hall] or Peace Memorial Park. We are aiming to get rid of the gloominess [*kurasa*]. It is not desirable to bring in any political color, for people are allergic to it.

This statement of the administrator who has been taking various initiatives in the city's cultural projects betrays the powerful associations among the bomb politics, and the signs of peace. His statement also reveals the very strategies with which he and other urban planners have been and will be attempting to reconcile the images of peace/the bomb with the city's new features. To be sure, he is not discrediting the significance of the tourists who visit Hiroshima to "think about peace." Most of those involved in city planning do acknowledge the valuable resources that the city can draw from the past, including the Atom Bomb Dome and Peace Memorial Park. What he is proposing here is a spatial segregation of historical representations and urban practices whereby the inhabitants and visitors are channeled onto a differently defined topography.

On the other hand, some have sought to retexture the concept of peace itself.[4] A local automobile company, for instance, proposed to erect a spectacular monument in recognition of the centennial of the municipal administration in 1989, an occasion officially announced as a marker of a new historical stage.[5] The "Peace Tower," as it was initially named, was planned as the world's tallest tower, to be marveled at as a symbol of new Hiroshima, "a symbol of *akarusa* [brightness and joviality] and local prosperity."[6] The plan proposed the placing of "a light of peace" at about the same level where the bomb exploded. At ground level, there was to be a communal center for entertainment, including a world shopping and festival plaza and an international youth center. In his interview with a newspaper reporter, an executive of the automobile company remarked, "We certainly do not mean to deny the Atom Bomb Dome. But isn't it about time to pursue not only the misery but also pleasures of peace [*heiwa no tanoshisa*]?" (*Asahi shinbun,* 12 March 1989).

This essay explores the various dimensions of city planning in the past decades, which include the promotion of tourism, different projects for urban renovation, and the production of a community festival. As will become clear, the Expo and "Peace Tower" plan are just two among many urban projects that have been transforming the memory site of the nuclear holocaust into one that celebrates "bright and jovial peace" (*akarui heiwa*). But what happens when a space of death is converted into one of conviviality? What becomes of the memories of mass destruction and suffering in a renewed landscape? And why and how should such transformations concern us at all? Through closely examining the ways in which city planning has been re-representing the urban landscape for the approaching twenty-first century, I seek to unravel the politics of memory in Hiroshima's urban renewal.

The re-visioning of Hiroshima's future has indeed incited controversy over representations of the past. Kurihara Sadako, a survivor and well-known poet and social activist, wrote the poem quoted at the beginning of this essay in protest against the increasing marginalization of atom bomb representations in the urban landscape. To be sure, the conflict between the desire to move beyond the holocaust memory and the desire not to overcome the past is not at all new. In one of the most important studies of the atom bomb survivors, Robert Jay Lifton observed that similar contradictory feelings filled the city nearly thirty years ago: "Hiroshima has been particularly plagued with the problem of carving out a new city identity while trying to avoid becoming nothing but an A-bombed city" (Lifton 1967: 310). Arguing that, for at least some survivors, "the new attractiveness is associated with 'selling the bomb,' gaiety and sensuality with forbidden pleasure; and all such vitality becomes an insult to the dead" (263), Lifton interpreted such resistance to pleasures and affirmation of life as a manifestation of the survivors' "guilt-saturated antipathy to pleasure" (313). The guilt-ridden survivors, he concluded, are caught in the ambivalence of whether to continue to remember the atom bomb destruction and to remain faithful and responsible to the dead, or to suppress the trauma in order to affirm and find pleasure in life.

However, unlike Lifton's work, which interprets these tendencies toward cherishing of the past and loyalty to the dead as a working of an assumed universal human psychology or sometimes as the symptoms of essential "East Asian" cultural traits, I problematize the political and cultural ramifications of such pursuits for and resistance against "brightness" in Hiroshima's urban renewals. The conflict between forgetting and remembering in the production of official memoryscapes reveals more than the "deep" psychology of the neo-Freudian or the "underlying" Japanese culture.[7] In analyzing the current milieu of memories about the war and the atom bomb, I believe it is crucial to question even the most familiar and naturally accepted notions such as life or death as well as categories of emotion, including pleasure, comfort, or gaiety, in order to discern how such concepts are in effect shaped and manipulated through the production of dominant discourse of and on Hiroshima. Even the innermost ambivalent emotions torn between the atom bomb memories and the pleasures of life are perhaps as much laden with power as saturated with guilt.

The engineering of "bright" Hiroshima, above all, is predicated upon the hegemonic modes of thought, ways of living, and styles of expression in Japan today, a cultural paradigm that one can arguably characterize as postmodern (Miyoshi and Harootunian 1988; see also Jameson 1984). The features we can observe in the discourse of/on Hiroshima's urban renewal—especially the pervading sentiments of moderation and comfort and the emphasis on cleanliness and the aspiration for *akarusa* (brightness, joviality and lightheartedness)—all contribute to Japan's dominant cultural condition, which, for instance, privileges "atmosphere" and images over substance (Field 1988; see also Berman 1989: 41), constantly transforms knowledge into mass commodities (Ivy 1988), and incessantly flattens and trivializes history (Fujitani 1992). The decentering of memories of the war and the atom bomb, I argue, is inextricably linked to this much larger process of the nation's postmodernity.

In exploring the marginalization of memories of the war and the atom bomb and its political and cultural implications, I attempt also to demonstrate the productive and transformative nature of space (see Soja 1989 and Boyarin in this volume). On the one hand, I portray the ways in which the cityspace is treated as a static object that urban development projects can re-landscape and alter (see Zukin 1991). At the same time, the reformulated cityspace can in turn provide a new "container of power" (Harvey 1989: 213), which further carves out new knowledge and consciousness, as well as amnesia, about history and society. The nation's increasing forgetfulness and the yearning for "brightness," I argue, are intricately inter-twined with the manufacturing of spaces that can in effect produce sub-jectivities conducive to the dominant tendencies of late-capitalist con-sumer culture. It is precisely this power of space, which can at once illuminate and mystify, which can produce and "hide consequences from us" (Soja 1989: 23), that makes urban renewal such a central agendum of contemporary Hiroshima, toward which those in power wittingly or un-wittingly steer their energy and resources.

The transformations of urban landscape, furthermore, generate con-tentions over representations of the past and historical awareness. Such bat-tles over memories have not only materialized *as* but, more importantly, developed *out of* and mediated through the struggles over actual space. In this essay I will identify the dominant processes of spatial containment, the forces that demarcate the boundaries and define the proper territories for memorialization, prescribing whose experiences should be remembered and when, where, and how they should be invoked. At the same time, the analysis alludes, though very briefly, to what may be called the strategy of deconfinement, that is, the practices individuals employ to counter the forces that segregate and suppress contesting representations of Hiroshi-ma's history and identity.

Remapping History

A series of urban renewal projects I discuss below, including those de-signed for the 1989 observance of the municipal administration's centen-nial, illustrates the varying and sometimes contradictory ways in which the strategies of spatial containment are actualized. These projects, failed or realized, epitomize the ways in which the knowledge about the city's past and present is reformulated through the remapping of history onto a renewed urban space.

In the process of urban redevelopment, the meanings of different sites are produced in relation to those of other sites. The Hiroshima Contem-porary Museum of Art, for instance, is constructed in contrast with those that signify Hiroshima's past. According to the city's office of tourism, the museum was designed to express the new, bright image of peace, contrast-ing sharply with the dark, gloomy image of the Atom Bomb Museum. In the Atom Bomb Museum, in the Peace Memorial Park, photographs and remnants of objects destroyed by the bomb are exhibited. Conversely, in the white, clean architecture of the Contemporary Museum of Art, the images of Hiroshima are presented through various contemporary art forms. The museum is intended to manifest the future, bright and full of potential, not the dark misery of the past. "If other cities [such as Kyoto or Nara] dwell upon tradition and historical heritage, we will advertise ourselves with everything that is new," explained a city official at the office of tourism.

Although some may see it troubling to exploit history in searching for the city's future image, others apparently have succeeded in excavating its past without risk of summoning up memories of the war and the atom bomb. A tourist pamphlet demonstrates how the atom bomb memory has become decentered in representing history (see Hiroshima-shi Kankô Kyôkai, n.d.). On the second page, headlined "Historical Fugue," one finds pictures of the Hiroshima Castle and some temples. The text reads:

> High waves called "The Trend of the Age" have rolled over
> Hiroshima, as they have over other places. These historical
> buildings, still standing, have witnessed history itself, and can tell us
> its meaning over the ages.

While remaining uninformed about how the castle was completely destroyed by the atomic bombing, tourists will "breathe the great passage of time in such historical places." The city also celebrated the quadricentennial of the castle's construction in conjunction with the municipal administration's centennial. If the museum exemplifies the future of Hiroshima, the past may be thoroughly summed up by the castle.

Some, indeed, criticize the strange forgetfulness involved in the manufacturing of nostalgia for the castle. It is overlooked that the castle, which became the foundation for the development of a feudal castle town in medieval Japan, was turned into a military headquarters during the Sino-Japanese War. It was celebrated as Emperor Meiji's temporary residence as commander in chief. For those who problematize the militaristic nature of the city during the modern era—the period when Hiroshima flourished as a "military capital" (*gunto*)—the castle's history manifests a clear causal link between the prewar development of the city as a major military center and the atom bombing as its consequence. They also point out that in Hiroshima Castle militant imperial symbols are displayed even today;

the National Defense Shrine, where the war dead are enshrined as Shintoist deities, is in the castle, and other war monuments there glorify war criminals and celebrate the war of invasion against neighboring Asian countries. For these observers the castle is an unsettling site of patriotic and chauvinist memories that are not yet reconciled with the memories of those killed by the atom bomb. For the tourist promoters and perhaps for most tourists, however, the Sino-Japanese War and prewar Japanese militarism belong to a sufficiently distant past. These memories are, at least in their eyes, remote enough to be recollected with a sense of romance and nostalgia.

Concerning the image of the castle, the Motomachi redevelopment project deserves a detailed examination. The project, strongly promoted by the recently privatized telecommunication company, is to celebrate both the four-hundred-year-old castle town and the twenty-first-century high-tech megalopolis. A close look at how the project was advertised reveals the ways in which marginalization of the atom bomb memory can occur through self-exoticization of urban space.

Not surprisingly, the young employees of a real estate corporation that subcontracted the promotion of the Motomachi redevelopment project explained to me that publicizing the project was difficult because they could conceive of "nothing representative of Hiroshima other than the notion of peace," and particularly "because there haven't been any nice recent images attached to the Motomachi District," which was once named by the mass media as "the atom bomb slum" district.[8] In the 1950s and the early 1960s, this stretch of riverbank was crowded with temporary and illegal residences of war survivors, the economically disadvantaged, and people excluded from the city's postwar housing projects. In a search for replacements for the image of "the atom bomb slum," the distant past of the Motomachi District was reexcavated. Everyday scenes of the Edo castle town, for instance, were depicted on street murals. To represent the Motomachi's recent history, anecdotes about the introduction of electricity, telephones, and locomotives—the romantic signs of the turn-of-the-century "Civilization and Enlightenment Era"—were introduced, in place of acknowledgments of the military use of the castle and nearby fields.

A planned thirty-six-story skyscraper is expected to transform the area northeast of downtown into a center for business and entertainment—"the main stage for the International Cultural City." The building is to be equipped with multipurpose spaces: hotel accommodations, *messe*/convention halls, plazas for various "cultural activities" and sports, television and radio studios, theaters, shopping arcades, and restaurants. The aim is to remodel the entire stretch of landscape that extends from the downtown transportation center to the western riverfront, integrating into the project the castle and existing public facilities such as a museum, gymnasium, and libraries, as well as the new monorail station now under construction, and resulting in a space of "information, twenty-four hours of internationalization, comfort, and amusement."[9]

One of the workers in the promotion office, a man in his early forties who grew up in the Motomachi District, claimed that Motomachi has been considered a dangerous, lawless place ever since the war. The residents, he explained, were those who lost practically everything to the bomb. In order to gain some pocket money, he and his friends used to collect metal fragments on the riverbed and sell them. They dug for lotus roots and caught frogs in the castle moat. "We brought the frogs to a Chinese restaurant on the way to school. We were paid pretty well." He now thinks that the area has changed a great deal. For one thing, it is safer.

> I see young lovers in Motomachi Park even after ten or eleven at night. In the older days, there were no lovers hanging out near the castle, although lovers were always present in the Peace Memorial Park. The Peace Park has been well maintained for a much longer time.

He definitely denied any positive feelings for his natal town. "There is nothing I hope to maintain among the images of old Motomachi. Those who grew up in the area hold only abhorrent and dark [*kurai*] memories," he concluded.

In the renewed urban imageries, however, even the worker's memory of poverty can create a moment in which mundane scenes become exotic and exciting. A woman in her midtwenties, full of energy, bright and gifted, explained how she cherishes her fascination with making new discoveries from the familiar and tries to exploit surprising analogues in the advertisements. When looked at carefully, she said, scenes of barracks and the figures of the homeless at the riverbanks near the railway station can "almost remind me of Southeast Asia, maybe Hong Kong, or could it be Venice?"

During the late 1960s, the period of Japan's rapid economic growth, the barracks and shacks of squatters were burned down through a number of what people remember as "suspicious fires" and were gradually replaced by functional and contemporary-looking high-rise apartment buildings. Although this immediate postwar housing project may simply have been designed to hide the undesirable (see Hiroshima-shi 1983: 148), the redevelopment project of the early 1990s is aimed at converting the entire meaning of the area through displacement and dispersal. The future Motomachi urban space will blend the views of high-rise apartments — the residue from the post-atom-bomb economic recovery — smoothly into the bright and pleasurable scenes of the future. It seeks not merely to wipe away stains from the past but to recast the very meanings that they might elicit. It is such spatial cleansing that mystifies history. I will return to this point in discussing the preservation of atom bomb ruins.

Decentering of the atom bomb memory in the redesigning of the official cityscape also occurs visually in how the city's name is written. While "Hiroshima" has often been written with *katakana,* a type of Japanese phonetic system that is today used mainly for transliteration of foreign words, tourist pamphlets now use *kanji* (Chinese characters) or, more often, *hiragana,* another type of Japanese syllabary.[10] Hiroshima in the older *kanji* recalls the old castle town and the prosperous city of late-nineteenth-century industrialization and militarization, whereas Hiroshima in *hiragana,* with its rounded and soft curves, evokes scenes of *furusato* (see also Robertson 1991), the nurturing hometown. In contrast, "Hiroshima" in *katakana,* which is derived in part from the transliteration of an English slogan, "No more Hiroshimas" stands for the more abstract conceptualizations that crystallize out of the atom bomb experience. It summarizes ideas that encompass prayers for those killed by the atom bomb, oaths for peace, and protests against nuclear war and violence. *Katakana* can best represent such abstraction. But because *katakana* is most typically used for foreign words, "Hiroshima" in *katakana* is also condemned as a nonindigenous concept — an alien notion, imported, especially from the West — that could not speak for the natives' feelings. "Hiroshima" in *katakana,* a sign of antiwar and antinuclear feelings, is an inappropriate image for the city in the era of regionalism: it is too distant, too foreign.

The illumination project, or the "lighten up" (*raito appu*) project, is yet another example of efforts to make Hiroshima "bright and jovial."[11] The three-year project, begun in 1989, was to illuminate some major tourist attractions, including the Atom Bomb Dome, several other popular peace memorials, buildings, and monuments along the riverside near the Peace Park, and downtown streets, parks, and shops. It is hoped that the neon lamps and bright shop window displays will turn the city into an attractive site for after-hours entertainment and will provide the citizens with new urban pleasures.

While people in the tourist and commerce industries welcomed the project as a significant effort to improve nightlife in Hiroshima, some have cast doubts on its intent. Detractors argue that the local electric company has pushed the city to raise nighttime electricity consumption in order to justify further construction of nuclear power plants. Others fear the environmental impact of excessive illumination. Some survivors understand the project as yet another conspiracy of "lightening" atom bomb memories, a trivialization of experiences of enormous gravity, of death and life.

One well-known survivor and storyteller, a retired home economics teacher who lost her leg to the bomb, gave me a copy of a newspaper article in which she was interviewed as a representative of survivors. In it she commented, "Let [the park] rest in peace at least through the night. I feel as if Hiroshima's past is fading away in the glaring lights." The article concluded by quoting a city official: "Precisely because it is a site from which 'the spirit of Hiroshima' [*hiroshima no kokoro*]" is delivered, we must change the present circumstances in which the place is closed in darkness, repelling people." The storyteller added, as she handed me the article, "This is the typical attitude of the city that always says, 'For peace,' 'For peace.'"

"Just because it is a sacred site, it need not be submerged in darkness," countered an official of the city's office of tourism. "There are ways to illuminate things while presenting them solemnly." When I asked him about opposition from the survivors, which had been reported in the newspaper, he criticized the mass media for "misconveying" survivors' opinions. "I think the media reporters must have stretched the responses of people like the interviewed survivors when in fact they expressed only a few doubts about the project. I think it all depends on how we do it. If we do it properly, they will be convinced." Apparently, it was difficult for this official, whose mother was a survivor and who was himself one as an infant, to imagine that the very notion of "properness" is being questioned by other survivors.

The tourism official further tried to alleviate my fears that the city's tourist administration may be effacing the memories of the atom bomb by uncritically subscribing to consumerism:

> Promotion of the tourist industry is ... the very act of pursuing peace. Those who visit Hiroshima to seek an experience of peace can be defined as tourists. It is the same as a pilgrimage to a temple [*otera mairi*]. The town that exists at a sacred site, a mecca of peace, is the same as one of those towns that develop nearby famous temples or shrines, that is, *monzenmachi*. So those who visit such sites can be regarded as tourists.

Here, Hiroshima's sacredness is transformed into another merchandisable object, just like any other attractive destination for tourists. Hiroshima now rests on the same relative spectrum as other cities, such as New York or Kyoto. The difference between the site of the world's first nuclear holocaust, the glitter of cosmopolitan urbanity, and the eminence of ancient "Oriental" tradition, is no longer critical.

To be sure, he did not deny the importance of conveying the atom bomb experience to others. "But one cannot be thinking about peace or about the survivors twenty-four hours every day," he emphasized. The memory of the war and the atomic bomb must be invoked "properly," at an appropriate place and moment:

> One needs *kejime,* to draw lines. Just as in the conservation of cultural treasures, there is no limit to the argument as to how much one should preserve. In this respect, the idea of a museum offers a compromise.

The aspiration for brightness, furthermore, becomes naturalized as an element of a timeless Japanese mentality. "To build a war museum did not seem to gain much popularity," he concluded:

> I think the Japanese people generally cannot bear to see something grotesque. There is even a plan to relocate all the remains of the atomic bomb, including the Atomic Bomb Museum. ... Building a war memorial park would be an alternative. It might be accused of being a bit gloomy, though.

The other half of the photocopy the retired home economics teacher gave me was another newspaper report about the new waterfront redevelopment project, the Hiroshima River Cruise Project. According to the original plan, the cruising boats would leave from a dock southwest of the Peace Memorial Park, proceed north along the park, pass beneath the Aioi Bridge (the original intended target of the bombing), and make a U-turn to their launching point. The plan also included on-board presentations by survivors of their atom bomb experiences. The cruise was designed in conjunction with the illumination project so that tourists on night cruises could appreciate the illuminated peace memorials, the Atom Bomb Dome, and other buildings alongside the rivers.

The boats are appropriately named Suisui and Runrun: *Suisui* is a mimetic word that describes smoothness, particularly in swimming, and is also used to highlight effortlessness of various actions. *Runrun* is a word one associates with the sound of humming, stemming also from fairly new usages of the Japanese word, such as *runrun kibun*. It connotes a cheerful mood or lightheartedness. Such an exploitation of the river by the tourist industry invited criticisms from the survivors and others who felt that their atom bomb experiences were being commodified and trivialized. Another storyteller, a retired factory worker and mother of two daughters, asked me rhetorically what sorts of atom bomb stories I would expect to hear on boats with names like these. A housewife in her thirties reminded me that "the rivers in Hiroshima are very special," because, as also recalled by many others, "enormous numbers of people have drowned and died there."

Celebration of Peace

> *Will it make me forget?*
> *No. But it will make you not mind remembering.*
>
>   (An exchange from the science fiction film *Logan's Run*)

In May the pleasant days of late spring arrive in Hiroshima. In the fresh breezes and bright sunlight, the people enjoy the verdant cityscape. The mild warm weather continues for a short while, to be followed first by the seemingly interminable rainy season and then by the oppressive heat of summer. Early May is also a period of successive national holidays, a period usually referred to as the Golden Week. The two national holidays in the first week of May — Constitution Commemoration Day on 3 May and Children's Day on 5 May — are often combined with weekends to make a long holiday, which for many overworked Japanese becomes a perfect occasion for short trips and outdoor activities. In recent years, various events, including new exhibitions and traditional folk festivals, have been held throughout the country during this time of the year. In Hiroshima an annual three-day Hiroshima Flower Festival takes place. Since its start in 1977, this festival, which involves not only the municipal community but also the neighboring region, has attracted as many as one and a half million spectators.

On 3 May 1989 I arrived at the Peace Park area shortly before noon. The opening ceremony was just about to begin. Little Cub Scouts, Boy Scouts, and girls in white lace ballet costumes stood along the long pathway from the park entrance to the central memorial. A chorus sang joyful music on the stage, accompanied by a huge orchestra and brass band. The mayor and other executives waited to light a torch on top of a cone-shaped flower tower, ten feet high, to signify that the festival had begun.

The transformation of the Peace Memorial Park's entrance area had started a few days earlier. The flower tower appeared in front of the Atom Bomb Museum and several arcades with colorful signs stood along the Peace Boulevard at regular intervals. A vast "main stage" was built at the park entrance. The newspapers and television stations announced that during the event traffic would be entirely blocked on a portion of the boulevard. Peace Boulevard, which runs on the south side of the park, is one of the major traffic routes through the core of the city. The blocking of traffic and the physical transformation of Peace Boulevard indicated the scale of the event.

As I walked past the stage at the entrance and moved toward the Peace Park's central cenotaph, I saw a few groups of tourists who offered prayers and incense and tried to take pictures with the cenotaph and Atom Bomb Dome in the background. It was not clear to anybody what was about to begin. "What is happening?" "How come these people are lined up?" It was difficult for the pilgrims to realize that a festival was about to start because the main stage was too distant to be seen from the cenotaph. The Boy Scouts tried to keep the tourists from standing in front of the cenotaph. When the Scouts finally succeeded, with assistance from adults, in creating a small open ceremonial space at the cenotaph, a young woman and man walked up together with a torch in their hands. At exactly noon everyone present for the opening ceremony, including the young couple and children, paid one minute's silent tribute to the atom bomb victims.

The couple bowed to the cenotaph, turned around, and proceeded down the long passageway, which was lined with children, and brought the flaming torch to the mayor, who waited at the festival's main stage at the park entrance. The mayor, lifted by a crane, lit the torch on top of the tower, opening the festival. This rather long and drawn-out period of transition, a ritual performance that transferred public attention from the cenotaph in the park's center to the park entrance, separated the two spaces. The dead were enshrined and calmly watching over the living from inside the Peace Park, while Peace Boulevard became the space where the festivities unfolded.

The parades held on the first and the second day were the high points of the event. During the three days of the festival, while marchers paraded over the 1.5-kilometer stretch on the Peace Boulevard, arriving at their final goal built in front of the Peace Park, various events unfolded at small stages and plazas that were set up along the boulevard. On these plazas were exhibits and performances: music shows; folk dance performances, both Japanese and non-Japanese; tea ceremonies; sake tasting; and bonsai and garden arrangement exhibits. On the side streets, small stands sold soft drinks and foods typical of neighborhood festivals. Smells of roast corn dipped in shoyu filled the area. Booths were everywhere, with *okonomi yaki* pancakes, *tako yaki* dumplings, and cotton candy for sale.

The festival offered as much opportunity for publicity for corporations that had factories and branch offices in Hiroshima as it did for the city and various organizations related to tourism. The corporations participated in the festival by entering floats, cheerfully embellished with flowers and colorful letters forming company names. To be sure, efforts were made to play down hints of commercialism as much as possible. Although encouragement of the community's recovery from the recession was in fact one strong motive behind the initial implementation of this extravaganza (*Chûgoku shinbun*, 3 May 1977; see also Hiroshima-shi 1983: 263), advertisements seemed restrained. Instead, the ways in which certain corporations and their products contributed to peace and community welfare were highlighted. A transportation company with a branch in Hiroshima entered a giant float displaying professional samba dancers from Saõ Paulo. A giant sphinx float passed by with a huge red sign reading, "I feel Coke." A telecommunication company also entered a float on which a wedding ceremony was portrayed, suggesting the role of technology in creating intimate and significant human relationships. The local salt company's float displayed the name of their product, "Kitchen Salt," with the slogan "We create the richness of human hearts."

Between the floats, brass bands, and baton twirlers, some of whom were police officers, various children's sports teams and students from private junior high and high schools marched down the street. Other organizations participating included jazz dance clubs, a Japanese folk song circle, a group of taiko drums, and volunteer welfare associations. In an attempt to lure tourists away from the city, people from neighboring towns and villages joined the procession and gave samples of their own "indigenous" festivals. The local association of Korean residents performed a Korean agricultural folk dance.

Perhaps because I was standing near the procession's terminus, there were irregular intervals between the arriving floats and marches. The flow of the procession had to be adjusted; some hurried quickly only to pass by, but others were made to stay longer, repeating their performance routines over and over. Police had to interrupt the parade to let people cross the street. Restrictions and instructions shouted through megaphones disturbed the supposedly relaxed and festive atmosphere. Constant interference to control both performers and spectators dampened the crowd's excitement. Although most spectators around me apparently enjoyed themselves as they anxiously waited for their families or friends to appear in the procession, a few young people who came to the festival expecting a carnival atmosphere expressed some disappointment. However, the green landscape, the fresh air from the ocean, and the late spring sun over the rivers greatly enhanced the joyfulness of the event, which might otherwise have left people with a feeling that the moment had been anticlimactic and artificial.

The festival, first held in 1977, was modeled after an event in which three hundred thousand people spontaneously appeared on the streets to celebrate a victory of the Hiroshima Carps, the nation's only local franchise baseball team, in the 1975 championship series. About a month before the first Hiroshima Flower Festival, newspapers reinvoked memories of this ecstatic homecoming parade of the baseball team as evidence of the citizens' strong longing for a harmonious and jovial communal event. The collective experience at the 1975 homecoming parade was remembered to have fostered "a new consciousness about the native home town [*kyôdo ishiki*] and a communal solidarity" (*Chûgoku shinbun*, 25 March 1977). A citizen's remark shows the thirst for cheerfulness (*akarusa*) among the citizens:

The alienated and atomized urban people's souls became one for the Carps. When one speaks of Hiroshima, the gloomy image [*kurai imêji*] of the atomic bomb pervades. For the first time in the thirty years since the end of the war, the citizens were united by pleasurable news [*akarui wadai*]. (*Chûgoku shinbun*, 25 March 1977)

Despite strong initiatives by the corporations, various efforts were made to characterize the festival as the birth of a new event "contrived and generated by the citizens" (*Chûgoku shinbun*, 7 May 1977 and 24 March 1977). The media and municipal public relations team emphasized the citizens' spontaneous participation in the making of the festival. A newspaper company, one of the major contributors to the festival, advertised it as a stage on which "the citizens are the main performers [*shimin ga shuyaku*]" (*Chûgoku shinbun*, 24 March 1977). University professors and folklorists stressed the importance of people's spontaneity and the involvement of every segment of the citizenry (*Chûgoku shinbun*, 1 January 1977). Shortly before the first performance of the Flower Festival, a special newspaper article publicized the event:

The new festival is coming. Three days from 3 May, amid the tender spring greenery, the entire area of the Peace Boulevard (Hundred Meter Road) and the Peace Park, the symbol of Hiroshima, the atom-bombed city, will turn into a single "plaza." In flowers, greenery, and music, citizens will cherish together the glory of peace.... One of the major goals of the festival is to nurture the "bud" of a new local community, growing through people's mingling and enjoyment. (*Chûgoku shinbun*, 23 March 1977)

Thus the idea of the festival came about. In this process people were again to confront the dilemma that the notion of peace was inseparable from that of the war and the atom bomb. But the producers of the Flower Festival appeared to be able to proclaim peace as a foundation of their community without evoking "dark and gloomy" atom bomb memory. A sugar company president, one of the developers of the festival, described to me how he had solved the dilemma by conceptually separating the two faces of Hiroshima, the city that was bombed and the city that has miraculously recovered and is now flourishing economically:

When one speaks of peace in Hiroshima, it means the atom bomb. Therefore [the image of peace has been] gloomy [*kurai*]. My opinion is that it is okay to keep the Atom Bomb Dome.

Hiroshima is indeed a city that once burned to death. But it is a city that also emerged out of that experience — with vitality, that is. To be able to present the city as such, peace as such, and energy as such is what I have pursued.

This effort to reconcile the city's atom bomb experience with the desire for a new, joyful, and festive occasion for the community is demonstrated eloquently through the actual production of the festival, especially as business elites and intellectuals carved out the official ideology of the new event. One newspaper summary of a round-table meeting led by these corporate leaders and other participants showed that the planners have just begun to depoliticize the concept of "peace" by trying to separate the atom bomb memories from the new festival of flowers, greenery, and music (*Chûgoku shinbun,* 31 October 1976). Throughout the discussion, the participants repeatedly emphasized that the spirit of this festival "should include consolation of the souls of the atom bomb victims [*genbaku no irei*]." The statement was, however, quickly rephrased: "Peace here means peace in a bright [*akarui*] sense, not with a dark [*kurai*] image," reemphasizing that "the spirit of the festival is peace, and its symbols are flowers and music," not the atom bomb (*Chûgoku shinbun,* 31 October 1976).

Some group members cautioned against further elaboration of the notion of peace. The chair of the executive committee asserted that even though "the International Peace City theme cannot be dismissed," the concept does not have to be spelled out in any official slogan "because it is already embedded in the spiritual background of Hiroshima." The members carefully dismissed factors that might provoke critical views on the issue of peace. They defined the festival as an opportunity "to express what peace means at the citizens' level" (*shimin reberu no heiwa towa nani ka*), that is, at the mundane level, apart from the conventional political arena. In other words, "it is not an occasion to think seriously [*kataku*] about ideologies [*ideorogî*]." The moderator of the round-table meeting summarized the members' opinions as follows:

So-called peace discussion is associated with various complicated issues, but the festival shall hopefully demonstrate a true happiness, a true peace, and a true festivity. To put it differently, the festival is an occasion to praise happiness and entrust flowers with the feeling [*kimochi*] of peace. (*Chûgoku shinbun,* 31 October 1976)

The notion of "citizens" and the signs of "flowers and greenery" served as key elements in enhancing the harmonious nature of the Flower Festival as a convivial communal occasion.[12] The official ideology of the festival overflows with innocent images of "flowers and greenery" that are constructed as the "authentic" signs of harmony and the well-being of urban community.[13] One planner at the meeting just described stated, "It is quite timely that the festival takes place right after May Day, since it shall be a joyful occasion for laborers [*rôdôsha*] as well, who will be able to continue to participate [after their May Day rally]" (*Chûgoku shinbun*, 31 October 1976). The "citizens" replaced the category of "laborers," effacing economic hierarchies and inequalities. Uniform and classless, "citizens"— who are at least in this instance liberated from "ideological strife," free from political divisions, and not in the least plagued by such concerns as economic exploitation or oppression—constitute subjects who celebrate a harmless peace festival.

The new festive event not only pacified and harmonized the community of the living; it also domesticated the community's relationship with those killed by the atom bomb. It is interesting to observe how the event has been contrasted with the Peace Commemoration Ceremony of 6 August.[14] Since it was first held, the Flower Festival has been advertised as an attempt to restore a positive sense of community and harmonious relationships among citizens—the two fundamental elements that were deemed to have been lost to the bomb from the "original" community. The aspirations for a new communal event, initially expressed by a handful of business leaders, gained strong support from the municipal government. In preparing for the first festival, a high-ranking city official stated, "The 8/6 Peace Commemoration Ceremony has taken root. However, a *matsuri* (festival) that every citizen can equally enjoy still needs to be invented" (*Chûgoku shinbun*, 17 July 1976).[15]

The media, furthermore, characterized the two municipal ceremonies as follows: "If the day of prayer, 6 August, is a celebration for 'stillness' [*sei*], the new festival celebrates 'activeness' [*dô*]" (*Chûgoku shinbun*, 15 September 1976).[16] August sixth is a day of mourning and prayer for the dead; Flower Festival in May is a day of joyous glorification of the living. The term *dô* connotes dynamism, potency, vigor, and animation; *sei* refers to the static and the silent.

For many, to be sure, "8/6" is never "static," nor are the dead ever

"silent." During the early postwar period, Hiroshima's 8/6 Peace Commemoration made the city a place for vocal protests against the escalating
arms race between the United States and the Soviet Union and against
Japan's post–Korean War remilitarization as part of the U.S. cold war strategy in East Asia. The right-wing terrorist attack on the Gensuibaku kinshi
sekai taikai (Ban on Atomic and Hydrogen Bomb World Conferences)
also escalated, as the Liberal Democratic party began to denounce the So-
cialist and Communist parties for manipulating the conference for their
own political interests, and subsequently pressured the Hiroshima prefectural government to cut subsidies for the conference in 1959. In 1963 radical students, demanding a ban on nuclear testing, attempted to take over
the site, only to be dispersed by riot police. During the 1970s the 8/6
scenes became extremely radicalized because of Japan's cooperation with
U.S. military aggression in the Vietnam War. When the late Prime Minister
Eisaku Sato attended the 1971 commemoration ceremony—in the first
participation by a current prime minister since the ceremony began—
groups of youths aggressively protested his support of U.S. military action.
Fifty-nine students were arrested. In sharp contrast to Nagasaki, which has
been associated with survivors' "prayers" (*inori no Nagasaki*), partly reflecting the city's large Christian population, Hiroshima has been characterized by its "anger" (*ikari no Hiroshima*).[17]

For the survivor poet Kurihara Sadako, quoted at the beginning of
this essay, the dead souls enshrined at the central memorial must scold and
awaken the living out of their indulgence in affluence and pleasure. She
argues, for example, that the recent emphasis on "bright" peace, including
advertisements for the Flower Festival, creates the illusion that peace has
already been accomplished. For such survivors "8/6," and not the Flower
Festival, manifests the "authentic" Hiroshima. The 8/6 Commemoration is
a reflexive and revitalizing moment whereby survivors and others are reim-
pelled by the memorialization to act further toward the yet unattained
peace. Prayers are given to appease the souls, but the act is far from making the victims impotent.

The Flower Festival has been defined and redefined not only by what
it is but also by what it excludes, what it is not. A festive event in which
people "respect peace and praise the pleasures of life" (*Chûgoku shinbun*, 3
May 1989) is different from an occasion in which community members remember the war and observe the dead. It is an event in which apolitical

"citizens" participate, not organized union laborers or activists; it is a festival in which police officers march in brass bands, not as law enforcers but as contributors to the moral community. It is also an occasion when the Cub Scouts and ordinary people, not the riot police, control the crowds. It is an event for the community, not a ceremony in which thousands of outsiders participate. The 8/6 Peace Commemoration Ceremony, to be sure, was originally designed to serve as a communal festive event, but it turned out to be only an occasion that revealed the conflicts in political attitudes and social ideals rather than encouraging consensual involvement of all citizens as a whole. A successful communal event must, by definition, be able to enhance a Durkheimian collective effervescence and a sense of unity, not disagreements, within the community.

Moreover, a festival for peace must be a "joyous" occasion: anger is not an appropriate sentiment. As the young president of a steel company maintained, the new communal event succeeded in representing the city of peace, but by clearly differentiating the notion of peace from the issues of the atomic bomb:

> Peace is the face of Hiroshima. Not the atom bomb, but peace,
> must represent the city. What is peace? When people get together
> and have fun, that is what I call peace.... The festival demonstrates
> an incarnation of peace [*heiwa no gugenka*], but in this case peace
> means that which is detached from ideological strife.

The inventors of the Flower Festival seem to have succeeded in yet another process of transforming the texture of the notion of peace. Today, the festival appears to offer a perfect occasion to celebrate the new official representation of Hiroshima, the site not of the nuclear holocaust but of peace and prosperity. The parade is a salute to commodities and affluence; it celebrates the multinational corporate culture. The festival also hails diversity in harmony. Different generations, classes, regions, nationalities, organizations of diverse political orientations — all of these are present. But such different groups, ordered and compartmentalized, would not interact or engage in dialogue so much as they might impress the spectators. The festival, above all, helps tame the concept of "peace" while decentering atom bomb memories in the city's official representation. The association among the themes of peace, the bomb, and politics, which apparently tormented the city administrator who was responsible for the prefectural exposition, is no longer present. At least in the discourse of the Flower Festival, peace is a sign of innocence and harmlessness. It masks and excludes questions that may include those of class conflict, oppression, military violence, or corporate exploitation, the issues to which "people are allergic."

Clean Surfaces

> *Mummies do not decay because of worms: they die from being transplanted from a prolonged symbolic order, which is master over death and putrescence, on to an order of history, science and museums.*   (Baudrillard 1983: 20–21)

A series of attempts to remove the ruins of atom bomb destruction can perhaps best illustrate the spatial containment of history in the renewal of cityscape. During my stay, a number of architectural remains from the bombing, including office buildings, banks, and bridges, were razed, one after another, for site renovation.[18] To be sure, the massive removal of atomic relics has met resistance from survivors and other citizens. Unlike the young steel company president, they maintain that the city has been totally neglecting the city's most important historical experience. The opponents of the renewal projects have formed groups to arrange various events, such as walk rallies, sketching festivals, and symposiums, to raise public concern about the disappearing atomic bomb ruins. Petitions for the preservation of several buildings were also submitted to the city. Three such controversies—those regarding the preservation of the Hiroshima Red Cross Hospital, the Nippon Bank Building, and the Atom Bomb Dome—show how the meanings of these sites have been produced, challenged, and transformed.

The Hiroshima Red Cross Hospital, or the "Atomic Bomb Hospital," as it is commonly referred to, was utterly destroyed by the bomb; only the outer walls of the buildings remained. Shortly after the war, the hospital was rebuilt, but with the retention of an iron window frame, warped by the atomic blast, and a white wall, pierced and scarred by pieces of broken glass. A new plan for the renovation and enlargement of the building, however, required the removal of these remains. The hospital managers decided to donate the ruined wall fragment and the window frame to the Atom Bomb Museum.

The preservationists organized groups and protested that the hospital should keep the remains as an organic part of the new building. A retired national railway worker, a survivor who lost his left eye to the bomb at age nineteen, was an active member of one of these citizens' groups. When I asked about his opinion on the matter, he stressed the significance of retaining a visible site/sight that can then provide a didactic space for memories:

> It is meaningful to have [the remains] preserved as they were
> bombed, in order for others to understand how destructive the
> weapon is. The role of the atomic ruins as witnesses to the
> bomb is becoming exceedingly important, especially when the
> human witnesses are aging. That which loses shape also loses spirit.
> When it disappears from our sight, it disappears from our
> memory. To take down the atom bomb ruins means to erase their
> history.

In the ten years since his retirement, this man has been searching on his own for what he calls "the atom bomb claw marks" (*tsumeato*), that is, the relics of the bomb, and compiling their photographs and his detailed handwritten explanations into a booklet. He takes with him almost everywhere a hefty high-tech camera, splendidly equipped with automatic focus and zoom and wide-angle lenses. His photographs are neatly organized, often pasted in commonplace notebooks, and the texts include descriptions of the objects, notes on their locations, and the photographer's own comments about the presumed conditions affecting the objects at the time of the bombing. It is as if, through his tenacious search for the "claw-marks," he is reconfirming his own life, the fact that he had survived, although with irreparable impairment: the camera substitutes for his lost eye. He criticized the city's attitude: "I feel as though I must continue to take pictures of the ruins so that I can help protect the human rights of the dead" (*shisha no jinken yûmon o mamoranya*).

At one of the public meetings the preservationists organized, a woman from a neighboring prefecture, who had been a student nurse at the hospital when it was bombed forty-four years before, was invited to give an eyewitness account of the bombing. In a soft but clear voice, she read what she had previously written down, sobbing at times and often pausing momentarily between the lines:

I was in my second year. In those days, we students were all
suffering from chronic malnutrition. But the wartime tension kept
our minds clear. As I stood facing the window that looked out over
the courtyard, a yellow-white illumination, like burning
magnesium, suddenly spread all over the window with a roaring
sound. It was still as death. I probably stood up immediately. The
ceiling had collapsed. The windows were broken. There was no
one moving. A patient passed by. . . . We tried to rescue a student
nurse who had been hospitalized. She was buried underneath a
crushed wooden building. But we were unable to move even a leg.
Like the rush of a tide, the wounded survivors rolled into the
hospital. Soon, the medicine ran out. . . . With outside help, we
cleared the inside of the hospital.

The town of Hiroshima fell into pieces so completely that I
could even view the far-off station; and it began to burn. The
buried students were unrescued; Hiroshima continued to blaze
brightly.

. . . On the morning of the seventh, we gathered in the
courtyard. Only thirteen of us were present among approximately
one hundred and fifty students who were at the hospital. The
wounded people packed into the entranceway began to die, one by
one. In about a week, everyone was gone. We burned the corpses
in the courtyard. We put in envelopes the bones that were still
burning inside. It continued day after day. . . . At every footstep,
bones cracked under our feet. The phosphorus flames continued to
burn, as if people were calling to let us know that they had died
there.

The defeat in the war was a great shock for us youth. Everything we received through education crumbled away. Only empty
feelings remained. The ruins before our eyes and the pain of the
deep wounds in our hearts — only from there, I believe, may
grow an unyielding will never to repeat war and never to use the
atomic bomb. I remember the white town I saw from the top of
Hijiyama for the first time since I recovered from ten years of
illness [caused by the radiation]. I remembered the town before it
had been burned. I also remembered the town that had turned
into ashes. And I saw the streets today. I now wish I could have
preserved the town of crumbling ruins, fencing it off with a chain.
I wished I could have frozen the flames of phosphorus that continued to burn, reminding us that people were dying here. I wish
so even to this day.

... All wars made people suffer, despite the differences in their
gravity.... It is not easy to defend peace. The hospital shouldn't be
completely renewed, but instead it must be handed on to the
generation that did not experience the war.... We must make the
right decision. For lives are at stake.

A readers' column in a local newspaper introduced an opposing view.
In contrast to the woman's memory, which was underpinned by strong
feelings for a lost collectivity, a sixty-one-year-old man who also remembered the hospital at the time of the bombing expressed no such nostalgia:

My father, too, was lying beside the entrance hall of the
hospital.... He died on the night of the ninth. As I close my eyes, I
can still remember vividly the scene at the hospital entranceway.
Several corpses were floating in the pond; nearby a few naked
bodies of female students lay cold. As I stepped into the hallway, I
saw an even more appalling picture. There were more dead people
than those who were alive. It seems like a miracle that I could find
my father in such apocalyptic circumstances.

But for me it is sufficient that the horrific scene is kept to my
own memories. I do not wish to return to the spot. Moreover, I
will by no means hope to explain to others about my father's
condition. The atomic bomb misery has already been recorded in
various ways. Isn't it better if the aging hospital should be drastically
renovated so that it can serve those of us who survived? At least
from watching the TV, the explanation given by the hospital
management personnel sounds reasonable.... The Atom Bomb
Dome alone is quite sufficient as a remains that records the atom
bomb experience in Hiroshima city. (*Chûgoku shinbun,*
26 January 1990)

Along with the Atomic Bomb Hospital, the Nippon Bank Building
also attracted the public's concern over preserving buildings that survived
the bomb. The European-classical-style structure, on one of the major
downtown avenues, came through the bombing despite being less than
400 meters from the hypocenter; it has continued to operate for business
during the postwar period. Following the bank's relocation plan, the decision was made to dispose of both the lot and the building, at the estimated
price of approximately 20 billion yen. Citizens who lobbied for the preservation of the Nippon Bank Building demand that the city purchase the building and remodel it into a public facility that would serve simultaneously as

a library, a commemorative hall, and a historical museum of literature related to the atom bomb.

A city assembly member's remark concerning the preservation of the bank building is helpful in understanding what is excluded in the renewed space of amnesia:

> [To turn the atom bombed buildings into] a small theater would be an interesting idea as well—a small space where the audiences can have an intimate and heartfelt experience, where people can talk about peace in an intimate and heartfelt way. Better to be smaller: the smaller the space, the more sensitive one can be. Even if they may be small in number, I want people to experience something heavy and deep. I want to make [the building] into a space where people can cherish their personal encounters with each other.

She continued, "It went through the bombing, survived, and has persistently lived through the postwar years. It is living its history." As a "living witness," it tells people its history, "how the space was used, what people saw and felt in it, and what kind of condition it was in at the time of the bombing."

Her narrative, with its central notion of "living-ness," differs sharply from the discourse of the Flower Festival, in which 8/6 memories have been retextured as the static and the dead. Clearly the bank building for her is not a static ruin. Even the literary artifacts are not merely objects for display: "It would be nice if we could have some place where both citizens and visitors could find literature that was written with specific emotions or under particular historical conditions." Here, literary works are understood not as texts that can be dislodged from contexts, but rather as memories inextricable from the space and history in which they were produced. Such "living-ness" of the specific historical moment, together with the rootedness of its memories in the particular space, might deter the accelerating forgetfulness and help place the past in constant dialogue with the present.

In contrast to the polemic controversies concerning the preservation of the hospital artifacts and the bank building, a remarkable public consensus was reached on maintaining the Atom Bomb Dome—the remains of the former Industrial Promotion Hall, which stands at the northern riverbank across from the Peace Memorial Park. The dome is also located on the park's north-south axis, a line that divides the park into near-symmetry, and it can be seen in the distance through the U-shape central cenotaph. In the fall of 1989 work began on permanent preservation of the Atom Bomb Dome, a "trace" of the nuclear holocaust. The fundraising campaign for the conservation of the relics, which began in May, reached the targeted amount of 100 million yen, one half of the entire expected cost of renovation, in less than a hundred days. By the beginning of 1990, the total donated amount exceeded 390 million yen. The major survivors' associations, antiwar and antinuclear organizations, and labor organizations succeeded in large-scale fundraising; many individuals donated their meager savings; children contributed from their allowances; and some seniors gave most of their retirement savings. Students collected donations at their homerooms and housewives did so among family members and neighbors.

The campaign made some long-buried sentiments resurface. Memories of the atomic bomb and the war, as well as postwar experiences that reached beyond generations, appeared in the media.[19] A woman said she donated money in order to console the souls of her close kin who were victims of the bomb. She expressed her strong attachments to the dome, which "remains standing even when its skeleton is exposed" (*Chûgoku shinbun,* 26 December 1989). A fifty-seven-year-old man remarked that donating money became a turning point, a start for his new life as a *kataribe,* a storyteller who could narrate to others the immediate atom bomb experience (ibid.). A seventy-one-year-old man remembered the day when he found the remains of his father-in-law, who had been working in the dome at the time of the bombing. He claimed, "Now that the city has completely changed its appearance ... it is only the dome that can convey to us the apocalyptic situation" (*Chûgoku shinbun,* 6 August 1989). A woman, according to her sixty-three-year-old daughter, would often claim throughout her lifetime that the dome reminded her of her late husband and son, victims of the bomb, who wished her to "live their years for them as well" (*Chûgoku shinbun,* 2 May 1989). A seventy-four-year-old woman whose husband was killed by the bomb while he was working at the dome recalled her surprise when her son once painted a picture of the dome, although he was too young to have remembered his own experience of the bomb (*Asahi shinbun,* 12 May 1989). A forty-six-year-old man who had not known that he was a survivor until ten years ago, when his mother obtained his health certificate, said, "If the dome is preserved, my two daughters who are now indifferent to the issues of war may remember some day in the future that their father used to talk about the atom bomb" (*Asahi shinbun*, 1 May 1989).[20]

Unlike the enthusiasm that involved the entire nation as well as concerned people abroad, the initial attitude of the city government toward the campaign was mixed—not about whether or not to retain the ruin, the dilemma Robert Jay Lifton had observed over twenty years before, but rather about how. The mayor, along with other city officials and several city assembly members, was reluctant to rely on a mass fundraising campaign. Such a campaigning style, it was feared, would tend to be dominated by supporters of the opposition parties, communists and socialists, and would most likely be manipulated ideologically (*ideologî undô ni riyôsareru*), distorting the "pure motives" (*junsui na kimochi*) of the donors (*Asahi shinbun*, 2 February 1989).[21]

Although the donations would be motivated by individuals' "pure" sentiments, it remains quite doubtful whether city officials and others could have felt comfortable about the flood of painful memories that filled the public arena. Contrary to their worries, however, the degree of the public's enthusiasm for the dome, incomparable by far with anything that had been expressed about other memorials or other atom bomb remains, allowed the city to prove that the dome, together with the Peace Memorial Park and the Atom Bomb Museum, is now the only legitimate and proper receptacle of atom bomb memories.

The Atom Bomb Dome, now a museumized object, comfortably situated in distant ceremonial scenery visible from the central cenotaph in the Peace Memorial Park, depicts the atomic horror as if it were a remote, almost fictional incident. Its sharp contrast with the background scenery of magnificently recovered urban space assures people of the peaceful, prosperous, and clean world. Through its permanent preservation, the Atom Bomb Dome became an officially designated site of memory for the collective experience of the atomic bomb. It will outlive all other atomic remains: the hospital wall, the bank building, and many others. The dome will then serve like Baudrillard's Disneyland for the postnuclear world. Though perhaps leaving in people's mind a slight uneasiness and doubts about the reality of nuclear condition, the neat confinement of atom bomb memories—unlike what the former railway worker called "claw-marks of the atomic bomb," scattered throughout urban surfaces—

obscures one's vision of a world that may in fact be thoroughly contaminated by nuclear weaponry.

Conclusion

Brightness, comfort, and cleanliness are the ruling aesthetic in Hiroshima's urban renewal. For the majority of young Japanese who grew up after the periods of rapid economic growth, the postindustrial reality presents itself through sanitized and comfortable images. Their knowledge about the era of heavy industrialization and modernization, an era that began in the late nineteenth century, is filled with painful stories of urban alienation, poverty, labor disputes, and industrial pollution. But today, electricity, "clean" energy, substitutes for oil and sooty coal. High-tech industry solves environmental problems; for working women, pleasant office automation replaces backbreaking labor in textile factories. The clean, bright, and comfortable urban scenery, moreover, rests upon the position of the nation in the present global political economy. The waterfront redevelopment project, for instance, which would change the coastal area from a center of heavy industry to an urban resort space, cannot be carried out without the actual removal of the industrial sector to other areas of the world and by virtually transferring the accompanying pollution and industrial wastes. The sanitized urban space is brought about in part by the nation's wealth and the transnational power that enables the physical displacement of the dirty and unpleasant.

Such an aesthetic of "brightness" does not simply describe the visible qualities of things or events. As we have seen, things and events also create cultural forces that direct action and emotion, prescribing the way we at once perceive and act upon the various dimensions of social life. They moreover shape our awareness of history and understanding of the world. It may well be argued that the resistance to the "lightening up" of urban scenery and cleaning up of "atom-bomb clawmarks" is as much residual sentiment (see Williams 1977) toward the fading memories as an objection to such governing aesthetics that aspire to superficial tidiness and their implications for ways of seeing—or, more crucially, not seeing—the world.

Through exploring the recent rearticulation of Hiroshima's self-image, this essay analyzed the politics of memories within the cultural conditions of late capitalism in Japan. Hiroshima's urban renewal is a part of the process whereby the city's political and economic power elites have attempted to determine, temporally and spatially, the official territory for memorializations of the war and the atom bomb, while simultaneously redesigning the landscape into one that uncritically assumes Japan's power and affluence and accelerates amnesia about the nation's recent past. By the marginalization and appropriation of representations concerning the war and the atom bomb, Hiroshima's urban renewal in effect creates a state in which any element or incident of the society becomes naturalized and non-upsetting, and thereby serves to maintain the society's existing arrangements of culture and power. In short, what we find in the engineering of "bright" Hiroshima is a purging of critical thoughts, a process of depoliticization attained through taming the memoryscape.

It is perhaps important to note that the promoters of urban development unanimously express strong reservations toward the opinions that discredit the city's recent transformations. The sugar company president in particular criticized those nationally acclaimed "scholars and cultural elites" (*gakusha, bunkajin*) who, when asked for public comment, almost without exception stressed the significance of Hiroshima as a site of atom bomb memorialization, rather than mentioning the city's other properties.[22] Such opinions of the "outsiders" are irresponsible, he aptly complained, for the commentators themselves do not need to face the consequences of what they propose. Indeed, if Hiroshima's "natives" choose to remain silent about the bomb, if they wish to avoid any further political turmoil over the war and the bomb or about nuclear issues in general, and if "they" choose to rebuild "bright and jovial" cityspaces, how can anyone convincingly argue that we onlookers, whose lives are not immediately affected, are entitled to speak against such ambitions? Isn't it rather audacious and unfair for those of us who temporarily visit Hiroshima to hope that the city and its people remain different from the rest of us so that we can experience what we believe to be the authentic Hiroshima?

Yet, I submit, demarcation of the insider/outsider boundaries can never be consistent, nor is it ever completely attained. The world is subjected to forces that increasingly accelerate the permeating of borders and the intermingling of money, information, merchandise, and people. Officially defined as an international *messe* and convention city, Hiroshima cannot escape the intrusion of multitudes of "alien" elements and heterogenous encounters. Such an orientation in urban planning rests upon the nation's wealth, the celebration of which undoubtedly fosters cultures that occlude the process whereby material affluence is obtained, obscuring questions regarding such issues as poverty, death, exploitation, and oppression. But the same conditions simultaneously allow the influx of elements that provoke an awareness of problems external to the given scope of cultural/political imagination. In a similar vein, the approaching observance of the fiftieth anniversary of the bombing in 1995 certainly will provide another setting for further contestations, especially between those who aim for a closure of war memories and a reconciliation with the past and those who seek for ruptures in the dominant temporal and spatial discourses.

While being fully aware of such possibilities for resistance enabled by the same condition of postmodernity (Foster 1983; Ivy 1988), in this essay I focused primarily on the process of domination.[23] As officially represented, Hiroshima will continue to transform itself into a site of pleasure and urban entertainment. It is becoming a future-oriented megalopolis and an international site of commerce and consumption, which remembers its four hundred years of castle town tradition. In the dominant logic of late capitalism, the designing of Hiroshima's twenty-first-century cityscape assumes that, as the "dark and gloomy" turns into the "bright and jovial," hardships will be replaced by comforts, disputes by consensus, pains by pleasures, and perhaps even Hiroshima's anger by conviviality. Fully entertained by the multiple dimensions of Hiroshima-ness, we will then enjoy the pleasures of peace without being discomforted by the potential for wars or nuclear terrors.

Through spatial reformulation and the enclosing of wartime histories, Hiroshima's urban renewal attempts, not to erase, but to reregister atom bomb memories. Containing them securely on a "proper" terrain, both temporally and spatially, it celebrates peace in its weightlessness. There peace becomes an icon for the harmlessness and the well-being of postwar Japan. At least in the official cartography of memory, seldom is it a reminder of death, anger, sorrow, or pain. Yet, even within the ruling imageries of the renewed cityscape, Hiroshima is a palimpsest of memories. Memories and sentiments, though now contained and submerged, await moments to reemerge, threatening to break their confinements. As de Certeau remarks, "Any autonomous order is founded upon what it eliminates: it produces a 'residue' condemned to be forgotten. But what was excluded reinfiltrates the place of its origin—now the present's 'clean' [*propre*] place" (1986: 4).[24]

Notes

This essay is a product of research conducted periodically between 1986 and 1990 and was originally drafted for the 1991 workshop "Space, Time, and the Politics of Memory," sponsored by the Social Science Research Council and the John D. and Catherine T. MacArthur Foundation, in Portsmouth, New Hampshire. The research and writing were supported by the Department of Anthropology at Stanford University, Hiroshima Stûdo University, a Social Science Research Council and MacArthur Foundation Fellowship in International Peace and Security, and a MacArthur Foundation Summer Grant, as well as a write-up grant from the Center for International Security and Arms Control at Stanford University. Young-hae Jung, Masanori Kobayashi, Hiroto Kuboura, Chiyoko Kuwahara, Suzuko Numata, Keizaburo Toyonaga, and many others generously shared their views on Hiroshima's current condition, although I am solely responsible for the content of the essay. Many thanks to the MacArthur fellows who were present at the workshop for their helpful suggestions. The essay also benefited from the following individuals' support and critical commentaries: Harumi Befu, Jane Collier, Takashi Fujitani, Marilyn Ivy, Masao Miyoshi, Renato Rosaldo, Miriam Silverberg, and Sylvia Yanagisako. This essay will be included in my book, currently in preparation, on the politics of Hiroshima memories.

All quotations without identified written sources are from personal interviews and conversations I had during the period of research (1986–90).

1. The official translation is: "Let all the souls here rest in peace; for [*sic*] we shall not repeat the evil" (Hiroshima Heiwa Bunka Sentâ 1978: 43). The usual lack of a subject in the Japanese phrase generated a well-known public controversy as to "whose" evil it was. The debate became especially heated in 1952 when an Indian jurist condemned the United States for its responsibility for making the decision to use the bomb. The city settled the case by publicly announcing that the subject is each individual who stands at the cenotaph and vows not to repeat the evil. The majority of survivors' opinions that appeared in newspaper columns during the 1950s were unsupportive of the phrase. They insisted that the phrase did not adequately express survivors' anger toward the bomb. In 1970 another public controversy was triggered by a group of right-wing intellectuals and politicians who demanded that the city change the inscription. They argued that the inscription manifested a shameful attitude, as if the massacred were apologizing for what had been done to them. Out of the controversy, it became clear that the majority of citizens support the phrase as is (Jichitai Mondai Kenkyûjo and Hiroshima Kenkyûkai 1982: 249–54).

2. This quotation from Kurihara's poem is taken from *Asahi shinbun* (20 August 1989).

3. It is also subtitled "The City of Water, Greenery, and Culture that Contributes to World Peace" (*kokusai heiwa bunka toshi — sekai heiwa ni kôken suru mizu to midori to bunka no machi*). A year later, detailed plans for achieving this official slogan were outlined for citizens in an easily accessible monthly newsletter published by the municipal Public Relations Department. See the summary of the Third Hiroshima Basic City Planning (Hiroshima-shi 1983).

4. Despite the pervasive association among the three signs mentioned above, the meaning of "peace" is far from being stable or transparent. For the national Conservative party leaders, for instance, Hiroshima's past stands as a proof of rapid economic growth and the country's affluence and prosperity, which have been achieved since 1955 under nearly forty years of one-party rule. Likewise, for Hiroshima's local power elites, the annual commemoration of 6 August offers an occasion to pay respects to the dead communally while also appreciating the city's successful postwar recovery. For them, Hiroshima's atom bomb memory is weathered and obsolete. Moreover, for those in positions of authority, defending peace might mean maintaining order and harmony. Hiroshima's past experience of the war and of

the atom bomb, on the other hand, are often articulated in gendered discourse as a sign of patriarchy and militarism. Many of those who oppose the official historiography claim that the experience of Hiroshima and Nagasaki has served to mystify the nation's history. In conjunction with the overall effacing of the war in Asia from state-crafted historical writings, including school textbooks, the collective memory of Hiroshima and Nagasaki enhances the image of Japan in the nation's historical consciousness as a victim, rather than an aggressor, in the war of invasion. And for the Korean minority, members of the so-called "discriminated villages" and other marginalized groups of people, Hiroshima's atom bomb memory illustrates the ultimate consequence of an autocratic state, while peace serves as a metaphor for struggles for civil rights and equality.

5. During this year, thirty-one Japanese cities celebrated the centennial of their municipal administrations, the commemoration of the 1889 local government ordinance (*shichôson rei*), which reformulated the regional administrations under the reign of the emerging modern nation-state.

6. At the time of this report, the prospects for building the tower were bleak because of various obstacles, including the lack of financing, a suitable location, and its cause. Naturally, there were strong protests from the survivors. Later, another newspaper article predicted the difficulties (*Chûgoku shinbun,* 29 December 1989).

7. In criticizing the usage of the spatial metaphor of depth/surface in the conventional anthropological conceptualization of closed, bounded, and essential identity, Dorinne Kondo discusses the need to move away from the notion of self as "the inner, reflective essence of psychological consciousness" (1990: 12). My critique of Lifton's analysis resonates with Kondo's warning that such theoretical assumptions about human psychology often preclude the understandings for "an open, shifting multiplicity of meanings, constituted in and by a changing field of discourses and forces of power" (14–15). The earlier conceptualization of self and emotion as sociocultural constructs embedded in a nexus of power was articulated by Michelle Rosaldo (1984). For more recent development of such approaches, see Catherine A. Lutz and Lila Abu-Lughod (1990) and Geoffrey M. White (1992).

8. For detailed historical and sociological research on the transformation of the Motomachi District, see Hiroshima-shi (1983: 110–48). It not only summarizes the development of the urban planning but also introduces, through literary representations and ethnographies, the recollections about the actual lives that unfolded in the space that was once called "the atom bomb slums" or "the aioi street."

9. The project is described thus in the promotion pamphlet *Mirai e habataku machi wo mezashite: miryokutekina toshikûkan zukuri.*

10. One example of the use of *hiragana* can be found in the tourist campaign pamphlet issued by the prefectural government "Sun Sun Hiroshima: Do *yû* Hiroshima." "Sun" and "Do" are written in alphabets as in the original English words; "Hiroshima" is written with *hiragana* both times it appears. "*Yû*" is written with a Chinese character as a translingual homonym, meaning both "play" and an English word, "you" (see Hiroshima-ken Kankô Kyanpên Jikkô Iinkai Jimukyoku n.d.).

11. See the campaign pamphlet issued by the city, *Hikari kankaku toshi Hiroshima kêkaku.*

12. Since the beginning of the festival, the newspaper has consistently emphasized two themes: citizens as the main actors of the festival and the symbolism of flowers. The 1989 Hiroshima Flower Festival used the slogan "Can you hear flowers singing?"; the following year there was, "Let's converse with flowers about our dreams and about our future." For the 1989 Flower Festival, a newspaper headline repeated the sentiment, "The main actors are the citizens."

13. Robert Jay Lifton observed a similar aspiration for greenery among the people in

Hiroshima in the 1960s, but he did not question how natural it was to appropriate such images. Lifton commented: "Even fourteen years after the bomb a commentator spoke of the city's 'nostalgia for greenery' and longing for the 'forest city' of the past (though when postwar allocations have been carried out, there will be a much higher percentage of land used for parks than there was in the prewar city). For . . . the hunger for it is a hunger for authentic symbolism of life" (1967: 265).

14. When the planning of the festival began, newspapers publicized it as follows: "A new festival is born in Hiroshima. Thirty-two years after the atomic bombing, a day to celebrate together the glory of peace is born in Hiroshima, the city where beforehand there was only the day of prayer, 6 August. The new festival is a day to 'praise peace' " (*Chûgoku shinbun,* 7 May 1977).

15. The head of the executive committee emphasized the need for a new festive occasion, claiming that Hiroshima, unlike other prefectural cities, has had "no *matsuri* that is firmly grounded in local history and tradition, or that can receive a consensus of the entire citizenry" (*Chûgoku shinbun,* 23 September 1976). The article also argued that while the annual summer Shôkon sai (festival for welcoming the dead souls) at the National Defense Shrine is often remembered as a festival celebrated by the entire community, it also has a strong association with the nationalistic and militaristic character of the prewar state. Several attempts to create festivals after the war, such as Hiroshima Matsuri or Minato Matsuri, it is argued, equally failed in involving the entire municipal community because they lacked rootedness in local history or because their concepts did not catch people's interests (*Chûgoku shinbun,* 30 March 1977).

16. This contrast of the August Peace Commemoration and the Flower Festival has appeared in the media several times since the initial conception of the event (*Chûgoku shinbun,* 31 October 1976, 28 April 1977, 4 May 1977, and 6 May 1979).

17. Nagasaki, however, has emerged as a locale of struggles against the national government since 1988, when Mayor Motoshima Hitoshi referred publicly to the war responsibilities of the late Showa emperor, and was later attacked by right-wing terrorists because of his statement. Nagasaki, together with Okinawa, is now a major counterstate locus in Japan's political geography today, whereas Hiroshima's administration is consistently compliant with state policy. Although in Nagasaki the mayor's commemorative speech has included references to the atom bomb victims in Korea and other countries, Hiroshima's mayors had remained silent until very recently not only on the issues of Japan's colonial aggression and war of invasion but also on the atom bomb survivors who are not nationals. The newly elected mayor, Hiraoka Takashi, a corporate executive and former journalist who has written extensively on the issue of Korean atom bomb survivors, has been more aggressive in clarifying Japan's war responsibilities and colonial rule over Asia. How such changes should be interpreted against the milieu in which the discourse on Japan's history of aggression is becoming hegemonic in national politics needs to be further examined, especially in relation to the development of debates on the status of the Self Defense Force and other constitutional issues. See also Field (1991) for further discussion on Mayor Motoshima.

18. Out of 142 major public buildings within five kilometers of the bomb's hypocenter, about 80 suffered only minimal damage. During the last 45 years, many of these surviving buildings have been taken down and only 29 of them are still standing (*Asahi shinbun,* 8 December 1990). For a brief description in English of the current state of the atom bomb ruins, see Shôno (1993).

19. Many donors attached letters to their money. Over three thousand letters received by the campaign office were to be edited and published by the city in the 1991–92 fiscal year.

20. Besides what appeared in the media, people in general often contrasted the Atom Bomb Dome preservation campaign with the first campaign held twenty-two years before. They argued that when the mayor stood in the front line of the street fundraising campaign, it was the city administration, not the survivors, that eagerly supported the Dome's preservation (compare Lifton 1967). "It was an important resource for the city's tourist promotion, you know," a middle-aged housewife told me in casual conversation, "so it is ironic that those people who are now campaigning for the preservation of the dome and other things—even the former head of the survivors' association—were in those days reluctant to retain the building. They thought the dome would only remind them of their painful memories." A national newspaper that openly supported the preserving of atom bomb ruins also called for the public's attention: "Let us not forget that in the past even the dome barely escaped from being demolished" (*Asahi shinbun,* 7 December 1990).

21. The newspaper report gave other reasons why the city assembly members hesitated to rely on a public fundraising campaign. Some asserted that the city should be financially responsible for the preservation; others worried that people might feel deceived if the campaign called for "permanent" preservation a second time. Out of over 390 million yen donated, the city decided to use 100 million, as was initially planned, and with the rest create a fund for the future cost of repairs.

22. An earlier instance of such an exchange between an outside celebrity and the insiders can be found in Kenzaburō Oe (1981). Oe quotes a letter he received from a survivor doctor who implicitly criticized Oe's portrayals of suffering survivors, expressing doubts about the politicization of Hiroshima. Oe responds: "I noted that its harshest criticism was reserved for passages written by me, an outsider to Hiroshima" (16).

23. Readers may wonder how one could possibly formulate any sort of resistance to such dominant structuring of the cityscape. Difficult though it may be to evaluate their effectiveness, readers should be reminded how critical the survivors' presence and their practices are. Although I cannot discuss it here in detail, their space of storytelling, such as the one we have seen in the recollection by the former nurse who survived the bombing in Hiroshima Red Cross Hospital, posits a powerful location in which voices of objections and resistance can be generated. Such tactics of insubordination within Hiroshima's politics of memory may be analogous to what Michel de Certeau observed of the space of popular stories: "This space protects the weapons of the weak against the reality of the established order. It also hides them from the social categories which 'make history' because they dominate it. And whereas historiography recounts in the past tense the strategies of instituted powers, these 'fabulous' stories offer their audience a repertory of tactics for future use" (1984: 23). Elsewhere (Yoneyama forthcoming), I discuss at length such spatial as well as narrative tactics of insubordination and other possible forms of resistance that unfold in contemporary Hiroshima.

24. Marilyn Ivy drew my attention to this remark and to its relevance to the context of Hiroshima's urban renewal.

Bibliography

Asahi shinbun. Osaka: Asahi Shinbunsha.

Baudrillard, Jean. 1983. *Simulations.* Trans. Paul Foss, Paul Patton, and Philip Beitchman. New York: Semiotext(e).

Berman, Russell A. 1989. *Modern Culture and Critical Theory: Art, Politics, and the Legacy of the Frankfurt School.* Madison: University of Wisconsin Press.

Chûgoku shinbun. Hiroshima: Chûgoku Shinbunsha.

de Certeau, Michel. 1984. *The Practice of Everyday Life.* Berkeley and Los Angeles: University of California Press.

———. 1986. *Heterologies: Discourse on the Other.* Minneapolis: University of Minnesota Press.

Field, Norma. 1988. "*Somehow*: The Postmodern as Atmosphere." *The South Atlantic Quarterly* 87 (3, Summer): 551–70. (Reprinted in Miyoshi and Harootunian 1989.)

———. 1991. *In the Realm of a Dying Emperor.* New York: Pantheon Books.

Foster, Hal. 1983. "Postmodernism: A Preface." In *The Anti-Aesthetic: Essays on Postmodern Culture,* ed. Hal Foster. Seattle: Bay Press. ix–xvi.

Fujitani, Takashi. 1992. "Electronic Pageantry and Japan's Symbolic Emperor." *Journal of Asian Studies* 51 (4, November): 824–50.

Harvey, David. 1989. *The Condition of Postmodernity.* Oxford (England) and Cambridge, Mass.: Basil Blackwell.

Hiroshima Heiwa Bunka Sentâ. 1978. *Hiroshima dokuhon.*

Hiroshima-ken Kankô Kyanpên Jikkô Iinkai Jimukyoku. N.d. "Sun Sun Hiroshima: Do *yû* Hiroshima."

Hiroshima-shi, ed. 1983. *Hiroshima shinshi: Toshi bunka hen.* Hiroshima: Hiroshima-shi.

Hiroshima-shi. 1989. *Hikari kankaku toshi Hiroshima Kêkaku.*

Hiroshima-shi Kankô Kyôkai. N.d. *Tabi no uta ga kikoeru: Hiroshima.*

Hiroshima-shi Shichôshitsu Kôhôka. 1989. *Shimin to shisei,* no. 893 (1 July).

Ivy, Marilyn Jeanette. 1988. "Critical Texts, Mass Artifacts: The Consumption of Knowledge in Postmodern Japan." *The South Atlantic Quarterly* 87 (3, Summer): 419–44. (Reprinted in Miyoshi and Harootunian 1989.)

Jameson, Frederic. 1984. "Postmodernism; or, The Cultural Logic of Late Capitalism." *New Left Review* 146: 53–92.

Jichitai Mondai Kenkyûjo and Hiroshima Kenkyûkai, eds. 1982. *Hiroshima Hiroshima: Daisanji Hiroshima shisei hakusho.* Hiroshima: Hiroshima-shi Shokium Rôdô Kumiai.

Kondo, Dorinne. 1990. *M. Butterfly*: Orientalism, Gender, and a Critique of Essentialist Identity. *Cultural Critique,* no. 16 (Fall): 5–29.

Lifton, Robert Jay. 1967. *Death in Life: Survivors of Hiroshima.* New York: Basic Books.

Lutz, Catherine A., and Lila Abu-Lughod, eds. 1990. *Language and the Politics of Emotion.* Cambridge: Cambridge University Press.

Mirai e habataku machi wo mezashite: Miryokutekina toshikûkan zukuri. NTT Motomachi biru kaihatsu keikakuan.

Miyoshi, Masao, and H. D. Harootunian, eds. 1988. Special issue: *Postmodernism and Japan. The South Atlantic Quarterly* 87 (3, Summer).

———. 1989. *Postmodernism and Japan.* Durham: Duke University Press.

Oe, Kenzaburō 1981. *Hiroshima Notes.* Trans. Toshi Yonezawa. Ed. David L. Swain. Tokyo: YMCA Press.

Robertson, Jennifer. 1991. *Native and Newcomer: Making and Remaking a Japanese City.* Berkeley and Los Angeles: University of California Press.

Rosaldo, Michelle. 1984. "Toward an Anthropology of Self and Feeling." In *Culture Theory: Essays on Mind, Self, and Emotion,* ed. R. Shweder and R. LeVine. Cambridge: Cambridge University Press. 137–57.

Shôno, Naomi. 1993. "Mute Reminders of Hiroshima's Atomic Bombing." *Japan Quarterly* 40 (3, July–September): 267–76.

Soja, Edward W. 1989. *Postmodern Geographies: The Reassertion of Space in Critical Social Theory*. New York: Verso.

White Geoffrey M. 1992. "Ethnopsychology." In *New Directions in Psychological Anthropology*, ed. Theodore Schwartz, Geoffrey M. White, and Catherine A. Lutz. Cambridge: Cambridge University Press. 21–46.

Williams, Raymond. 1977. *Marxism and Literature*. Oxford: Oxford University Press.

Yoneyama, Lisa. Forthcoming. *The Dialectics of Memory: Hiroshima*. Berkeley and Los Angeles: University of California Press.

Zukin, Sharon. 1991. *Landscape of Power: From Detroit to Disney World*. Berkeley and Los Angeles: University of California Press.

5

Hegel's Zionism?

Jonathan Boyarin

THIS ESSAY IS an attempt to articulate some of the modern European assumptions about history and national existence that underlie early secular Zionist thinking. These assumptions still seem to be in force among Israel's academic elite and among the leaders of many of its political parties. They help to shape the discursive field within which the makers of Israeli policy and opinion conceive possible resolutions of Israel's conflict with the Palestinians. Thus this essay will repeatedly juxtapose critical discussion of Hegel and other early modern thinkers with symptomatic citations of Zionist thought. I will make explicit the shared nexus of fundamental ideas about history, nation, and state that Hegel's thought shares with Zionism, but the connection I am describing is neither exclusive nor genetic. As the question mark in my title is meant to suggest, my main goal is to interrogate assumptions shared by chauvinists and liberals, and thus help establish an area of discussion beyond the questions of strategy, justice, and compromise between two self-contained "nations."

My theses are four:

1. History, in Hegel, is conceived as the progressive embodiment of spirit in the state (Soja 1989: 46, 86).

2. This absolute model of history as the progression of the world spirit obviates the option of panchrony (Weinreich 1980) — an empathic, imag-

137

inative identification with previous generations—as a basis for Jewish collective identity.

3. Zionism is an attempt to act upon the prediction of the Hegelian progressive-statist ideal, paradoxically using Hegelian thinking about history, identity, and the state.

4. In the Zionist case, Hegelianism is confounded by, among other things, the unexamined slippage between the possible evolution of a "universal liberal" (but covertly Christian) state and a projected "liberal Jewish state."

If these four points, which fairly well encompass the various considerations taken up below, are borne in mind, they should help the reader make sense of this preliminary treatment of a vast, nebulous, and vitally important topic.

The discussion is divided into sections on the specificity of Hegel; Hegel, history, and the state (these first two sections relate primarily to the first and second of my theses); Problematics of modern Jewish identity (relating mostly to my third thesis); Zionisms and the state (dealing chiefly with theses 3 and 4); and preliminary conclusions.

The Specificity of Hegel

The link between the progressive unfolding of Reason and the embodiment of that progress, first in loosely defined "nations" or "worlds" and ultimately in bourgeois Western European states, is a basic theme in Hegel, especially in *The Philosophy of History*. Hegel is so important and so revealing a figure because he formulates nation-statism per se, rather than just being an Enlightenment Figure or a particular nationalist. Both intellectually and chronologically, he seems to be a vital linchpin between Enlightenment progressivism and romantic nationalism. The combination of an ideology of progress with the view that its culmination is manifest in the various European states has served a variety of political visions. Because Hegel's glorification of the Germanic world was not founded on racism, the structure of his philosophy of history was available for any number of nationalist projects of the Right and Left, including those of Jewish-state nationalists. The worthiness of a statebuilding project was noted by the British Conservative Lord Balfour, who extolled it as an alternative outlet for the destructive energies expended by Jewish revolutionaries (Talmon 1980: 234).[1] On the other hand, through Marx, a Hegelian logic could be applied to a leftist view of Zionism as well (Avineri 1981) — especially given Hegel's Orientalist denigration of Asia as immature and unprogressive (Turner 1978: 25–38).[2]

Nevertheless, an objection can be raised as soon as I claim a privileged link between that theme and the problematics of Zionism. To what extent is Hegel merely emblematic, an unusually verbose and vigorous propounder of these modern ideas? The answer is that if we are merely content to brand Zionism as a variety of European nationalism, there is no lack of theoretical or historical models, German, French, and English. If we regard Zionism only as an aspect of colonialist ideology, justifying its repression of local populations outside Europe through an ideology of "progress" that spreads outward from an advanced Europe, here again Hegel is certainly not unique. Precisely what makes the link between Hegel's *Philosophy of History* and secular Zionism so important is that both share a territorialist and statist conception of national identity as well as a supersessive view of history — the notion that the intellectual limitations of the past are always overcome in time. Unlike other nationalist movements, neither is grounded primarily in a vision of the *restoration* to its proper "state" of a glorious, eternal national essence. What Hegel applied to Germany as the pinnacle of world history up to the time of his writing, the early Zionists applied to Jewish history at the turn of the twentieth century and to the project of colonization in Palestine.

Likewise, historians may well object that the eighteenth-century Enlightenment was one thing but primarily romantic nineteenth-century nationalism quite another. Inasmuch, however, as both Hegel's *Philosophy of History* and the founding texts of classical, Western Zionism[3] share the Enlightenment belief that modernity is becoming progressively wiser than "tradition," along with the nationalist belief that individual identity is properly realized in wholehearted participation in the territorially defined nation-state, then the Enlightenment, modernity, and nationalism do seem to form a coherent intellectual complex. These ideas were held, for example, by the pioneering Hebrew lexicographer Eliezer Ben-Yehuda, for whom

total liberation from the burden of Torah and the commandments [*mitzvot*] [was] a mandatory step in the struggle to revive the

Hebrew language. Religion is the source of the Jews' excessive "spirituality." It has usurped the role of land, language, and state — the three pillars of national identity and life for every people. This led to Ben-Yehuda's call for nationalism without religion. (Luz 1988: 13)

There are a number of ways that a critic of rationalist, statist Zionism might relate this stance to Hegel's heritage: first, by regarding Hegel as an intellectual forerunner, a prophet before his time; second, by regarding him as an intellectual progenitor, one of the unacknowledged intellectual ancestors of Zionism; third, by taking him crudely as a convenient whipping boy, a sort of source of all evil, the locus of thinking gone wrong; or, fourth, by viewing Hegel's thought as an unusually self-confident and clearly articulated example of a well-defined (but not necessarily continuous) structure of feeling. It is primarily the last attitude toward the *Philosophy of History* that I am striving for here. Despite references below to specific genetic connections that at least one scholar (Shlomo Avineri) has drawn between Zionism and Hegel's theory of history and the state, I am not trying to identify the intellectual origins of Zionism, but rather to elucidate some of its unspoken assumptions.

Despite my almost exclusive concentration on ideas here, I certainly think both Hegel's writings and Zionist ideology need to be placed within the context of the formation of national states in nineteenth-century Europe. This is another reason for deemphasizing the first three attitudes I outlined above. I do not argue that consciousness determines history. Rather, in the kind of relation explored by Robert Wuthnow (1989), the social contexts of Europe after the French Revolution and of that same Europe after the Dreyfus case in France and the 1881 pogroms in Russia served as fertile grounds for new ideas that both framed the crises of their times and transcended them in powerful visions. Hegel sought to reconcile idealist thought with the reality of the Prussian bureaucratic state. The Zionists sought both to foster Jewish security in the face of Christian European xenophobia and to reinvent Jewish collective existence on new grounds. The consequences of those visions, rather than the anatomy of their enabling contexts, are my subject here. I hope to surprise a constellation of ideas our own intellectual discourse shares with Hegel and the Zionists, and thus to clear some space for the imaginative transcendence of that constellation.[4]

Hegel, History, and the State

In the interpretation of Hegel on which my line of inquiry rests, he is the prophet of the state as bearer and apotheosis of history. Hegel scholars have become somewhat defensive about this notion of late. Thus Duncan Forbes, at the beginning of his introduction to the main text of Hegel I will be using here, remarks that

> It contains the notorious phrases about the state being the divine
> Idea on earth, reason ruling the world and so on, which have been
> made to mean precisely the opposite of what Hegel intended.
> (Forbes 1975: vii)

Forbes, it turns out at the end of his introduction, is arguing quite specifically against the view that Hegel's *Philosophy of History* was an extended apology for the existing Prussian state. Whether or not Hegel was a deliberate apologist for the Prussian state of the 1820s, the universal and "scientific" cast of his rhetoric made it available, as I have said, for any number of projects linking state structures to the cunning of history.

A passage from a late interview given by Jean-Paul Sartre first led me to think of Hegel as a key source for the identification of history with state history. In the course of several comments about Jewish identity and history, Sartre and his interviewer Benny Lévy touched on Hegel thus:

SARTRE: ... When I said that there is not any Jewish history, I was thinking of history in a well-defined form: the history of Germany, the history of America, of the United States. That is, the history of a sovereign, political reality with a homeland and with other similar states. When one should have thought of history as being something else, if one meant that there is a Jewish history. It was necessary to conceive of Jewish history not only as a dissemination of Jews throughout the world, but also as the unity of the diaspora, the unity of the dispersed Jews....

LÉVY: In other words, the history that Hegel put on our landscape wanted to get rid of the Jew, and it is the Jew who will allow us to get out of this history that Hegel wanted to impose on us.

SARTRE: Absolutely.... (Lévy 1980: 178)

I have cited this exchange before, in a paper taking up these questions from a different angle (Boyarin 1992). However, when I originally sub-

mitted that paper for publication, the editor insisted I remove Benny
Lévy's remarks about Hegel and Sartre's affirmative rejoinder. Doubtless the editor read Lévy's remarks as an implication that Hegel was in
some sense philosophically responsible for the Nazi genocide, an argument I hardly want to take up here. On the contrary—and this is the
link between my third and fourth theses stated above—to a large extent the very exhaustion of the liberal-nationalist ideal that Hegel
helped articulate produced the ideological turmoil in which Nazism
flourished.

There is another reason why this exchange is so haunting. Decades
after Sartre, in *Anti-Semite and Jew,* accepted and celebrated Zionism as "authentic" Jewish self-expression, here he seemed to have seen a very different potential Jewish social contribution. Sartre's hint at an altogether different way of conceiving history—his claim that by taking the claims of
Jewish history in diaspora seriously, he has gained insight into our usual
assumptions about the constitution of history—is congruent with the
poststructuralist ideal of identifying the limits of thought and hence enabling their transgression (see Ashley 1989: 284). One of these limits, a
heritage more generally of the Enlightenment but certainly passed down
to us by Hegel, among others, is "the cult of reason" (Marcuse 1966). Indeed, part of the Hegelian legacy with which poststructuralism struggles is
the difficulty of formulating History at all without recourse to an underlying, supreme, progressive Reason.

A second indication of the importance of Hegel to the relation between Jewish collective identity and the state is the title of a book by the
academic theologian Emil Fackenheim, *The Jewish Return into History: Reflections in the Age of Auschwitz and a New Jerusalem* (1978). Clearly, there
is a conception here of History with a capital *H,* a brightly lighted stage
that a nation can be either on or off. Although Fackenheim's title suggests
that this History is not necessarily triumphant, and he elsewhere ultimately demurs from Hegelianism, the dénouement whereby this tortured
"return" is completed in the accomplishment of a Jewish ethnic state is
quite consistent with Hegel's criteria for historical existence. In fact, a
strict reading of Hegel on the grounding of history would suggest that
were it not for the establishment of the state of Israel, the Nazi genocide
would be "historical" only for those states that committed it, not for the
people who suffered it:

Family memorials and patriarchal traditions have an interest only within the family or tribe itself. . . . But it is the state which first supplies a content which not only lends itself to the prose of history but actually helps to produce it. . . . It thereby creates a record of its own development, and an interest in intelligible, determinate, and — in their results — enduring deeds and events, on which Mnemosyne, for the benefit of the perennial aim which underlies the present form and constitution of the state, is impelled to confer a lasting memory. (1975: 135–36)

All of this is not to suggest that Hegel was a protototalitarian or consistently anti-Jewish. Rather, Hegel's unquestionable valorization of the state can be linked more prosaically to Robert Wuthnow's explanation of the unique opportunities intellectuals enjoyed in the Prussian state of the eighteenth century (1989: 244). In Prussia, indeed, it apparently was the intellectuals' task to harmonize Enlightenment with a bureaucratically run monarchy.

Certainly there is a chauvinistic cast to Hegel's philosophy of history. As Shlomo Avineri summarizes, "The stages of history, which for Hegel represent stages of consciousness, are objectified in a succession of cultures" (1972: 222), and Hegel speaks of the "Germanic" nation (within which he seems to include all of Western Europe) as representing the culmination of history and consciousness (1956). Less commented on, however — perhaps because it has been shared by virtually all of Hegel's commentators — is not his ethnic chauvinism but what might be called his chauvinism of the present, a consignment of the past, whatever may have been its virtues in its time, to the dustbin of history (see, for example, Hegel 1975: 138). For Hegel, once a nation has fulfilled its world-historical role, it is no longer *interesting* except in the all-important process of deliberate reconstruction of world history. Furthermore, in all his glorification of the Germanic world, he is hardly a precursor of the German romantics who reinvented Teutonic myths. For Hegel, the ancient "heritage" of a nation is not especially significant before the nation plays its historical role. A nation plays that role during the epoch in world history when it helps to realize spirit by progressive exercise of secular power.

There is no room in such a view of history for a sense of identity grounded in Jewish communities that did not depend on state sovereignty for their collective identity, whatever other repressions and weaknesses they may have entailed. That kind of identity relies on the contingent narrative associations between generations that are coming and those that are going. This is quite different from the idea of an entire "people" entering and leaving history, which makes sense only if one assumes that certain human experiences are ontologically privileged above others. In the course of some prefatory remarks to a critical analysis of "the new historicism" in literary theory, Joel Feinman argues that Hegel's grand schema of world history leaves no room for anecdote (and indeed Hegel derides the merely "accidental" aspects of what happens). To Feinman, this airtight rationale for history is effectively ahistorical, atemporal, noncontingent:

> Hegel's philosophy of history, with its narration of the spirit's gradual arrival at its own final self-realizing self-reflection, is the purest model of such an historical *grand récit.* . . . Properly speaking, such a history is not historical. Governed by an absolute, inevitable, inexorable teleological unfolding, so that, in principle, nothing can happen by chance, every moment that participates unto itself, is thereby rendered timeless; such moments, we can say — and here I am influenced by Jean-Luc Nancy's discussion of this issue in a paper on Hegel and "Finite History" — exist, for all intents and purposes, precisely because they are intentional and purposeful, outside of time, or in a timeless present, and this because their momentary durative appearance is already but the guaranteed foreshadow, the already all but realized promise of the concluding end of history toward which tendentiously, as but the passing moments in a story whose conclusion is already written, they tend. (1989: 57)

Feinman does not comment on the link between this foreshortening of historical contingency and the grounds of the modern nation-state, but others have, as I will discuss.

Hegel, Enlightenment, and the Problematics of Modern Jewish Identity

So far I have discussed the key complex of ideas in Hegel's thought that I find remarkably congruent with secular Zionism. The next step in this roundabout argument will be a consideration of the ideological dilemmas of Jewish modernity for which Zionism proposed a solution.

One aspect of the intellectual prehistory of Enlightenment, vital to my argument, is what Richard Ashley calls "the Cartesian practice of spatialization" (1989: 290, 296–97, 306). Ashley's concern is with a turn toward a spatial (rather than, for instance, genealogical) organization of political domains, with a logic of both inquiry and polity based on "absolute boundaries between inside and outside." (Hence, for instance, a social scientist would reject this essay as a hopeless venture, since I have failed to "delimit the object of inquiry.") The implications of this objectified "politics of absolute space" are elaborated in an essay by R. B. J. Walker, although he does not refer specifically to Descartes:

> After Machiavelli ... the principle of state sovereignty came to be framed within the context of the Euclidean-Galilean principle of absolute space rather than the complex overlapping jurisdictions of the medieval era. (1989: 42)

Walker's main concern is with the implications of a unitary, spatial logic for the discourse on relations *between* spatially defined sovereign polities. But the logical grounds for eliminating "overlapping jurisdictions" — which include not only feudal nobilities but also the special corporate identities of the church, trading colonies, and legally-chartered Jewish communities — appear within the same "politics of absolute space" that grounds the elaboration of "international relations."

This reification of space is consistent with the Hegelian reification of History. Now it is possible to refer to a group of people living not only "outside of history" but "outside of space" as well, as in the introduction to a recent collection of essays on the differing situations of Jews inside and outside Israel:

> A proto-Zionism, or an appreciation of the role of Jewish space, was a fundamental component of diaspora Judaism through the ages. And this despite the fact that the Jewish people lived outside of space, and that space was a conceptual category, limited to a sacred history of the distant past and future. (Levine 1986: 5)

This quotation partakes both of a rigid conceptualization of pure space — a "politics of absolute space" — and of several of the Hegelian assumptions referred to earlier.[5] The first striking point is the very category of a Jewish people, continuing to exist, whether in possession of a sovereign territory or not. Once the "people" is defined as the fundamental unit, how could they possibly be seen to have an existence "in space" unless they lived en masse? Such a synoptic ideological view has no room for what Hegel would call "accidental" aspects of history:[6] there can be no account of everyday life as *domestic space*, or of Jewish communities as existing in *social space*, rather than globe space.[7] In a curious way, "realism"—the rhetoric of critique, exposing as a mere "conceptual category" the empathetic means by which Jews outside of the Jewish commonwealth in space *and* time drew on its memory to sustain their identity—thus leads to a hypostatization of the nation as a noncontingent "Jewish people" and a concomitant effacing of the everyday existence of Jews. The term "proto-Zionism" is revealing, as it implies Zionism as the telos or the fruition of a previously immature Jewish existence. Revealingly, Levine's article also employs the rhetoric of "hosts" and "minorities," which for perhaps centuries now has betrayed the popular assumption that there are indeed "absolute spaces" rightfully associated with certain "nations" and not others.

Nevertheless, the recognition of a tension between space and time as grounds of collective identity—a tension that perhaps becomes explicit only in modernity and helps to define modernity (the distinction between space and time characteristically begins to collapse in a postmodern mode)—can help me to overcome the temptation to join in a pessimistic version of the grand Hegelian scheme, to see the chronology of modernity as leading logically and ineluctably toward Nazism and genocide. In order to avoid the argument that Hegel was merely a protototalitarian (the consequences of his ideas are more complex than that), I have to preserve some distance between his two motivating convictions: the progressive revelation of the world spirit (through time) in nations, and its (spatial) embodiment in the state. Hegel seems to have no interest in *ethnic* exclusivity or unity, which may help to explain his explicit defenses of Jewish emancipation. The aspect of Western European statebuilding that draws on the ideal of ethnic-national independence had such broad roots that it hardly needed Hegel as a promoter (see McNeill 1986). The emphasis on the state is much more properly Hegel's. Perhaps, in fact, this very deemphasis of any polluting intermediate collective authority (other than the family, which is a smaller analogue of the state) between the individual and the state is what is so distinctive, so very modern, in Hegel. He seems passionately to have desired a perfect realization of the analogy between the individual person and the state as individual: "In world history, however, the individuals we are concerned with are nations, totalities, states" (Hegel 1975: 36).

The temporal implications of this combination of progressivism and statism do not seem to lead directly to the glorification and invention of a mythic past, as in Nazism (see Lacoue-Labarthe and Nancy 1989). Hegel's ideal is to be distinguished both from the ethos of traditional panchronic, textual communities, for whom "the past" did not exist as a rigidly separate category (Stock 1990; Carruthers 1990), and from the powerful romantic version of nation-state ideology, which was not so much panchronic as explicitly oriented toward a past "golden age" and the project of its revival.

The liberal state relies rather on the novel ethos of *simultaneity*: the creation, originally through printed literature, of an awareness among the population of itself as a collective in space all working together at the same time to enable each other's individual lives (Anderson 1983). Anderson and other recent theorists are well aware of the importance of the romantic promotion of folk heroes, folklore, and the like in the project of nation building, but they see these primarily as the props of a new common sense among the *living* residents of the national territory. Consistent with this view, I will suggest that the view of Zionism as an attempt to reconstruct an imagined ancient polity misses its thoroughly modern nationalist thrust and its progressive, Enlightened prejudices. Whereas we are used to seeing nationalism in terms of an identification with a hypostatized collective past, Zionism entails an explicit rejection of an immediate past that no longer works as the ground of Jewish identity. Its founding texts are those of "Western" or "Westernized" intellectuals with faith in the future and little use for the past. Thus one of them, the onetime hugely successful popular philosopher Max Nordau, who had nothing but contempt for Hegel, still shared Hegel's belief in a "reality" from which primitive Man had been woefully distant:

> Fantasy, hardly impeded by the attention, which was as yet but little developed artificially, and limited by no consideration of reality, known or unknown, dominated the whole realm of brain activity, and developed with a luxuriance never found in the disciplined reason and trained observation of civilized man, except when his mental balance is disturbed by disease and he raves under the influence of acute mania, or of alcohol, opium, hashish, or other poisons. (1910: 341)

It is possible to specify a bit more about this theoretical and ideological tension between the projects of inventing a national past and creating a sense of national simultaneity, for part of the project of statebuilding, as Hegel knew, is the construction of an official, rationalized national history, rigorously separated from oral tradition and local textualized memories. Thus the contemporary academic Jewish historian Yosef Hayim Yerushalmi has retraced and reinscribed the break between "Jewish history and Jewish memory" (1982). His reification and implicit glorification of professional historiography, as something occurring only at the point of a decisive *break,* where consciousness is shocked into seeing reality, carries echoes of Hegel's "owl of Minerva flying at dusk." Yerushalmi's stance as a critical, individualist historian alienated from the lulling tales of Jewish "memory" reinforces the modern delegitimization of panchrony, and masks its own grounding in the state through its representative, the secular university.[8]

Against Yerushalmi's claims for proper, modern history's residing in the disaffected individual, against Hegel's claims that it resides in the state, Amos Funkenstein argues for its continuity with other forms of calling forth the past: "Western historical consciousness does not contradict collective memory, but rather is a developed and organized form of it" (1989: 19). But this view is necessarily *post*modern, inasmuch as it argues against a modern conception of history—Hegel's—that has held the field for a century and a half. The history that is created for and in the name of nation-states is a past intended to define a bounded territory. It has no room for unofficial memory's "overlapping jurisdictions." The rigid separation of rationalized national histories from folkloric memories accompanied the demolition of feudal corporate identities.

Unfortunately for the Jews of Western Europe, the "absolute spaces" of modernity are not neutral spaces. If in the general context of the Enlightenment the Jews, as Talmon says, were "a test case and a touchstone," sometimes it seemed more as though they were caught between the hammer and the anvil.[9] The links between the ideology of realization of spirit in the individual, on the one hand, and Protestant statism, on the other, are fully elaborated only in Hegel. Already in Kant, however, there is discussion of the evolution from Judaism to Christianity as an allegory of the evolution from "immaturity" to enlightenment. As Steven Smith argues, discussing Kant's distinction between statutory law and moral law,

> Kant everywhere treats Judaism as a stand-in for a purely statutory, ecclesiastical faith while Christianity is treated as a moral religion of our practical rationality. (Smith 1991: 93)

This is not to deny that liberal thinkers such as Hegel believed in the individual's freedom of religion. The problem for Jews was, first of all, that it was hard to prove themselves enlightened (and hence worthy of citizenship) while clinging to a "statutory, ecclesiastical faith," and second, that the modern world is

> deeply and in its essence the bourgeois-Protestant world which has announced that all men can be free.... Thus the Jews may find a home in the modern state but at the price of being socially and spiritually marginalized in it. For Hegel, every historical people has its peak moment of creativity on the world stage and by now the Jewish moment is long past. To the extent that Judaism has survived at all, it is a relic, a vestige of a once vital but now superseded civilization.... [The] recognition of free choice as the core of religion is itself a Protestant idea and has no basis in Jewish experience or tradition. The liberal solution to the Jewish question, then, is predicated upon a recognition of the hegemony of a largely Protestant culture. (Ibid.: 101)[10]

For Western European Jews, therefore, the modern dismantling of the resources of Jewish panchrony and the corporate identity of Jewish communities left (or, what amounts to the same thing, appeared at the time to leave) virtually no other basis for Jewish collective existence *except* the land—that is, a Jewish nation-state. This is another way of saying that the attack, both external and internal, on Jewish *cultural* or *communal* distinctiveness left no metaphorical "ground" for Jewish existence except Palestine.

Zionisms and the State

What we think of as Zionism, despite the existence of a World Zionist Organization and then a Zionist state, is in fact a catchall for numerous, often mutually contradictory currents of thought. All the varieties of Zionism, however, are based on arguments about the best means to guarantee the physical security of the Jews, and the best means to guarantee their collective identity. I am focusing on the latter issue—that is, to the degree that the two can be separated. Some postmodern critical theorists argue that states maintain their identities, and hence their borders, by continually re-producing the ideological threat of the barbarian behind the walls (Ashley 1989). Of course, this supposed danger does not obviate the physical threat to the stranger, "abnormally" located inside the walls. On the contrary, it accentuates that threat.

Nevertheless, the ideological range of Zionist visions of Jewish iden-tity is (or was) relatively wide. There were, quite early, religious Zionists who saw the emigration program as a messianic project; liberal Zionists who saw it as a constructive colonial scheme; Marxist Zionists who saw it as the only basis for a "normal" class struggle; and Revisionist Zionists who saw it as the only way to get away from the goyim who were out to kill the Jews anyway. The question of how much the varieties of Zionism need to be differentiated for different purposes is open and contentious.

There is another reason to underscore the point that I am not trying to identify Hegel as a proximate "cause" of Zionism. The Zionist movement did not spring up contemporaneously with Hegel, but in the context of a decidedly non-Hegelian anti-Semitic reaction toward the end of the nine-teenth century. Again, although the issue of physical security that came to the fore at the fin de siècle arose within the same broad modern context as the issues of identity that came to prominence in the era of Enlightenment and Jewish emancipation, the two cannot be easily collapsed into each other.

Individual Zionist thinkers did not have to accept Hegel's combina-tion of spiritual progress with its culmination in the state. Max Nordau explicitly denied the claims for moral progress in history, reserving prog-ress strictly to the technical sphere of satisfaction of human wants and adding his belief in national regeneration and safety (1910: 343). Nordau rejected Hegel's philosophy of history as mystical gobbledygook, an ut-terly transparent apologia for Christianity:

> And this is what is put forward as the philosophy of history — these
> ravings that might have fallen from the lips of a delirious monk
> whose brain was fevered by the writings of the Dominicans. Hegel
> is indeed one of the most appalling figures in the intellectual history
> of the human race. (1910: 79)

What Nordau shares with Hegel — and the link is significant without any need to claim derivation *from* Hegel — is the sense that only in the context of a national existence on their own soil are the people truly alive:

> Zionism has awakened Jewry to new life, morally through the
> National ideal, materially through physical rearing. But Zionism
> also makes a sharp division between the living and the dead;
> only now can we estimate the fearful devastation which eighteen
> centuries of captivity have wrought in our midst. (Nordau
> 1941: 88)

The idea that there are epochs when the members of a nation are collectively "alive" and others, lasting millennia, when they are "dead," fits
well into a series of dichotomizing rhetorical judgments of history. One
of these that has critical effects is Hegel's argument that history can be divided into the essential and the accidental. Another is the central Zionist
idea that Jewish existence in "Exile" has been "anomalous," and that there
is a "normal" form of collective existence that should be the "state" of the
Jews as well.

This Zionist notion of normal existence is both psychological and national. It rests on what Nancy calls "the axiom that unity in general is personal, and that the person is unitary" (1982: 488). At the time when the
state starts making strong identity claims, one cannot live "normally" in a
state with which one does not identify. The affinity with Hegel seems quite
clear here. Even if Hegel can be read as tolerant of diversity among individuals, for him, each *person* is supposed to be realized or to realize herself
in *one* collective. The individual can be happy, reconciled to history, only
when his actions are in harmony with the historical force of the nation
(1975: 81). In order for the individual to be able to recognize himself and
be realized in the nation, however, the link between them must be carefully defined and guarded:

> Individuality is awareness of one's existence as a unit in sharp
> distinction from others. It manifests itself here in the state as a
> relation to other states, each of which is autonomous vis-à-vis the
> others. (Hegel 1952: 106)

In classical secular Zionism, the link between the assumptions that
the person is unitary and that genuine existence is uninational and collective is almost ubiquitous. In the beginning of *The Making of Modern Zionism,* Shlomo Avineri stresses the issue of identity rather than the issue of
physical security as a motivation for the "assimilated" early Western European Zionists. He asserts that they "responded ... to the challenge of their
identity, looking for roots" (1981: 13). What other conclusion can follow

except that Zionism was the coming-into-existence of a "normal" existence for them—indeed, a shedding of their "accidental" Europeanness
and a realization of their "essential identity"? David Ben-Gurion, the "father" of the state of Israel, dreamed in turn of the day when all the citizens of Israel would realize their inner essence in the state, when they
would finally become "a sovereign, state-bearing people, lovingly and willingly carrying the duties and burdens of independence" (quoted in Avineri
1981: 214). In this aspect, as well as in the notion of the *Machtstaat,* the
powerful state that inspires the respect of its neighbors (Droz 1966: 131),
Ben-Gurion shared Hegel's ideal.

   Whatever critique may be mounted of Hegel's model of the state in
the abstract, different problems remain regarding its application to the situation of the Jews. Hegel's ideal was especially powerful in a state where,
first of all, the territorial *ground* of unique national identity was fundamentally uncontested, and second of all, Protestant Christianity provided
both a sweeping rationale for the course of history and a rationale for the
individual rights of unbelievers. For Zionism to establish a unique ground
of territorial identity, a population of resident Arab Others had first to be
excluded (first ideologically, then physically).[11] Second, notwithstanding
the image of the Jews taking their place "among the family of nations,"
Zionism could not avail itself of a Jewish equivalent to Protestantism. The
closest thing to such an equivalent—Reform Judaism—was explicitly
anti-Zionist. Lacking, therefore, Hegel's easy identification of their "own"
group's interests with universal interests, and lacking as well the traditional
resources of Jewish "identity," the traditions they invented had much in
common with other Western European nationalisms of the time: "Political
Zionism promoted such things as dueling fraternities, songs and marches,
and a rather atavistic notion of nationalism" (Avishai 1985: 25). Indeed,
Herzl later recalled the period when he was writing *The Jewish State* in
these terms: "My only recreation was listening to Wagner's music in the
evening, particularly to *Tannhäuser,* an opera which I attended as often as
it was produced. Only on the evenings when there was no opera did I
have any doubts as to the truth of my ideas" (1973: 17–18).

   There is yet another difficulty in the direct application of Hegel's philosophy of history to the Jews: Zionism could not borrow the scheme
wholesale, since in it the Jews have been passed by.[12] But what it could
adopt was the notion of the state as the culmination of history, and the
notion that each nation has its genius to contribute to world progress. On

the most prosaic level, Hegel may have been an important validation for the radical claim of the early Zionists that the Jews were indeed a nation. On the other hand, if the Jews (for Hegel, part of the Oriental world) have had their moment at the forefront of history, then what would the content of Jewish culture be for secular, loosely "Hegelian" Zionists? Here we may see the crux of the debate over whether Zionism is properly seen as a *new and modern* phenomenon or as the realization of an ancient desire: again, in the Hegelian schema, the question is posed yet undecidable, because resurgent Jewish nationalism is strictly "accidental."

Despite all these conundrums—and, indeed, despite the fragmention of the putative Israeli "collective identity"—some Zionist writers still hold out for the Hegelian ideal of "normal," territorial, progressive, public, and unicentral Jewish life: "Today, due to modernization and secularization, Israel is the normative expression of this collective existence of the Jewish people, of *Klal Yisrael*" (Avineri 1981: 221). Like Avineri, Michael Walzer continues to hold to the vision of "a Jewish state (where 'Jewish' is a weak or liberal modifier)" (1989: 127)—that is, a state that would be Jewish as France is French, with a dominant cultural identity that does not exclude the rights of minorities. Walzer realizes that there are problems with the analogy to France, let alone the United States, but he locates these in the fact "that the Jews are a religious as well as a national entity" (ibid.), which strikes me as both a false distinction and a red herring. The difficulty Arabs will ever have "joining with goodwill in the singing of 'Hatikvah'" (ibid.) hardly stems from the fact that the longing expressed in that song has "religious" roots, but rather that the formulation of that longing is inimical to their collective interests. Walzer, with universalist ambitions but Hegelian-statist notions of collective identity, poses the issues, admits he can't answer them, and claims to be able to "imagine a number of accommodating and liberal answers" (ibid.) to them. He does not spell them out.

I do not mean to dismiss Walzer as a political theorist or claim that the prime concern of his scholarship is the ideological defense of the Jewish state (compare Said 1988). Nor yet, and more importantly, is it my point that the Jews should be the first to give up their state, as they were among the last to get one. My point is rather that the problems inherent in Hegelian statism appear sharply in the problematics of the Jewish state, as they did in the problematics of Jewish identity in the nascent modern Western European states.

Preliminary Conclusions

Symptomatic of Hegel's discussion of "the geographical basis of history" (1956) is his reading of the East as the "dawn" of history. In other words, his "geographical basis" is a metaphoric and highly stereotyped version of ecological determinism. This conception of geography, however, excludes any discussion of the territorial basis of the state. There seems to be a logic to this exclusion and stereotyping that needs to be teased out further.

Hegel's geographic determinism is part of his *grand récit* of the "essentials" of world history discussed in the passage from Joel Feinman I cited earlier in this essay. On the most general level, the analogy between Hegelianism and Zionism that I want to draw is based on Hegel's linked desires to call a halt to the vagaries of history by "foreclosing the future" within a comprehensive narrative of Reason (Plant 1983: 236) and "to demonstrate that the modern world can provide a sense of being at home in the world" (207).

My claim is that Zionism, more than the atavistic or restorative movement toward an ancient vision or the revolutionary irruption into history of a messianic promise, represents an altogether modern, "Hegelian" attempt to fix, eternally, Jewish identity by grounding it in territory. There is a much more than superficial link between Hegel's desire to allow the Germanic peoples to be "at home" in history and the literalized Zionist rhetoric of enabling the Jews to be "at home" on the globe, once modernity had stripped them of their "portable homeland" of memory. For both, the idea of history as a sequence of constant supersession of the past "leaves no possibility for a resting place for the mind" (Kemp 1991: 161).[13] Thus the desire for a geographical "fix" is inseparable from the loss of that other "homeland." It can be related both to the syndrome of a disorienting, anxious experience of a fleeting succession of "transient pasts" (Koshar 1990) and to secular Jews' "alienation from texts and textual messages" (Funkenstein 1989: 22).

What has been called the rise of Israeli "fundamentalism" is a much more complex phenomenon than a simple return of outmoded forms of "religious" authority. In the decades since 1967, the Gush Emunim settler movement, with its emphasis on the biblical base of Jewish rights to all of the "Greater Land of Israel," has in fact stepped into the breach left by the exhaustion of Labor Zionist pioneer ideology. It is grounded simultaneously in the original pioneering ideology and in yet another reworking of the triumphalist portions of the biblical conquest narrative. Its modern, rather than "preliberal," nature is indicated by its spokespeople's explicit rejection of Western liberalism (Lustick 1988). Its appeal indicates the weaknesses of a liberal notion of collective identity grounded in a limited sovereign state.

The self-image of Labor Zionism is consistent not only with Hegel's progressivist geographical determinism but also with his split between the Occident and the Orient. Zionism's statist displacement of the inhabitants of Palestine is justified in the language of European modernization, a recent reworking of the concept of progressive realization of spirit externalizing itself in the world. But it is essential to note that this justification does not work only against non-Jewish Palestinians. It is grounded in the reification of "traditional" Judaism as an Other whom history has passed by (see, for example, Avineri 1981: 24). During the founding period of the state, this resulted in active denigration of the religious rights of Orthodox Jews. Now it leaves liberal Israelis with only the barest understanding of the background and motives of militant Orthodoxy.[14] A similar heritage of prejudice hampers the relations of liberal Israelis of Ashkenazi extraction with the "Oriental" Jewish majority. During the period of mass absorption, they were subjected by the ruling Labor Party to a policy of forced acculturation, and deliberately slated to become the proletarian base of the "normal" class structure of the new Jewish state (Shohat 1988; Swirski 1989). During the years between 1977 and 1992, Labor was unable to draw mass Oriental support from the right-wing Likud party or the "Sephardi" Oriental party Shas. Labor's slim victory in the 1992 elections was partly due to Oriental Jews' double anger at Likud's slighting of their practical needs in favor of settlements in the Occupied Territories, and at the demotion of David Levy, a Moroccan Israeli high in the Likud leadership.

Such are the inevitable dilemmas of an attempt to fix collective identity in the modern world as a "unit in sharp distinction from others," resting on a geographical base. Israel may be able to live with the delimmas for some time, but at present, they are hardly an adequate answer to the "Jewish question" still posed by the modern state system. Overcoming those dilemmas will entail the dismantling of many of the sharp distinctions that have been constructed over the last few centuries, on which rest not only Zionism but modern collective identity in general—between one nation and another, between tradition and Enlightenment, between the essential and the accidental in history, and, perhaps most of all, between the living and the dead.

Notes

1. Curiously and most regrettably, although Talmon devotes a large chapter of his book *The Myth of the Nation and the Vision of Revolution* (1980) to the plight of the Jews under modern European nationalism, he says nothing about the rise of Zionism as part of this larger phenomenon.

2. Beyond the question of Zionism, Hegel's argument for the embodiment of progress in the national spirit seems to have been picked up by intellectuals around the globe. One example of this is the combination of Westernism with Japanese nationalism through a Hegelian spyglass that produced the rationale for modern Japanese high pictorial art (Tanaka 1990).

3. An analysis starting from the somewhat autonomous Eastern European roots of Zionism might look quite different. The mass base, and a great deal of the Jewish content, of Zionism is anchored in Eastern Europe. Still, the ideology of the secular Jewish state, as it has been established, largely conforms to the ideology of the bourgeois Western European nation-state.

4. Edward Said articulates the imperative I am responding to here: "This is where we are now, at the threshold of fragmentation and specialization, which impose their own parochial dominations and fussy defensiveness, or on the verge of some grand synthesis which I for one believe could very easily wipe out both the gains and the oppositional consciousness provided hitherto by these counter-knowledges. Several possibilities propose themselves, and I shall conclude simply by listing them. A need for greater crossing of boundaries, for greater interventionism in cross-disciplinary activity, a concentrated awareness of the situation—political, methodological, social, historical—in which intellectual and cultural work is carried out. A clarified political and methodological commitment to the dismantling of systems of domination which since they are collectively maintained must, to adopt and transform some of Gramsci's phrases, be collectively fought, by mutual siege, war of maneuver *and* war of position. Lastly, a much sharpened sense of the intellectual's role both in the defining of a context and in changing it, for without that, I believe, the critique of Orientalism is simply an ephemeral pastime" (1985: 107; emphasis in original).

5. It might be objected here that for Hegel space is the inert and neutral ground of nature, whereas the history of nations unfolds in time. As Hegel's analogy of the unfolding of history from East to West to the progress of the sun in the sky suggests, however, *The Philosophy of History* seems deeply implicated in an imperial discourse that first identifies peoples by geographical determinants and then builds a chronological narrative around the assumptions made on the basis of that geography.

6. Cassirer brings the following citation from Hegel's *Encyclopedia of the Philosophical Sciences,* paragraph 6: "We must presume intelligence enough to know … that existence is in part mere appearance, and only in part reality. In common life, and freak of fancy, any error, evil and everything of the nature of evil, as well as every degenerate and transitory exis-

tence whatever, gets in a casual way the name of reality. But even our ordinary feelings are enough to forbid a fortuitous existence getting the name of the real" (1946: 261).

7. By domestic and social space, I mean the smaller and more circumscribed areas within which the bulk of a self-identified community's interactions take place, and also (not quite the same thing) the space of daily life as perceived by the members of that community. For the members of local Jewish populations following Jewish law, salient features defining the community as a social space include the presence of a cemetery and the maintenance of a physical boundary marker (*eyruv*) inside which Jews are permitted to carry things on the Sabbath. For more general treatments of "social geography," see Pred (1990) and Soja (1989).

By "globe space," I mean precisely that conception of territory that is expressed on classroom globes: discrete, sovereign spaces large enough to be recognizable on a small-scale representation of the earth's surface.

In both cases there is a link among authority, space, and collective identity. Where Jewish collectives are able to define themselves in social space, they are generally still functioning as "textual communities" (Stock 1990) — their shared sense of authority is rooted in a set of founding, infinitely interpretable texts. When the authoritative basis of the textual community was eroded in the atmosphere of Enlightenment and modern nationalism, the sovereign authority of the nation-state became a compelling alternative ground for collective identity. Avineri, for instance, does not even seem to recognize the possible authority of textual communities, as evidenced by his emphasis on the formal, normative, official existence of Israel compared with other Jewish populations: "Other Jewish communities are merely aggregates of individuals, and as such they have no normative standing as a public entity. Israel, on the other hand, is conceived not only as an aggregate of its population, but its very existence has immanent value and normative standing" (1981: 221).

8. None of this should take credit away from Yerushalmi for his crucial achievement of having started a genuine critical reflection on the relation between the creation of history and the dynamics of Jewish collective identity.

9. Talmon is referring here to the Jews as a test case for the extension of *les droits de l'homme* to previously disenfranchised groups within the rationalizing nation-states. It would be worthwhile to compare the rhetoric about the Jews' putative existence "outside of" history, or their lack of a history of their own, to the discourse on "peoples without history" (Wolf 1982) in the colonized world. The "solution" of the Indian problem by the creation of reservations, for example, seems consistent with my argument about the imperial, universalist background of the territorial solution to the Jewish problem.

10. Jean-Luc Nancy backs this argument with a quotation: "One could in any case appeal to the end of the Remark at 552 of the *Encyclopedia*: Philosophy exists in the end only as the State, as that State that develops the truth of the Protestant religion" (1982: 483; see also Turner 1988 on the concept of the "nation-church-state").

Hegel explicitly contrasts Protestantism with Catholicism in this regard, referring to "the foolish attempts made in our own times to devise and implement constitutions independently of religion. The Catholic religion, although it is akin to Protestantism in so far as they are both forms of Christianity, does not permit that internal justice and ethicality in politics which the more profound principle of Protestantism embodies" (1975: 103–4).

In quoting Smith, I do not mean to argue that a state understood as being rooted in Protestantism necessarily *is* an effective guarantor of religious freedom. Nor do I mean to suggest that a Jewish state has no room for religious tolerance. (No matter how much many of the founders of Zionism may have wished for a Jewish state just like Germany, I'm not arguing that Israel's problem is its failure to be more like Germany.) The key fact remains, as

Smith points out, that the individualistic ethos of Protestantism is not shared by Judaism. The consequences of this difference for state structures are a more complex issue than I am capable of treating at this time.

11. Here it is necessary to insist again that there are, or have been, many Zionisms, some predicated on binational coexistence on the same territory. I am trying to explain here that if they failed, it is not solely, nor is it necessarily primarily, on account of Arab "intransigence." It can be argued that Palestinian nationalism, which has crystallized around resistance to Zionist encroachment, follows the same logic of territorialism and "Othering" as does Zionism. Thus Henry Louis Gates has recently written in response to an article by Edward Said, "As Said knows, the territorial conception of the nation—centered on the self-determining homeland of that (gendered) indigene—is historically no more 'nature' to the colonized than to the European colonizer" (Gates 1990: 326). But of course what the Palestinians would have done or will do remains altogether hypothetical, since they remain more or less powerless vis-à-vis the Israeli state.

12. On this, see Avineri on the philosopher Krochmal's resolution of the aporia of a Jewish Hegelianism (1981: 14–22).

13. Max Nordau held that with the onset of modernity the pace of change had simply become too much for our ancestors to bear. Stephen Kern glosses and cites Nordau's book *Degeneration:* "He believed that people can respond to most demands made upon them if there is time for gradual adaptation. But the onset of modernity came too fast: 'No time was left to our fathers. Between one day and the next, with murderous suddenness, they were obliged to change the comfortable creeping gait of their former existence for the stormy stride of modern life, and their heart and lungs could not bear it'" (Kern 1983: 125).

14. Such reification is hardly confined to Zionists. For example, the relentless Israeli social critic Israel Shahak claimed in a recent interview that the ultranationalist, chauvinist "religious" forces in Israel today represent a "return to original Judaism," to a "Judaism that existed some generations ago" (Veeser and Jerry 1990: 98). Shahak, who explicitly grounds his comments in an "antireligious" perspective, fails to see the ways in which "Judaism" is fundamentally changed by the accession to state power—much as Christianity changed upon being adopted as the state religion of the Roman Empire.

Bibliography

Anderson, Benedict. 1983. *Imagined Communities: Reflections on the Spread of Nationalism.* London: Verso.

Ashley, Richard K. 1989. "Living on Border Lines: Man, Poststructuralism, and War. In *International/Intertextual Relations: Postmodern Readings of World Politics,* ed. by James Der Derian and Michael J. Shapiro. Lexington, Mass.: D. C. Heath and Company (Lexington Books). 259–321.

Alvineri, Shlomo. 1972. *Hegel's Theory of the Modern State.* Cambridge: Cambridge University Press.

———. 1981. *The Making of Modern Zionism: The Intellectual Origins of the Jewish State.* New York: Basic Books.

Avishai, Bernard. 1985. *The Tragedy of Zionism: Revolution and Democracy in the Land of Israel.* New York: Farrar Straus Giroux.

Boyarin, Jonathan. 1988. "Waiting for a Jew: Marginal Redemption at the Eighth Street

Shul." In *Between Two Worlds: Ethnographic Essays on American Jews,* ed. Jack Kugelmass. Ithaca, N.Y.: Cornell University Press. 52–76.

———. 1992. "Palestine and Jewish History." In *Storm from Paradise: The Politics of Jewish Memory.* Minneapolis: University of Minnesota Press.

Carruthers, Mary. 1990. *The Book of Memory: A Study of Memory in Medieval Culture.* New York: Cambridge University Press.

Cassirer, Ernst. 1946. *The Myth of the State.* New Haven: Yale University Press.

Chatterjee, Partha. 1986. *Nationalist Thought and the Colonial World: A Derivative Discourse?* London: Zed Books.

Droz, Jacques. 1966. *Le romantisme allemand et l'état.* Paris: Payot.

Fackenheim, Emil. 1978. *The Jewish Return into History: Reflections in the Age of Auschwitz and a New Jerusalem.* New York: Schocken Books.

Feinman, Joel. 1989. "The History of the Anecdote: Fiction and Fiction." In *The New Historicism,* ed. H. Aram Veeser. New York: Routledge. 49–76.

Forbes, Duncan. 1975. Introduction to Hegel 1975. vii–xxxviii.

Funkenstein, Amos. 1989. "Collective Memory and Historical Consciousness." *History and Memory* 1 (1): 5–26.

Gates, Henry Louis. 1990. Critical Remarks. In *The Anatomy of Racism,* ed. David Theo Goldberg. Minneapolis: University of Minnesota Press. 319–29.

Hegel, Georg Wilhelm Friedrich. 1952. *The Philosophy of Right.* Trans. T. M. Knox. Chicago: Encyclopaedia Britannica, Inc.

———. 1956. *The Philosophy of History.* Trans. J. M. Sibree. New York: Dover Publications.

———. 1975. *Lectures on the Philosophy of World History — Introduction: Reason in History.* Trans. H. B. Nisbet. Cambridge: Cambridge University Press.

Herzl, Theodor. 1973. *Zionist Writings: Essays and Addresses.* Vol. 1. New York: Herzl Press.

Kapferer, Bruce. 1988. *Legends of People, Myths of State: Violence, Intolerance, and Political Culture in Sri Lanka and Australia.* Washington, D.C.: Smithsonian Institution Press.

Kemp, Anthony. 1991. *The Estrangement of the Past: A Study in the Origins of Modern Historical Consciousness.* New York: Oxford University Press.

Kern, Stephen. 1983. *The Culture of Time and Space, 1880–1918.* Cambridge: Harvard University Press.

Koshar, Rudy. 1990. "Building Pasts: The Language of Historic Preservation in Twentieth Century Germany." Paper presented to conference on Public Memory and Collective Identity, March, at Rutgers University.

Lacoue-Labarthe, Philippe, and Jean-Luc Nancy. 1989. "The Nazi Myth." *Critical Inquiry* 16 (2): 291–312.

Levine, Etan. 1986. "Introduction: The Jews in Time and Space." In *Diaspora: Exile and the Contemporary Jewish Condition,* ed. Etan Levine. New York: Steimatzky/Shapolsky. 1–11.

Lévy, Benny. 1980. "Today's Hope: Conversations with Sartre." *Telos* 44: 155–80.

Lustick, Ian. 1988. *For the Land and the Lord: Jewish Fundamentalism in Israel.* Washington, D.C.: Council on Foreign Relations.

Luz, Ehud. 1988. *Parallels Meet: Religion and Nationalism in the Early Zionist Movement.* Philadelphia: Jewish Publication Society.

McNeill, William H. 1986. *Polyethnicity and National Unity in World History.* Toronto: University of Toronto Press.

Marcuse, Herbert. 1966. *Reason and Revolution.* New York: Humanities Press.

Nancy, Jean-Luc. 1982. "The Jurisdiction of the Hegelian Monarch." *Social Research* 49 (2): 481–516.

Nordau, Max. 1910. *The Interpretation of History*. New York: Moffat, Yard and Company.

———. 1941. *Max Nordau to His People: A Summons and a Challenge*. New York: Scopus Publishing Company, Inc., for Nordau Zionist Society.

Plant, Raymond. 1983. *Hegel: An Introduction*. Oxford: Basil Blackwell.

Pred, Alan. 1990. *Making Histories and Constructing Human Geographies: Essays on the Local Transformation of Practice, Power Relations, and Consciousness*. Boulder, Colo.: Westview Press.

Said, Edward. 1985. "Orientalism Reconsidered." *Cultural Critique* 1 (Fall): 89–107.

———. 1988. "*Exodus and Revolution*: A Canaanite Reading." In *Blaming the Victims: Spurious Scholarship and the Palestine Question,* ed. Edward Said and Christopher Hitchens. New York: Verso.

Shohat, Ella. 1988. "Sephardim in Israel: Zionism from the Standpoint of its Jewish Victims." *Social Text* 19/20: 1–35.

Smith, Steven. 1991. "Hegel and the Jewish Question: In between Tradition and Modernity." *History of Political Thought* 12: 87–106.

Soja, Edward W. 1989. *Postmodern Geographies: The Reassertion of Space in Critical Social Theory*. New York: Verso.

Stock, Brian. 1990. *Listening for the Text: On the Uses of the Past*. Baltimore: Johns Hopkins University Press.

Swirski, Shlomo. 1989. *Israel: The Oriental Majority*. London: Zed.

Talmon, J. L. 1980. *The Myth of the Nation and the Vision of Revolution: The Origins of Ideological Polarisation in the Twentieth Century*. Berkeley and Los Angeles: University of California Press.

Tanaka, Stefan. 1990. Public Memory in Japan. Paper presented to conference on Public Memory and Collective Identity, March, Rutgers University.

Turner, Bryan S. 1978. *Marx and the End of Orientalism*. London: George Allen & Unwin Ltd.

———. 1988. "Religion and State Formation: A Commentary on Recent Debates." *Journal of Historical Sociology* 1: 322–33.

Veeser, H. Aram, and Marilyn Jerry. 1990. "Israel Today" (interview with Israel Shahak). *Z Magazine* (March).

Walker, R. B. J. 1989. "*The Prince* and 'the Pauper': Tradition, Modernity, and Practice in the Theory of Shapiro." In *International/Intertextual Relations: Postmodern Readings of World Politics,* ed. James Der Derian and Michael J. Shapiro. Lexington, Mass.: D. C. Heath and Company (Lexington Books). 25–48.

Walzer, Michael. 1989. "What Kind of State Is a Jewish State?" *Tikkun* 4 (4): 34 ff.

Weinreich, Max. 1980. *The History of the Yiddish Language*. Chicago: University of Chicago Press.

Wolf, Eric R. 1982. *Europe and the People without History*. Berkeley and Los Angeles: University of California Press.

Wuthnow, Robert. 1989. *Communities of Discourse: Ideology and Social Structure in the Reformation, the Enlightenment, and European Socialism*. Cambridge: Harvard University Press.

Yerushalmi, Yosef Hayim. 1982. *Zakhor: Jewish History and Jewish Memory*. Seattle: University of Washington Press.

6

The Reincarnation of Souls and the Rebirth of Commodities

Representations of Time in "East" and "West"

Akhil Gupta

IN 1984–85, WHILE doing fieldwork in a small village in northern India that I have named Alipur, I found myself the subject of an unlikely story. At that time, I didn't know quite what to make of it (I still don't), but it proved to be both profoundly unsettling and curiously affecting. The story was told by a young girl who was not quite three years old, perhaps even closer to being two. She was the youngest of four children of a relatively well-to-do high-caste (*Thaakur*) household of the village. In the course of my fieldwork, especially toward the end of my stay in Alipur, her father Sompal became one of my closest friends.

One day, shortly after having started fieldwork, I found myself talking to various people from the *Thaakur* neighborhood in front of Sompal's house. In the middle of a somewhat difficult conversation (I was still struggling to understand the local dialect), I heard a child's voice saying, "My brother Bobby has come." I couldn't see the child's face since she was standing on the windowsill behind the fine wire mesh screen that is commonly used in houses, and the sun was shining at an angle that made me squint and completely shadowed her. I paid no attention to it at that time.

161

It was unusual, though, that the child should have mentioned the name "Bobby." Although uncommon as an official name even in urban areas, one does find a number of products (everything from sunglasses to laundry detergent) named "Bobby," after the immensely successful Hindi film with the same title from the mid-1970s. No one in the village, of course, would have been given such a name.

During the course of becoming a regular visitor to Sompal's house, I learned more about the child, Nisha. She was at an age where she talked incessantly but very little of what she said made sense. The adults around disregarded her earnest efforts at conversation as nothing but a child's babbling. On rare occasions, though, she would utter clear and complete sentences.

I discovered that after my visits Nisha would go to neighbors' houses and excitedly tell them that her brother Bobby had come to see her that day. However, while I was there, she made no effort to talk to me or play with me. On the contrary, fond as I am of children, when I attempted to get to know her, she ran away and watched me, out of what seemed like shyness, from the adjacent room. At first, I placed her excessive shyness in the wider context of similar behavior exhibited by Indian children in the presence of unfamiliar visitors and didn't ascribe any significance to it.

This pattern persisted for a while. One day, when I was talking to her mother and grandmother, I asked them why she wouldn't play with me. They questioned her (she was, as usual, watching me from outside). Her response was that she was afraid of me. I was trying to think of what I might have done to have scared her. "Why are you afraid of him?" asked the grandmother. Nisha replied, "I was playing and my brother Bobby drove a car over me." Perhaps sensing my reaction, the old woman waved her hand dismissively in the air and said, "Don't pay any attention to her! She's just remembering things from a past life." Nisha's mother concurred.

I was so stunned that I didn't know what to think. How did the little girl, who had almost certainly never ridden in a car, and rarely seen one, come up with such a bizarre story involving a car? And why did she decide that *I* was Bobby? It was clear that it was not a passing fancy. From the instant she had set her eyes on me, she had consistently identified me as "Bobby." Intriguing as all this was, the reactions of her mother and grandmother were even more perplexing. They saw nothing extraordinary in the whole affair, dismissing it when it occurred, and seemingly paying no attention to it during the rest of my stay, although Nisha continued to refer to me as her brother Bobby.

I later learned a fuller account of her story. She claimed to have been playing outside their house when a monkey ran after her. Frightened, she sat under the car. "My brother didn't know that," she said. "It wasn't his fault." Her mother reported that when she would see an illustration in a children's book of a young man wearing spectacles or when she would encounter objects that I had left for their household, she would often start crying. Passing through the market town one day, she pointed to a building and blurted out, "Our house (*koThii*) was of that color." The elders present made fun of her, "Sure, you had a big house! Sure you had a car!" (*BaDii aayii koThii vaalii! H*aa*, jaruur kaar thii tere par!*) Her mother also told me that as she has grown older, Nisha's references to "Bobby *Bhaiyyaa*" have become less and less frequent.

One would expect a Western scholar to be completely shocked by such an incident. However, anyone who has grown up in India, as I have, has heard rebirth stories with such regularity that it should have been easy to assimilate this anecdote to a familiar genre. After all, the circulation of these stories itself depends on (and creates) an acknowledgment of both their possibility and their authenticity. But this tale crept under my skin. Perhaps it proved so unsettling because, unlike stories in which the strangeness of events was always distanced because it was happening to *other* people, this had happened to me.

Other stories of reincarnation narrated to me by villagers also emphasized a pattern of sudden and unexpected death. I was told that only certain types of people remember their past lives: those who died from snakebite, or whose death occurred by water or fire, those who were poisoned, and in some cases, even those killed by smallpox. The reason people such as these were able to remember their previous existence was that although their body was destroyed, their being (*praaN*) was still roaming about in an unconscious state (*acetan avasthaa*). If one dies after a long illness, the memory of the past is destroyed. But if one dies unexpectedly, the memory of the past is still alive after nine months in a new womb.

Almost all the important features of Nisha's story are also consistent with patterns commonly found by rebirth researchers. Most people are reported to remember events from their past lives around the age of three and to lose this ability by the age of seven; a surprisingly high proportion—about 49 percent—report dying violently; their ability to remember their past life is triggered by an incidental remark or event; and a fair proportion display phobias of the things that had caused their deaths (Chengappa 1988).

Before proceeding further, we should stop to ask how seriously these stories are taken by their narrators and audiences. Are they self-consciously presented as fables intended to instruct and edify but not a literal rendering of actual events with real effects? Although one could, of course, find a range of interpretive postures, I discovered that for the most part the belief in rebirth is taken extremely seriously by everyone concerned, especially those directly affected by it. A man from a nearby village who died in midlife was reborn in a place a little distance farther down the railway line. When he remembered his past life, he started telling everyone his previous name, the name of his wife, and the number and age of his children. He was taken to the village of his past and at once recognized his former wife (who was well along in years by then) and children. So strongly does he feel the bond with his previous family that he now supports both his current family and those who depended on him in his earlier birth, dividing his time between the two households.

Since most of these reports originate in India, one can ask a broader question: Is the belief in rebirth limited to India? And if so, why? One can begin to answer these questions by thinking of the way in which categories found in discourse shape experience. Before the latter part of the nineteenth century, for example, there were no perverts because the new understanding of disease, in which perversion appeared as a form of abnormality, was not yet in place (Hacking 1986: 222). Similarly, one might ask if rebirth is not experienced in the West because the categories through which that experience might emerge do not exist. Are American children's "make-believe friends," for instance, real relatives in the past lives of Indian children?[1] Or is equating the experiences of different cultures in this way misleading because it presumes a degree of translatability that does not, and cannot, exist?[2]

Another reason these questions are important is that representations of time have performed a central function in the construction of difference between Self and Other. Notions of rebirth and the concepts of cyclicality, rhythmicity, and concreteness have played a crucial role in Orientalist representations of an exotic and inferior Other opposed to the West.[3] In this essay, I do not employ the strategy of challenging the representation of the Other for its essentialism, exoticism, evolutionism, and culturalism, for explication would in itself belabor the point. Instead, I turn the gaze around and investigate the *partiality* of the self-representations of the West. By looking mostly at everyday life and the social science literature, I demonstrate that representations of the Western Self depend on the deployment of discourses on time that implicitly construct and reify differences in a manner that is homogenizing, essentialist, and evolutionary.

> *These were the first words Gibreel Farishta said when he awoke on the snowbound English beach: "Born again, Spoono, you and me. Happy birthday, mister; happy birthday to you."*   (Rushdie 1988: 10)

More than on anything else, the notion of rebirth seems to depend on the distinctively "Oriental" conception of the circularity of time.[4] I clearly recall the time when I was an undergraduate at a large midwestern university and one of my professors, drawing a straight horizontal line on the board, asked the students if time moved from left to right. Only two people in a class of forty didn't think it did: one of them was Vietnamese and the other was I. So he asked us how *we* saw the movement of time and both of us replied, more or less simultaneously, that it was circular. I give this example to illustrate two points. First, dominant representations of time are deeply embedded, even if they are not held consciously. As a seventeen-year-old, I had certainly never pondered the nature of time, yet I could effortlessly identify an "incorrect" representation. This was equally true of the other students who were sincerely amazed that time could be conceived in any other way but as an infinite line progressing from a charted past into an unknown future. Secondly, this exercise seemed to bring out rather clearly the obvious difference, even opposition, between "Western" and "Eastern" conceptions of time.[5]

If this opposition between East and West were employed to demonstrate that notions of time are differently constructed in diverse cultural contexts, it would hardly deserve comment. But because these essentialized differences between (allegedly internally homogeneous) areas of the world become so important to the civilizing mission of colonialism and the developmental mission of neocolonialism, they deserve closer scrutiny. The "circularity of time" turned out to be a powerful Western trope to chart, label, define, and criticize the Orient, and, finally, to rule it. Notions of rebirth, for example, have been interpreted to reveal a deep-seated fatalism in "the Indian psyche."[6] In the absence of the "disenchantment" of the world and the growth of a strictly secular realm of social life, fatalism found its way into many different activities. The unwillingness of the farmer to experiment with new technologies, of the poor underclass to revolt, and of the monied to take the risks necessary for industrial capitalism to thrive—all could be explained with reference to fatalistic attitudes.[7]

Postcolonial representations of India repackaged these attitudes in interesting new ways. Although very influential, modernization theory was the least creative in this regard. When fatalism does not appear explicitly in modernization tracts as a variable constraining development, it is replaced by factors such as a lack of a sense of punctuality or of an appreciation of the value of time. The "third world,"[8] in other words, is poor because it doesn't have a sense of time that streams into an unredeemable past, a valuable commodity that has to be preserved, treasured, and exchanged like money. If only they had a sense of time more like ours, the logic goes, they too would be rich. Variations of this theme can be found in representations of unchanging, traditional society in historical studies and of organically connected social and cultural wholes in functionalist anthropology.

> *Hegel remarks somewhere that all great, world-historical facts and personages occur, as it were, twice. He has forgotten to add: the first time as tragedy, the second as farce.*   (Marx [1852] 1959: 320)

It is ironic that the self-representation of the Western industrial economies as societies whose wealth is accompanied, if not explained, by an abstract, linear, and progressive notion of time finds unexpected confirmation in capitalism's sharpest critics. In his famous "Time, Work-Discipline, and Industrial Capitalism," E. P. Thompson (1967) persuasively argues that the experience of the first generation of English factory workers can best be understood in terms of conflicts due to the differences between their sense of time and that required for industrial production. Thompson labels the "inappropriate" sense of time that these former agricultural laborers brought with them to the factory "task orientation." Cyclicality and variability are its distinguishing features. It is a mode of organizing the activities at hand so that they are attuned to the "rhythms of nature." In agricultural work, bouts of intense activity usually alternate with long periods of idleness.

This, combined with the intermingling of labor and social intercourse, serve as the distinguishing features of task orientation.

As industrial laborers, these workers have to confront a completely new regime of time-discipline, one based on radically different presuppositions about the nature of time. Here time is abstract, labor a commodity, and tasks fragmented. What is created in factories results from the immense coordination of the activities of perhaps thousands of different workers. But the individual worker is not involved in a gigantic communal project; as Walter Benjamin put it, "the article being worked on comes within [the worker's] range of action and moves away from him just as arbitrarily" ([1939] 1969: 175).[9] The more general point is made by Marx: "It is a common characteristic of all capitalist production ... that the worker does not make use of the working conditions. The working conditions make use of the worker; but it takes machinery to give this reversal a technically concrete form" (cited in Benjamin ibid.). Exemplified by the assembly line, work with machinery involves the coordination of the workers' "own movements with the uniformly constant movements of an automaton" (ibid.). The automatic, repetitive, uniform activity required of workers as the manufactured part moves past imposes a rhythm of work that is arbitrary in relation to task orientation. But the pace of work is not arbitrary because it is set by calculated efforts to generate profits on the part of the capitalist. That work is now measured against a homogeneous, abstract, and linear notion of time is thus a necessary result of a process of production where labor is social but profits are private, where time is money because it represents the capitalist's profits, and where time can be "lost," "wasted," "spent," "utilized inefficiently," and so on, precisely because it can potentially be translated into additional revenue.

According to Thompson, the task-oriented sense of time served as a lively source of resistance to the discipline imposed on the first generation of the industrial proletariat.[10] Yet resistance was ultimately unsuccessful. A new consciousness of time slowly permeated the entire social fabric, so much so that the most intimate rhythms of peoples' lives came to be regulated by the clock.[11] Thompson was concerned with understanding this momentous transition because he believed that if humane alternatives were to be found to the alienating and self-destructive tendencies inherent in modern society, which pillages the past and mortgages the future, we would have to remember what alternatives have been given up in the name of "progress." But he was also deeply ambivalent about the value of time discipline, recognizing its productive potential while at the same time viewing its successful march over the "third world" not without a sense of regret:

> Without time-discipline we could not have the insistent energies of industrial man; and whether this discipline comes in the form of Methodism, or of Stalinism, or of nationalism, it will come to the developing world.(1967: 93)

Just as alternative ways of being, encoded in different conceptions of time, were lost in the move to industrial society in Europe, so too will the homogenizing effects of industrial time-discipline smooth out the varied rhythms of work and life in the developing world.[12]

There is something very disturbing about Thompson's heartfelt critique of capitalist time-discipline. By questioning something so "immediately given" as our experience of time, he makes us see the truth of Kafka's claim: "To believe in progress is not to believe that progress has already taken place. That would be no belief" (cited in Benjamin [1934] 1969: 130). Claims of progress, in other words, cannot be justified with reference to any permanent or objective measure, but depend instead on the dissemination of a particular belief, a belief in *one* among many possible types of change. For instance, is it progress if the life expectancy for individuals goes up but the species itself faces extinction due to nuclear war? In showing what has been lost in subscribing to the particular belief *of* progress that has come to characterize capitalist society, Thompson wanted to reaffirm the belief *in* progress, not to bury it.

And this is where Thompson's work proves disturbing. For his powerfully incisive critique of capitalism harbors a nostalgia for what it has replaced in the West, a way of life that in one swift move becomes identified with the "third world" today. Johannes Fabian (1983) has argued that this is a standard transposition in Western discourses on the "Other." By locating others in the past (a phenomenon that Fabian labels "allochronism"), what is usually being denied is not just the concurrence of their existence but responsibility for their continuing oppression. Furthermore, placing other societies in a prior stage of a narrative of linear development reinforces the dominant Western faith in progress.

It would seem unfair to tar Thompson with the same brush as the people he opposed. After all, Thompson didn't see in the "third world" an opportunity for self-congratulation or an excuse to exercise contempt for the poor. Rather, he employed it as a critical mirror that enables the West to reflect on what has been lost in the name of progress. However, while Thompson differed markedly from his opponents in his evaluation of the gains of industrial capitalism, he shared with them a belief that its notions of time are essentially different from those of either the societies that preceded it historically or the societies that accompany it today. Whereas time in industrial capitalism becomes abstract, homogeneous, empty, linear, and progressive, shorn of "nature's rhythms," and unconnected to the task at hand, historical and cultural Others construe time as concrete, cyclical, closely connected to nature, and experienced in the context of specific tasks.

> *Human beings who turn away from God lose love, and certainty, and also the sense of His boundless time, that encompasses past, present and future; the timeless time, that has no need to move.*   (Rushdie 1988: 214)

It would, of course, be foolish to deny that the far-reaching changes that accompanied the industrial revolution permanently and irreversibly altered Western notions of time. It is also true that dominant representations of time in the West *emphasize* its linear, continuous, unidirectional, and progressive character, its preciousness, and its interchangeability with money.[13] What I wish to question is whether the changes that occurred in conceptions of time are best understood as the move from cyclicality *to* linearity, from task-orientation rooted in concrete activity *to* an abstract passage disconnected from the flow of everyday life, and from a close synchrony with the rhythms of nature *to* an alienated homogeneity imposed by work-discipline. Rather than accepting this narrative as a plausible reconstruction of the Western past and a powerful prediction about the "third world" today, rather than acquiescing to the dominant portrayals of the difference between Self and Other that circulate widely in the Western world, we need to ask *why* discursively available representations of time in the West remain oblivious, despite easily observable evidence to the contrary, to features of cyclicality, concreteness, rhythms, and, yes, even rebirth. This silence is politically important because it allows the Western narrative of progress to go unchallenged and enables the continued management and surveillance of the "third world" in the guise of "development."

Before going further, let me state that the task of answering why hegemonic representations of time in the West are silent about cyclicality and rebirth lies beyond my competence. Nor have I done the ambitious ethnography of modern Western society that would conclusively demonstrate that the indicated paradox does in fact exist. What I want to do instead, through the use of a few examples, is to suggest that notions of time commonly attributed to the "third world," especially "the Orient," reside comfortably, if invisibly, in industrial capitalist societies.

Although the different features of time that I have identified are so intertwined that it is difficult to discuss one or the other in isolation, let me first take up the issue of cyclicality. Is cyclicality a property of time found only in preindustrial or noncapitalist societies? In a provocative article, Maurice Bloch has argued that the anthropological evidence reveals two notions of time:

> On the one hand we have concepts rather like our own folk
> everyday concept of linear durational time and on the other hand a
> concept of a static notion of time often referred to as cyclic, the
> two words referring to the same sort of evidence. (1977: 282)

Rather than be relativistic and attempt to locate non-Western societies in the category of the "cyclical," he says, if we observe the contexts in which circular and linear notions of time are employed, we find that

> at some time, one notion of time is used, and at others another, and
> we can immediately notice that the evidence for static or cyclical
> time comes from that special type of communication, which we
> label ritual in the broad sense of the term: greetings, and fixed
> politeness formulas, formal behaviour and above all rituals, whether
> social, religious or state. By contrast the contexts in which notions
> of durational time are used are practical activities, especially
> agriculture and uninstitutionalized power. (ibid.)

According to Bloch, anthropologists have reached the conclusion that notions of time are radically different across cultures by making a mistaken comparison. They take concepts of time from ritual contexts in other cultures and compare them with "*our* everyday practical" idea of time (1977: 290; emphasis in original). Thus, in answer to the question posed earlier, Bloch would probably say that cyclicality is not just a feature of noncapitalist societies. Unlike Thompson, Bloch denies that a fundamental shift occurs in moving from the exotic nonindustrial societies typically studied by anthropologists to the highly industrialized capitalist society of which he is a part. He does this by taking an essentialist position on production: everyday practical activities of production require a linear and durational concept of time, no matter what the cultural context. This is one strategy by which to resist the exoticization of the Other. It is a questionable one, however, because it assimilates the Other to one's own cultural constructions. In this case, the culturally specific, Western notion of "everyday production" (see Baudrillard 1975) is employed to assert cross-cultural similarities in concepts of time. Does Bloch not successfully avoid the pitfalls of Orientalism only to succumb to that old anthropological bugaboo, ethnocentrism?

Associating the concepts of linearity and duration with the process of production, although quite correct in some respects, is, on the whole, misleading: ever since Quesnay, the central metaphors employed to understand the capitalist economy have been ones of circularity. For example, Marx's analysis of capitalism rests on the circular process whereby money is turned into more money through the extraction of surplus value in the production and circulation of commodities. In fact, one can see that the entire Marxist analysis of crises, whether those of accumulation or those of overproduction, turns on the failure of the closure of the "circuit of capital." Nor is this way of thinking peculiar, somehow, to Marxism. Sraffa's famous reinterpretation of Ricardo emphasizes the circle of production in its very title, *Production of Commodities by Means of Commodities* (1960). In neoclassical theory, the circle is even tighter because distribution falls out of the picture. Here, production and consumption are locked in a perpetual market-clearing dance, providing returns to scarce factors on the one hand and satisfaction of desires on the other.

If one turns from the metaphors of economic theory to the more mundane interpretations that businesses and investors employ in their daily life, the presence of cycles is even more striking. Chief among these is the well known "business cycle," which has in the past displayed a mysteriously constant periodicity.[14] Another example is the "hog cycle" experienced by hog producers in the United States for nearly a century, which has a periodicity of about four years (Luenberger 1979: 162–65). Although the sacred texts might demur, the "little tradition" of the religion of business in modern-day America is pervaded by images that evoke cyclicality even when they don't explicitly state it. This is the language of upturns and downturns; of swings, shifts, and depressions; of boom and bust; of turning things around; of hitting rock bottom; and so on: all positions are pregnant with the possibilities of their opposite location in that circle of risk.

The discursive space may be thickly populated with metaphors of wave motion and of movement around a circle, but what does that tell us about the "lived experience" of time, about its phenomenology? Is the boredom and alienation of work endured as an interminable "stretching out" of time? Clearly, one can point to many facets of everyday life, especially working life, that are experientially linear. But just as "nine to five" marks the traversal of a straight temporal path, "Monday to Friday" marks its repeated cadences (the daily grind). Isn't the seemingly oppressive flow of time in assembly-line work but the necessary complement of the repetitiveness of the task? And what could be more infinitely circular than the silent rotation of the hands of a clock? The calendar can be seen as a device that marks the passage of linear time but it does so only by noting the *recurrence* of sacred festivals, national holidays, and on television and National Public Radio, the birthdays of popular stars.[15] It seems to me that the lived experience of time in the modern western world is poorly explained by postulating linearity and cyclicality as opposing and essential principles. I should quickly add, however, that I am not advocating a facile synthesis whereby the two principles are brought together into a dialectical spiral. My point, rather, is to question the employment of these reified representations of time in the construction of a particular kind of difference between Self and Other.

Another major contrast often drawn between industrial and nonindustrial societies is that in the former time is homogeneous, empty, and regular, whereas in the latter it is rhythmic and irregular.[16] The basis for this difference, often unstated, can be traced to the relationships of these societies to nature. Whereas agricultural, pastoral, and hunting-gathering societies are closely attuned to the "rhythms of nature," in industrial societies these bonds are severed. For example, much has been made in pop sociology of the fact that electric lights, three work shifts, all-night radio and television broadcasting, and twenty-four-hour restaurants, grocery stores, and laundromats—what might be called the "Denny's revolution"—are slowly blurring any meaningful distinction between night and day.

Once again, as with the case of cyclical time, we find a troubling set of essentialist dichotomies being constructed in which agricultural (and, more generally, nonindustrial) societies are identified with "nature," and industrial societies are identified with technology. Ecological and nostalgic critiques of industrialism that seek to overturn it through a "return to nature" implicitly end up legitimizing the dominant Western narrative of progress as a victory of technology over nature (and, simultaneously, of the West over the Orient). Instead of asking, "Do people in agricultural societies respond to nature instead of mastering it? Are they truly attentive to the sounds of nature and in tune with its seasons and rhythms?" we need to question the evolutionary narrative that identifies the historical trajectory of the West as moving from a state of nature to an age of technology.

One of the more important themes in this narrative is that the "natural" rhythms of work in nonindustrial societies are flattened, homogenized, emptied out in the transition to industrialization. Instead of intense bouts of hard labor alternating with periods of idleness, we get the steady, regular, normalizing beat of capitalist time-discipline. But in what way is the daily routine of commuters who leave their home at dawn and return at sunset any less rhythmic than the circular path traversed by the Nuer shepherd taking his herd out to pasture? In what sense are the seasonalities of work for the agricultural laborer in India significantly more pronounced than those of the construction worker in Minnesota or other colder parts of the United States?

It is significant that one place where rhythms are widely accepted in the West is in their association with nature, especially in the cultural construction of the human body (and particularly the female body) as a "natural" object. In fact, the body, constituted as a biological system in homeostatic equilibrium, is recognized as being in ill health by the irregularity of its cycles: hence "diseases" like arrhythmia, the irregular beating of the heart. Other examples might note the New Age technique of charting biorhythms (the monthly cycle of the emotional and physical states of the body) as well as concerns with the sleep cycle, the menstrual cycle, and so forth. Even so discerning a critic of physiological/medical metaphors of the human body as Emily Martin fails to distance herself from this association. In *The Woman in the Body,* she analyzes PMS (premenstrual syndrome) as being the result of the inflexibility of the demands of capitalist time-discipline in the face of a woman's "natural rhythms" (1987: 113–38).

The idea that time in the non-Western world is rhythmic because of the nature of agricultural or pastoral life also finds expression in another powerful opposition. Here the concrete nature of time experienced through the carrying out of specific tasks is contrasted with an abstract and empty passage of time measured against a scientifically determined standard. Concerning the Nuer, Evans-Pritchard says:

> The daily timepiece is the cattle clock, the round of pastoral tasks, and the time of day and the passage of time through a day are to a Nuer primarily the succession of these tasks and their relation to one another....
>
> ... The Nuer have no expression equivalent to "time" in our language, and they cannot, therefore, as we can, speak of time as though it were something *actual,* which passes, can be wasted, can be saved, and so forth. I do not think that they ever experience the same feeling of fighting against time or of having to coordinate activities with an abstract passage of time because *their points of reference are mainly the activities themselves,* which are generally of a leisurely character. Events follow a logical order, but they are not controlled by an abstract system, there being no autonomous points of reference to which activities have to conform to precision. Nuer are fortunate. (Evans-Pritchard 1940: 101–3; my emphasis)

No doubt the "good fortune" of the Nuer, as of other people whose lives are rooted in the concrete succession of tasks, is a thing of the past. In exchange for their subjects' land, labor, and raw materials, colonial governments all over the "third world" left them with an abstract system of time. But before taking this line of reasoning further, we should stop to ask if the contrast between time perceived as a succession of tasks and time perceived as an abstract concept best captures the genuine differences that may exist between Nuer and Western conceptions of time.

One reason why this opposition appears inherently plausible is that we assume task orientation to be the same type of activity in different contexts. Yet when one thinks about the form that task orientation would be likely to take under conditions of generalized commodity production, as in the capitalist world, one realizes that an "abstract" conception of time is but its chaperon. Some years ago, the most popular theory of management, MBO (management by objectives), had task orientation inscribed in its very name. In fact, if anything, capitalist societies have been accused of being *overly* concerned with task orientation. Habermas, for instance (1970), decries the process whereby questions of practical-moral import are increasingly formulated in terms of means-end relations, in terms of accomplishing technical tasks. Task-oriented and abstract conceptions of time, therefore, poorly fit prearranged positions in a system of polar opposites. If one thinks of Indian villages, where work is primarily agricultural; where many men wear watches; where radio programs, buses, and trains work on schedules made up in abstract time (or at least are supposed to); where reincarnation and transmigration occurring across incredibly large temporal units are considered a commonplace feature of everyday life (here I am thinking of the notion of *kalpa*s, or the four *yugaa*s), one is forced to abandon any simple opposition like that between concrete and abstract time.

I am concerned with refuting this opposition at some length because it serves as a master trope to distinguish the civilized from the primitive, cosmopolitan from rural, adults from children, and men from women. These disparate themes are unified in the narrative of progress embodied in the idea of development. Thus cognitive development, at least according to Piaget, is measured by a child's increasing capacity to think abstractly and generalize from repeated concrete occurrences to formal rules; moral development (I am thinking mostly of Kohlberg) is measured by the subject's ability to universalize abstract moral rules (a measure by which Mohandas Gandhi reached the highest or fifth stage but by which, Kohlberg found, most women reached only the third);[17] cultural and intellectual development is measured by the abstractness of the representations and theories that enable one to make "useful" distinctions; and, finally, economic development is measured by the production of generalized exchange values, by the growth of abstract measures like GNP and QLI (Quality of Life Index). In moving from concreteness to abstraction, one develops simultaneously along cognitive, moral, intellectual, cultural, and economic dimensions. It is through this play of oppositions, by which the primitive, the rural, children, and women are assimilated, rather than by simple assertion, that the dominance of the West becomes synonymous with the development of the cultivated white male.

There are secular reincarnations, too.   (Rushdie 1988: 17)

So far, I have attempted to demonstrate that cyclicality, rhythms, and concreteness are not features of time peculiar to the Orient (or, more generally, to non-Western noncapitalist societies). But surely, one might think, it would be foolish to make the same argument for reincarnation. Everyone "knows" that to experience rebirth, one needs to go to the "mystical East."

I want to argue that, farfetched as it may appear at first, the idea that forms of rebirth circulate widely in the West warrants further investigation. To anticipate a common misreading of the argument that follows, I would like to emphasize that I am not equating the rebirth of objects of art or of other objects with the rebirth of beings, but merely pointing to what is common in their conceptions of time. In "The Task of the Translator" Benjamin introduces the notion of the *after*life of objects of art: "The history of the great works of art tells us about their antecedents, their realization in the age of the artist, their potentially eternal afterlife in succeeding generations. Where this last manifests itself, it is called fame" ([1923]1969: 71). Famous works of art, as exemplified by the translated text, are not simply objects with elongated lifespans; rather, every time they are displayed, performed, read, interpreted, they are reborn. Benjamin animates the world of objects by reconceptualizing the idea of life: "The concept of life is given its due only if everything that has a history of its own . . . is credited with life. In the final analysis, the range of life must be determined by history" (ibid.). "The idea of life and afterlife in works of art," says Benjamin, "should be regarded with an entirely *un*metaphorical objectivity" (ibid.; my emphasis).

If works of art were the only objects that lent themselves to notions of an afterlife, my claim that such ideas circulate widely in the Western world might be reasonably disputed. However, one way to see the generality of the phenomenon is by considering what Igor Kopytoff has called "the cultural biography of things" (1986). By doing a life history of a commodity, one can trace its birth (that is, its invention and initial commoditization), the various rites of passage in its life (that is, its movement across spheres of exchange or its movement across different thresholds of exchangeability), its death (due to withdrawal from circulation), and, if applicable, its rebirth (due to recommoditization). I think one can see this process particularly clearly when one thinks of the currents in fashion, whether those of clothes and haircuts or those of cars and buildings. We speak easily of fashions being born, dying, and coming back to life. Popular magazines announce that "it's the 1950s all over again," that courtship and marriage "are back" (one wonders where they were circulating in the interim), or sometimes that "the 1920s are here once more." In fact, one way to understand what Jameson calls one of the central features of post-modernism, the "complacent play of historical allusion and stylistic pastiche" (1984: 55), might be to see it as a rash of rebirth.

The problem that notions of rebirth encounter in the West is perhaps reflected in a rhetorical question posed by Benjamin in "The Task of the Translator": "Is not the continued life of works of art *far easier* to recognize than the continual life of animal species?" ([1923]1969: 71; my emphasis). Here we have a sharply drawn conceptual polarity that is exceptionally influential in the Western world. Why is that the case? Why is the rebirth of *beings* so difficult to accept at the same time that belief in the rebirth of *things* has become second nature?[18] Of course, one reason is the assumption that commodities and persons are essentially unlike each other; in Heidegger's famous distinction (1962), one is ontic and the other ontological. Bringing these unfamiliar entities within the same framework would then seem to be a fundamental category mistake. Yet one need not trivialize the depth of feeling that characterizes the rebirth of beings as opposed to that of things, or claim that the two processes are experienced with the same emotional intensity, in order to point to the similarities in their notions of time. Nor does the mundane and everyday nature of the rebirth of things in any way diminish the profound effect it has on people's lives.

Kopytoff has radically challenged the self-evidence of the opposition between persons and things by considering its cultural and historical context:

> We take it more or less for granted that things — physical objects
> and rights to them — represent the natural universe of commodities.
> At the opposite pole we place people, who represent the natural
> universe of individuation and singularization. This conceptual
> polarity of individualized persons and commoditized things is
> recent and, culturally speaking, exceptional. (1986: 64)

I want to suggest that this recent — and culturally exceptional — conceptual opposition may help us understand why Westerners have so much difficulty with the notion that persons, like commodities, can be reborn.[19] To talk of the relative newness and cultural distinctiveness of the polarity between persons and commodities is, however, not to downplay its importance nor to explain its cultural invisibility. The idea that persons can be reborn in a manner analogous to that of commodities appears deeply threatening in the West precisely because it attacks the entire ideological edifice of capitalism. For if persons were not unique, individual, and singular in some primal sense, what would it mean for them to make promises, have wills, and *enter contracts*?[20] The whole ideology of democratic capitalism, of participation in an economy and in a polity, is predicated on the maintenance of this sharp and irrevocable distinction between persons and things.

Another reason for the Western difficulty with the rebirth of beings may be due to the fact that it involves reswitching between physical and nonphysical states. The transition from a corporeal state to a noncorporeal one and then back to a physical body seems to defy all the conventional dualisms: materialism versus spiritualism, realism versus idealism, and so forth. In finding similarities in "Western" and "Eastern" notions of time, I want to problematize the discourse through which the reincarnation of beings "naturally" appears as the polar opposite of the rebirth of commodities. Why is the circular movement from physical being to spiritual entity and the passage back more mysterious or more difficult to comprehend than the cycle that starts from individualized thing, goes to a generalized commodity, and then comes back?[21]

Ideas of rebirth explained to me by villagers in Alipur bore a striking resemblance to the way in which people in the West normally think of commodities. When people die, their *aatmaa* (loosely, "soul") sheds their physical body and wanders freely in the universe. At a later time, it attaches itself to another being, either human or animal. If people perform good deeds, they are reborn in a higher state, their *aatmaa* attaches itself to a higher being; otherwise, they may move lower down the hierarchy of life. Similarly, in the West, when things become parted from their owners, they enter a free-floating world of commodities. Here they circulate, entering into a series of movements, some lateral, some vertical, finally attaching themselves to new subjects. For a while, they are taken out of circulation. If their owners are famous, they reenter the world of commodities as things of value (for example, George Washington's axe or Lincoln's writing table), and are reborn as venerated objects.

> *History the intoxicant, the creation and possession of the Devil, of the great Shaitan, the greatest of the lies — progress, science, rights — against which the Imam has set his face.*

Bilal continues to address the darkness. "Death to the tyranny of Empress Ayesha, of calendars, of America, of time! We seek the eternity, the timelessness, of God. His still waters, not her flowing wines."   (Rushdie 1988: 210–11)

When we look at Western representations of India (and of the Orient more generally), we find that conceptions of time have played a very important role in the construction of difference between self and other. These differences are predicated on the opposition between the Western notion of time and Oriental concepts of cyclicality, rhythmicity, concreteness, and rebirth. By challenging these easy polarities, I do not, of course, wish to deny that genuine differences exist nor do I hope that they will one day be overcome. Rather, by defamiliarizing the familiar, I wish to emphasize the historical and political construction of these differences. What I want to question is a *particular* strategy of creating difference between Self and Other, namely that employed by Orientalism, which proceeds by taking a partial view of the Other and a partial view of the Self and exaggerating both. There is no reason to think, for example, that South Asian peoples live with a *unitary* sense of time or that the differences within the subcontinent can be successfully assimilated in counterposing them to the West. In fact, essentializing and exoticizing the Other is one way to avert the challenge of cultural difference. Thus, to treat Nisha's story (with which I begin the paper) as a prototype of the radical otherness of the Orient is to safely "bracket" it within hegemonic constructions of difference. I have instead tried to show how it destabilizes those established orders of difference.

There is now a growing body of literature that establishes the selectivity of Western representations of Others. To the extent, however, that these analyses accept the self-representations of the West, they remain limited in their ability to criticize them. My goal in this essay, therefore, has been largely to demonstrate the partiality of the self-representation of time in the West. By doing this, I wish to take away the ground on which distinctions have historically been constructed in the Western narrative of progress, distinctions that continue to justify, under the guise of "development," the subordination and management of the "third world" today.[22]

Is the deconstruction of Orientalist discourses but the first step in a new global metanarrative of homogenization? In the "global village," will cultural difference be reduced to performances enacted in front of tourists searching for authenticity? By now, it should be pretty clear that these are not our only choices. Although I have chosen to criticize one particular

construction of difference in this essay, that between "Western" and "Eastern" representations of time, the argument is obviously more general. One
could just as easily look at many other concepts, such as notions of the
capitalist "rational economic actor" versus the noncapitalist "economy of
affect," or of calculated maximizing behavior versus moral economy.

This leads me to my final comment, which is also one of the main
objectives of this paper. What we have to see is that the construction of
the self-evident differences between Self and Other grew out of, and served,
a particular political project. In rejecting this project, we have to be careful not merely to invert its evaluation of difference while preserving its
categories. Instead, we have to fundamentally reevaluate, rethink, and represent categories of difference so as to arrive at a genuinely antiimperial-
ist and non-Eurocentric critical practice.[23] Here, it might be useful to
turn, not to the metanarrative of global homogenization, but to multiple
narratives of what Ulf Hannerz has called "creolization" (1987), the invention and emergence of new coordinates of difference in the face of powerful global processes pulling in the opposite direction.

Notes

I would like to thank Purnima Mankekar, James Ferguson, John Peters, Renato Rosaldo,
Lata Mani, Jane Collier, Sylvia Yanagisako, Dipesh Chakrabarty, Martin Jaffee, G. Carter
Bentley, Brackette Williams, E. Valentine Daniel, Resat Kasaba, Diane Wolf, Karl Potter,
Elizabeth Perry, Ellen Fuller, Debraj Ray, Amita Shastri, and participants in the Comparative Religion Colloquium at the University of Washington, at which an earlier version of
this paper was presented on 18 April 1989. I am especially grateful to Tara Mohanan for
help with the transliteration. Fieldwork for this paper was conducted in 1984–85 and in the
summer of 1989.

1. This provocative question was suggested to me by Paul Brass.

2. Here I am thinking of the notion of "incommensurability" first put forward by Kuhn
(1970) and later elaborated by Rorty (1979) and Bernstein (1985).

3. "The West" is obviously no more of a homogenous and unified entity than "the
Orient." I use it because (1) one needs to reconstruct an Occident in order to critique Orientalism, thus introducing an element of strategic essentialism; and (2) I am referring to the
effects of hegemonic representations of the Western self rather than its subjugated traditions
(see also Mohanty 1988). I do not therefore use the term simply to refer to a geographical
space but to a particular historical conjugation of place, power, and knowledge.

4. I am using the terms "circular" and "cylical" interchangeably. It should be clear from
the context that circularity does not necessarily imply stasis.

5. Ellen Fuller pointed out to me that whereas the statement "History repeats itself" is
fairly common in the West, it is almost always employed as a negative example, as in George
Santayana's dictum, "Those who cannot remember the past are condemned to repeat it."

6. Although I speak here in the past tense, this is by no means a view of India that is behind us. Rather, it continues to play a powerful role in popularly circulated representations of India in the West.

7. Debraj Ray has pointed out to me that the belief in fatalism need not contradict the belief in progress. One could hold a fatalistic attitude toward progress, that is, believe that change is inevitable and there is little one can do about it, whether one likes it or not. Fatalism is therefore a phenomenon that is probably as widespread among the depoliticized citizens of advanced industrial capitalist states as among those of the third world. That fatalism is then invariably used to denote an unchanging, traditional, "Oriental" world itself says a great deal about its politics.

8. Many of the same caveats apply to my use of the term "third world" as to my use of "the West." It is neither implied that all countries so labeled are similar nor that "first" and "third" worlds exist as separate and separable spaces. In the postcolonial world-system, the idea of the "third world" has become the foil to the self-representations of "the West." It is important to recognize that; hence, the quotation marks (see also Mohanty 1988 and Ahmad 1987).

9. It was this fact that was so effectively exploited in the biting humor of the film *Modern Times*.

10. Thomas Smith (1986) has challenged the generalizability of this point by attempting to show that in the case of Japan, the conflicts between management and workers in early industrialization seldom involved clashes over notions of time.

11. Tristram Shandy, for example, could date his conception exactly, because his parents' sexual habits were so exactly regulated by the clock.

12. Interestingly, Thompson got his notion of task orientation from Evans-Pritchard's descriptions of the Nuer.

13. Here the link with the commodification of labor power in industrial capitalism is most explicit: time is money because labor power can be sold on the market, converting time to money.

14. It seems to me that the belief in such phenomena is no less "metaphysical" than the belief in witchcraft or extrasensory perception; yet I suspect this suggestion would be met by loud protest from believers.

15. This observation was made to me by John Peters.

16. That this opposition continues to be extremely influential can be discerned from Benedict Anderson's important recent study of nationalism (1983: 28–31).

17. See Carol Gilligan's forceful critique (1982) for details.

18. One must not exaggerate the difficulty that reincarnation faces in the West. The rebirth of Elvis Presley is a staple item in the popular tabloids usually found in supermarket checkout counters, becoming the contemporary counterpart to the belief in the second coming of Christ. Conversations with the dead through séances conducted by a medium also frequently find expression in popular culture. Born-again Christians and Shirley MacLaine share a belief in rebirth, however much their specific conceptions of it may differ. Brackette Williams has pointed out to me that folk theories of genetics, in which children are called the "spit and image" of someone in a previous generation or in which children are said to have "taken after" a dead relative, also implicitly acknowledge rebirth.

19. It would be interesting to work out the implications of this statement for the analysis of commodity fetishism but that is the subject of another paper.

20. I am grateful to Jane Collier for suggesting this point to me.

21. I am indebted to James Ferguson not only for the ideas expressed here but for the specific language employed as well.

22. See here the compelling critiques of "development" made by James Ferguson (1990) and Arturo Escobar (1984; 1988).

23. I am grateful to Lata Mani for suggesting this way of phrasing the matter.

Bibliography

Ahmad, Aijaz. 1987. Jameson's Rhetoric of Otherness and the 'National Allegory.'" *Social Text* 17: 3–25.

Anderson, Benedict. 1983. *Imagined Communities: Reflections on the Origin and Spread of Nationalism*. London: Verso.

Baudrillard, Jean. 1975. *The Mirror of Production*. Trans. Mark Poster. St. Louis: Telos Press.

Benjamin, Walter. [Various dates] 1969. *Illuminations: Essays and Reflections*. Trans. Harry Zohn. ed. Hannah Arendt. New York: Schocken Books.

Bernstein, Richard J. 1985. *Beyond Objectivism and Relativism: Science, Hermeneutics, and Praxis*. Philadelphia: University of Pennsylvania Press.

Bloch, Maurice. 1977. The Past and the Present in the Present. *Man* 12 (2): 278–92.

Chengappa, Raj. 1988. "Parapsychology: Clues to the Unknown." *India Today*, international edition, 31 December, 98–103.

Escobar, Arturo. 1984. "Discourse and Power in Development: Michel Foucault and the Relevance of His Work to the Third World." *Alternatives* 10: 377–400.

———. 1988. "Power and Visibility: Development and the Invention and Management of the Third World." *Cultural Anthropology* 3 (4): 428–43.

Evans-Pritchard, E. E. 1940. *The Nuer*. New York: Oxford University Press.

Fabian, Johannes. 1983. *Time and the Other: How Anthropology Makes Its Object*. New York: Columbia University Press.

Ferguson, James. 1990. *The Anti-Politics Machine: "Development," Depoliticization, and Bureaucratic Power in Lesotho*. Cambridge: Cambridge University Press.

Gilligan, Carol. 1982. *In a Different Voice: Psychological Theory and Women's Development*. Cambridge: Harvard University Press.

Habermas, Jürgen. 1970. *Toward a Rational Society: Student Protest, Science, and Politics*. Trans. Jeremy J. Shapiro. Boston: Beacon Press.

Hacking, Ian. 1986. "Making Up People." In *Reconstructing Individualism: Autonomy, Individuality, and the Self in Western Thought*, ed. Thomas C. Heller, Morton Sosna, and David E. Wellberry. Stanford, Calif.: Stanford University Press. 222–36.

Hannerz, Ulf. 1987. "The World in Creolization." *Africa* 57 (4): 546–59.

Heidegger, Martin. [1927] 1962. *Being and Time*. Trans. John Macquarrie and Edward Robinson. New York: Harper and Row.

Jameson, Frederic. 1984. "The Politics of Theory: Ideological Positions in the Postmodernism Debate." *New German Critique* 33: 53–65.

Kopytoff, Igor. 1986. "The Cultural Biography of Things: Commoditization as Process." In *The Social Life of Things*, ed. Arjun Appadurai. Cambridge: Cambridge University Press. 64–91.

Kuhn, Thomas. 1970. *The Structure of Scientific Revolutions*. 2d ed. Chicago: University of Chicago Press.

Luenberger, David G. 1979. *Introduction to Dynamic Systems: Theory, Models, and Applications*. New York: John Wiley.

Martin, Emily. 1987. *The Woman in the Body: A Cultural Analysis of Reproduction.* Boston: Beacon Press.

Marx, Karl. [1852] 1959. "*The Eighteenth Brumaire of Louis Bonaparte*" (excerpt). In *Marx and Engels: Basic Writings on Politics and Philosophy,* ed. Lewis S. Feuer. Garden City, N.Y.: Doubleday & Company, Inc. (Anchor Books). 318–48.

Mohanty, Chandra. 1988. "Under Western Eyes: Feminist Scholarship and Colonial Discourses." *Feminist Review* 30: 61–88.

Rorty, Richard. 1979. *Philosophy and the Mirror of Nature.* Princeton: Princeton University Press.

Rushdie, Salman. 1988. *The Satanic Verses.* New York: Viking Press.

Smith, Thomas C. 1959. *The Agrarian Origins of Modern Japan.* Stanford, Calif.: Stanford University Press.

———. 1986. "Peasant Time and Factory Time in Japan." *Past and Present* 111: 165–97.

Sraffa, Piero. 1960. *Production of Commodities by Means of Commodities.* Cambridge: Cambridge University Press.

Thompson, E. P. 1967. "Time, Work-Discipline and Industrial Capitalism." *Past and Present* 38: 56–97.

7

The Claiming of Space and the Body Politic within National-Security States
The Plaza de Mayo Madres and the Greenham Common Women

Jennifer Schirmer

> *Woman must put herself into the text—as into the world and into history—by her own movement.* (Cixous 1976: 875)

> *The body is . . . directly involved in a political field; power relations have an immediate hold upon it; they invest it, mark it, train it, torture it, force it to carry out tasks, to perform ceremonies, to emit signs.* (Foucault 1977: 25)

JUST AS STATES use ideology as a basis for hegemonic control of society, so, too, do states assert their power through the control of public space. In turn, just as such ideology is resisted through counterideological practices, so, too, is the state's control of public space resisted by forms of spatialized disobedience, primarily through the use of speech and the body. The mothers who have demonstrated at the Plaza de Mayo in Buenos Aires (called the "Plaza de Mayo Madres" throughout this essay) and the women protesters at Greenham Common peace encampment in England are two groups for whom space is not incidental but a central organizing theme

185

and an expression of collective identity. These women have re-presented speech and bodies as sites of resistance to their erasure in the modern state—an erasure that parallels the disappearance of victims of the national-security states (NSS) with their discourses of counterinsurgency and nuclear war. In so doing, these women are creating a double presence: for the literally and figuratively disappeared victims of their states and for themselves as women. By "interrogating the ruse of authority, interrogating its [very] constitution" (Butler 1991: 155), the Plaza de Mayo Madres and the Greenham Common women have come to spatialize their strategies of resistance and articulate a hope for a new social and political order. These activists challenge us to recast our visions of political space and women's agency in the form of a spatialized discourse of empowerment.

A Spatial Delineation of State Power.　Although state power is delineated by laws, codes, and institutions, it is also articulated spatially by way of its stately buildings; its resplendent plazas; its orderly, gridlike streets; and, most saliently, the strict uniformity of its military garrisons and bases. These ordered spaces and monumental buildings exist, to some extent, so that we may know where the state begins and where it ends.

This "bounding of order" is by no means accidental. As architectural historian Anthony Vidler points out, the planners and architects of the Enlightenment used geometry in our cities and streets as instruments of order and regulation. For the Enlightment state, and, in many places, for the state today, "the street itself [has] become Rational and equilibrious, supremely silent without people" (Vidler 1978: 42). Architecture and city planning were, as the French conservative *fonctionnaire* Jean-François Sobry maintained in 1805, indispensable arts for the maintenance of public order. They served to demonstrate to the citizen "the example of order, the happiness of order, the supremacy of order, the magnificence of order, the spectacle of order" (cited in Vidler 1978: 42). By containing and dispelling disorder, and by defining the physicality of legitimate politics as that which takes place off the streets (but not in the private sphere), the architecture of governance would become a precise map of its political perspective—a Map of Orderly Public Space—by the eighteenth century in Europe and by the nineteenth and twentieth centuries in many colonial cities.

Social Movements.　Space can be useful for emerging social movements as well as for the state. Claus Offe, for one, writes that in social movements,

"certain points in space are often charged with symbolic meaning and sin-
gled out as the foci of collective action (occupied houses for squatters in
Scandinavia and West Germany, nuclear energy plants for Swedish and West
German peace movements, and the Sanrizuka airport near Tokyo for Japanese protesters). Thus, rather than building their own organizational infrastructure, new social movements have been skillful in utilizing already
available nonpolitical public spaces and modes of communication to assert
their own political purpose[s]" (1984).

Moreover, Offe argues, the essential informality of the modes of action
of social movements makes these movements' continuity in time always
precarious. They try to overcome this difficulty by defining certain days as
occasions for public and spatially assertive collective action, such as May
Day, International Women's Day, and the Easter marches of the European
peace movement of the late 1950s and early 1960s.

Hannah Arendt has also connected "space" to "politics." She writes of
the "public spaces" of politics as a topographical figure of speech: constitutional government is likened to moving within a space "where the law
is like the hedges erected between the buildings and one orients oneself
upon known territory. Tyranny is like a desert: one moves in an unknown,
vast, open space, where the will of the tyrant may befall one like the sand-
storm overtaking the desert traveler." She later begins to distinguish such
controlling space from "associational space" where "men [*sic*] act together
in concert" and "where freedom may appear." These are "sites" of common
action and power coordinated through speech and persuasion (Arendt in
Benhabib 1992: 91–92).

A Gendered Body Politic of Space and Women's Erasure. The creation of an "orderly public space" not only has been seen as necessary for
control of the masses, but also has been directly identified with a particularly masculinist image of stable order and authority.[1] Coupled with this
image of the state of masculinist proportions is the assumption that an un-
restrained "feminine" presence in the public order represents disorder and
corruption, which threatens the very foundation of the "natural gendered
order" of the state. For Jean-Jacques Rousseau, for example, cities in eighteenth-century Europe represented an "excessively feminized"—that is,
disorderly and corrupt—political spectacle of the absolutist state. Ancient
city-states, for him, were "properly ordered publics of masculine speech,"
divided into a set of intransigent, immutable "universalities" of public/

private, male/female, nature/culture (Landes 1988: 71). For him (and Montesquieu), modern public women in France in the 1790s symbolized their "unnatural," willful public independence.[2] In fact, after the repression of disturbances and uprisings led by poor women in 1795 to demand bread and lower food prices from the Constitutional Convention, the convention decreed that women were disturbers of the peace and must remain in their homes; gatherings of more than five women would be dispersed by force (Graham 1976: 251). Women's public activism was equated with out-of-control mobs that needed to be restrained by both architectural and legal means, and "privatized" to the "shadowy interior of the household" in which the woman does not "act" but "merely behaves" (Arendt in Benhabib 1992: 108, 90).

Hence, while the theorists of Democratic Liberty and of modern Public Civility proclaimed freedom for thought, speech, and movement, they successfully banished women's public speech and outlawed women's political life. "Out of place" and without speech in the political arena, woman was told she is most virtuous when she knows her "proper place" and keeps silent, that is, when she is least public. Boundaries between the public and private, the political and social, the productive and reproductive, and justice and family were established, and justified by women's absence in the first and presence in the second. This exclusion transformed women into objectified, subjugated subjects, "subject[s] who compl[y] in becoming the *object* of an act of political representation ... [rather than persons] who embody the principle of a disinterested rational discussion [and thus] are so entitled to act (for themselves and for others)" (Landes 1988: 205).

At the same time but offstage from the central drama of political life, women nonetheless served and still serve as what we might call "sites of bodiliness" in public places — as objectified and abstract heroines and inspirational symbols, to be gazed upon and admired by men. As Norman Bryson has observed, "Women cannot produce an image of acting within male vision; all they can do is become the site of a male gaze that apprehends the female as passive before vision, the object of and for the male gaze" (1984: 73–74).

Women's political representation then is built upon a paradox: as "objectified subjects," they are simultaneously present and not present (a paradox that will arise again with the discussion of the "disappeared").

Yet women have occupied and still do occupy public space as protestors and as victims of state power. To the extent that women contest and renegotiate the boundaries between public and private, and between justice and family, by using women's bodyspeech as a site of resistance, women may be transforming the Orderly Public Space and thereby developing a new politics of empowerment.

Women and the Body.   While women's bodily presence may have been banished from public space, women are expected to be intimately involved in caring for the bodies of others—in childbirth, or when nursing the aged, young, ill, or wounded—in both public and private settings. Moreover, if women are denied access to a public presence, their being was and still is given particular significance as "body." Caroline Walker Bynum suggests, on the basis of new religious significance given the body between 1200 and 1500, and particularly, the "intense bodily metaphors" of female mystics who "received graphically physical visions of God," that the body itself may actually have a history (1992: 182). Medieval visions fused the genders, perceiving Christ's flesh as female, especially in its bleeding and nurturing, and allowing women more than men to imitate and fuse with Christ bodily, especially in the stigmata (1992: 204).

It is precisely this identification of women with flesh and bodiliness that lends consequence to women's public bodily actions. The conscious use of their bodies as sites of resistance may also have significant consequences for women's spatial politics. Women's protest can take the form of a bodily metaphor. They can wear photos of their disappeared relative pinned to their breast or hanging on a string around their necks—similar to soldiers' dog tags—to demonstrate the nonhumanity of war (appearing as replaceable parts, as luggage) and also to use the public grammar of war to counter it on their bodies as "intense bodily metaphors." This porousness of gender may help us understand how women's bodies, circling a plaza or as a blockade in front of a military gate, can be at once gendered (women) and politicized (men). Women often use their bodies as derisive metaphors to highlight viscerally the very lack of bodies in national security discourse.

The Body Politics of Space, Torture, and Nuclear War.   Along the "supremely silent streets without people" the human body, in occupying public space, becomes the point of exchange between power and knowledge, between subjectivity and objectivity (Foucault 1980). This constellation of the body and space is most dramatically demonstrated in the national-security state. The ability to make human bodies simultaneously present as figurative and literal targets and absent by complete disappearance, or total erasure on a mass scale, either by the actions of security forces or by nuclear bombs, is reflected in the national security discourse of Latin American militaries and the militaries of the Western Allies—the institutions trained to map and discipline the state's Orderly Public Spaces in the twentieth century.[3] The numbers of disappeared and assassinated in Latin America, believed to number close to 300,000, parallels the massive number of victims of the Hiroshima and Nagasaki bombings (330,000) and the 100,000 Iraqi victims in the Gulf War.[4]

In national security discourses about counterinsurgency or nuclear war, the ability "to destroy entire bodies of bodies" is matched by "a partial preemptive disappearance of the body" from representations of war (Gusterson 1991: 45). Atomic bomb victims, like torture victims, become objectified, disappeared as humans, and "read" as a kind of "collective text" for scientific signs of the mysteries of power of the bomb or regime. Aristotle held that under torture the body reveals "a kind of evidence, and appears to carry with it absolute credibility because a kind of constraint is applied" (quoted in Schirmer 1988b: 98). In the process of being "read," the human-body-as-subject becomes reconstituted as a "body of knowledge"—a "knowing" by the repressor through torture interrogation sessions, or a "knowing" by the nuclear/medical scientist observing the slow, painful disintegration of the body from radiation-induced cancers. Nuclear war might be seen as a form of coerced massive torture and execution: "Building missile silos is like building gas chambers. Only this time, they won't have to bring the people to the chambers; they will come to the people" (Kirk, interview with author, 1987).

Mapping the Masculinist State through National Security Discourse. The Manichaean bipartition of national security doctrine of the modern state, created to redeem Western and Christian civilization worldwide from communism, a bipartition that prevailed from the late 1940s until the end of the cold war, does not allow much ideological or physical space for difference. Otherness is tolerated only when it is conspiratorially adversarial, ossified, and recast as The Enemy. The Other/The Enemy is constructed by "interpreting them in a special way so that they may become truly offensive" (Sartre in Graziano 1992: 114)—in order to justify their erasure.

While distinct in their methods and degree of virulence to counter opposition (this difference cannot be overstated), national-security states maintain a threat mentality that is shared and interdependent. In one instance, the "invasion" of "foreign, subversive ideas" has already occurred, with the "foreign bodies eliminated" and "disappeared"; in the other, the "invasion" and annihilation of nuclear forces is imminent with the body-as-subject disappeared from the discourse. While cognizant of "threat" and "subversion," national-security states are oblivious to individual bodies, "compressing people increasingly together until they are formed into one" (Arendt 1968: 466). Bodies exist in space not as separate beings but as "cancers to be extirpated" or as "collateral damage." Yet these are not euphemisms for mass murder. Human bodies *are* eliminated with deaths collateral to the real issue at hand: winning a war.

A national-security mentality assumes not only the right to decide who is to live and who is to die but also the citizens' ignorance of where and when they may be forced to die. The space, timing, and disembodiment of death remains a state monopoly, hidden from the citizen in Argentina by laws of "Presumption of Death because of Disappearance,"[5] of Fullstop (*punto final*), of Due Obedience (*obediencia debida*)[6] — laws that admit to the inexorability of the past, terrible deeds, while reprocessing remembrance of that past — and by an Official Secrets Act in England with regard to a remote but terrifying future.[7] The paradoxical need of these states for a public secretiveness about an unthinkable yet recognizable unknown (the *desconocidos* and the mushroom cloud) allows national-security states to believe they can forgo public consensus in their Maps of Orderly Public Space and can censor past or future opposition to their "security." It is believed the "immature" citizenry are too little prepared for consensus politics and need to be restrained. None are asked by national referendum whether they want to be saved from communism, by torture and forcible disappearance, or from nuclear holocaust. Nor is survival a matter up for majority vote. Indeed, citizens of targeted cities are asked nothing at all.

National-security states, however, are also dependent upon publics that are conscientiously forgetful yet fearfully curious, unseeing yet voyeuristic. Their citizens must know there are secrets so terrible they must be kept secret, even while these states make it publicly known that secrets exist — a situation that the states hope will create precisely the climate of fear and paralysis in the citizenry they desire. It is a public, similar to women in their public occlusion, that does not "act" but "merely behaves" (Arendt in Benhabib 1992: 90). The logic of national-security states frames Hegel's words in a new light: "The well known is unknown, precisely because it is well known" (quoted in Benhabib 1992: 242). One can be aware and afraid of where the boundaries and sanctions of national-security states lie without knowing what those sanctions are: "Fear is the starting point, and given the dreadful potential of nuclear weapons, it is absolutely reasonable to be afraid" (Cook and Kirk 1983: 11).

Argentina: "Somos Derechos, Somos Humanos." The 1976 junta, under General Videla, subscribed to a cold war national security doctrine combined with a medieval religiosity.[8] The world was divided into two camps: the United States (West) and the Soviet Union (East). God's will required the military to preserve the natural order of the West. The International Conspiracy of Subversion was constructed by the junta regimes of 1976–82 as antidemocratic, anti-Christ, and, hence, anti-junta, for which "[The West] is today an attitude of the soul [of the state] and is no longer tied to geography.... God has decided that we [the juntas] should have the responsibility of designing the future" (Massera 1979: 50 and 102). Anyone even passively opposed to the juntas' agenda was viewed as anti-Argentina, a traitor who disowned La Patria (the Mother Country), and was seen as one of the "apátridas" (feminized and countryless) — a disease alien to the body politic that had to be "exterminated" (Graziano 1992: 217).

Massive numbers of civilians (up to 30,000 students, workers, professionals, and housewives) in Argentina became military targets for official, civilian-attired security forces to abduct, torture, and "disappear." A "forced disappearance" consisted of abduction by task forces (*grupos de tarea*) of usually six to ten heavily armed men in civilian dress. They would close off streets, black out and surround neighborhoods, and violently enter homes, workplaces, or restaurants to handcuff or tie victims' hands behind their backs, blindfold the eyes or cover the entire head with a hood (*capucha*) (sealing victims into their own private space of horror), and transport victims in a Ford Falcon, either on the floor or in the trunk, to one of the 340 torture and detention centers in which the great excess of torture became common practice (CONADEP 1984). Except for a small percentage of victims, the disappeared (*desaparecidos*) were tortured with a *picana electrica* (an electric rod with increasing voltage) on the breasts, anus, and sexual organs, and executed shortly after their abduction by being drugged and thrown alive, their bellies slit, out of an airplane into the sea, or shot at the edge of mass graves. Their bodies were incinerated and then covered over (Cohen Salama 1992). Some died incrementally under torture, but most were kept alive among what Partnoy calls the "walking dead" (1986). The body is so possessed by the state that the victim is continually resuscitated for pain and eventually for final destruction. "You're not going to be able to die," one victim was told at La Perla detention center, "here you're going to stay alive as long as we want you to" (Graziano 1992: 186). Stripped of identity ("You're nothing, you don't exist"),[9] the victim is denied the autonomy of her or his own death, "proving that henceforth nothing belonged to him and he belonged to no one. His death merely set a seal on the fact that he had never really existed" (Arendt in Graziano 1992: 97). Victims are erased from public memory. Like women erased from the public sphere, the disappeared are objectified, subjugated subjects with no agency of their own, made present only through their arranged absence.

The language of counterinsurgency itself is camouflaged and sanitized with euphemisms for torture and killing: "extracurricular activities," "tainted,"[10] "pacification," and "low-intensity conflict."[11] Domesticated imagery exists for killing as well: while the military dismiss the female relatives of the disappeared as "just housewives," they used the term *chupar* ("to suck"), and the words associated with it, to refer to both the methods of disappearance of the victims of the dirty war and the consequences of such actions. The Enemy was engulfed and digested by the body politic, "nourishing" it, until expelled, as though excrement, through execution and disappearance (Graziano 1992: 176–77; Perelli, this volume).

As in nuclear discourse, there is the conflation of civilian with military targets. The "immense task" the Argentine military took upon itself "expanded exponentially" so that 80 percent of the victims had no relation to terrorism (Graziano 1992: 33), much as the civilian victims of Hiroshima and Nagaski had little to do with the decisions of the Japanese military establishment, or the citizens of Baghdad had no means by which to stop Saddam Hussein. The symbolic value of innocent and arbitrarily selected civilian victims provided the Argentine regime with bodies as well as the benefit of a paralyzing uncertainty among the population (similar to the "shock value" of the atomic bombing of the Japanese). Here was a public yet silent recognition of clandestinity. In Argentina, the official discourse of denial, together with the cruel, uncertain dynamics of a culture of fear, placed family members seeking their "disappeared" relatives in a limbo of not knowing what constituted either effective or imprudent action in discovering their whereabouts.

There is, however, a difference between the finality of a death and the terror and wrenching angst from a "disappearance." This is eloquently explained by human rights lawyer Emilio Mignone, whose daughter was abducted from the family apartment in Buenos Aires in 1976: "[It creates] desolation and impotence.... A premeditated disappearance because a group of individuals of the system decides that a person must be kidnapped and will give no notice of the person's existence is something new, disastrous, and incredible. It is of no use to us, the relatives, then, that time passes" (Mellibovsky 1990: 47–48). Why, asks Graziano, make a spectacle of an abduction that will later be denied (1992: 41)? It was in order to discipline the public space of whole cities, to create involuntary spectators to staged, violent abductions, while the majority of the *desaparecidos* would remain "absent forever" (Lieutenant General Viola in Graziano 1992: 43).

"We Are Not in the Business of Killing":[12] The National Security Doctrine of the Western Allies.   Since World War II, cities have proven themselves "rewarding" military targets for plane-transported bombs in massed incendiary raids, and "in choosing cities as the targets for the first atomic bombs, the military were true to their assigned mission."[13] Truman believed to his own dying day that the bombing "was purely military action against military targets" (Bundy 1988: 80). Despite the massive killing of civilians in two major Japanese cities, the nuclear bombing was viewed as the "least abhorrent choice" in achieving the desired shock (ibid.).

As with the ideology central to counterinsurgent strategy, the world was divided into two camps: the United States (West) and the Soviet Union (East). Today the strategy of the Western Allies for the protection of "national security" involves the potential use of weapons of mass destruction. These include strategic and tactical "smart" nuclear weapons such as the "Euromissiles" (German-based Pershing II and British-based Cruise missiles) as well as the nonnuclear Scuds with guidance systems.[14] As in World War II, this strategy affixes the spaces of cities as military targets despite its civilian casualties. Such a strategy, albeit with nonnuclear weapons, was employed in the Gulf War, in which upwards of 100,000 Iraqis were "attrited."[15] While civilians become military targets in "humane bombings," the blood and destruction are wrapped in the metaphors of Orderliness, Decency, and Law in the world (such as U.S. Joint Chiefs of Staff Chairman Colin Powell's statement that sending missiles was a "delivery of an ordnance" to triumph over the violent, lawless Other [Butler 1991: 76, 78]).

Like counterinsurgency language, nuclear war discourse is camouflaged and sanitized with such euphemisms for killing as "collateral damage" and "attrited." Both discourses, moreover, are heavily gendered, even infantilized: although Argentine torturers worship the Mother, they refer to each other as "the Baby" or "the Little Apple" [*Manzanita*] (Ulla and Echave in Graziano 1992: 168). This recalls the "Fat Boy" and "Little Boy" bombs dropped on Hiroshima and Nagasaki (which mothered "daughter fission products") (Gusterson 1991: 49).

The Ambiguities of Disappearance and Spectatorship.   Under circumstances of "disappearance," national-security states appropriate their publics' "sight," making them, like women in the public sphere, spectators. Guiding them as blind "witnesses" in the presence of bodily absence, forcing them to "see" the unseen and come to the "appropriate" conclusion, this "spectacle" is designated as the sign of the omnipresent power of the state. Although there is a military recognition of bodily presence (the "chupados" of Argentine task forces or the "kills" of Allied pilots), there is also an ambiguous absence within the official denials ("There are no disappeared in Argentina," "We are not in the business of killing"). With bodies killed-and-erased either on the screen of war or on the streets of war, subjugation becomes unverifiable. Certainty is appropriated by the state only to be complemented by doubt:

> In a closed system without exits, public knowledge terrorizes as
> much as public ignorance. The boundaries between knowing and
> supposing, between knowing and denying, fade. The same
> totalizing repression that prohibited sight through the use of head
> coverings in the detention centers employed the reverse of that
> tactic for the public at large: sight of the abstract people was
> permitted, was mandatory, but the act of seeing and knowledge of
> what had been seen were used to terrorize and repress the seers.
> (Graziano 1992: 82)

Both the Plaza de Mayo Madres and the Greenham Common women[16] have somehow escaped being part of this muted spectatorship of Argen-

tine and English societies, part of these assumed audiences to past and future atrocities. The suspended animation — present but not absent — has
created a dissent, and a new subjective reality, among the Madres and the
Greenham Common women.

Women's Ironic Interrogations of the State

Woman's Body as Political Geography and Inscription.   In the mapping of the public sphere, women's bodies have served as the "critical
medium for the inscription and naturalization of ... power" in all its naturalized "truths" (Alonso 1992). Explored, mapped, conquered, and raped,
the female body and its metaphorical extension, the home, become the
symbols of honor, loyalty, and purity, to be guarded by men. Recent work
on the "body politic" emphasizes how "the State" inscribes its power on
woman's body as "the social skin" of political life (Turner in Alonso 1992:
418). The ways in which the Madres and Greenham Common women
utilize their "social skin" as sites of their resistance to the national-security
state and their adamant refusal to be "disappearing" bodies attest to our
need to reformulate our visions of the political usages of "the body in
protest" in public space, in particular, and in politics, in general.

The cultural and political conditions in Argentina and England are
decidedly different, but in both instances actions in the name of national
security created spontaneous, imaginative, and empowering movements by
women.[17] In Argentina, the counterterrorist doctrine practiced by the Argentine juntas between 1976 and 1982 to secure the nation against "foreign enemies" dislocated, dismembered, and disappeared the very families
it was claiming to protect. In England, a secret 1979 NATO decision was
taken to site U.S. Cruise missiles and U.S. military personnel on English
soil to maintain inter/national security against the Soviet Union. This decision necessitated both a site that remained off limits and activities that
were kept secret from the very citizens they were meant to protect. As was
stated earlier but bears repeating, the Argentine situation was far more
drastic in its immediate consequences for the population. The logic, however, of national security and its potential long-term consequences is similar.

Different as the contexts are in which they act and the historical conditions out of which they emanate, the Madres and the Greenham Common women hold concerns in common for making public the preserva-

tion of life, justice, and the right to know the truth. They openly and bodily challenge the state's move "to presume the right to kill others in our names" (Cook and Kirk 1983: 109). By claiming public space in order to demand the right to know the official truth of what has become of their relatives in counterinsurgency campaigns, or what may become of them in a nuclear war, these women defy the public secrecy of the state:

> I want to know where my son is, if he is alive or dead. I want them to finally tell me the truth about what happened, and if they killed him, I want to know when, where, why, and who did it. Only the day they have responded to all those questions will I stop fighting. (Plaza de Mayo Madre in Bousquet 1983: 150)

Finding themselves in circumstances in which "the obscene becomes the commonplace and the abnormal the normal" (Debray 1977: 360), these women confirm not the symbolic but the very corporeality of the "body politic." These women have made the public squares and streets their own, if only temporarily. As a result, not only is the governance of space and memory "up for contention" (Boyarin, this volume), but resistance to it may be more inclined to articulate itself as spatialized disobedience.

Women's spatialized disobedience at the Plaza de Mayo in Argentina and at Greenham Common in England represents a politics that initially had no clearly expressed strategy. The event instigated the idea, and the idea went beyond itself to "locate" and attach itself to a politically charged space to create a movement: the forced disappearance of their relatives in Argentina and the siting of nuclear weapons at Greenham Common. In both movements, as we shall see, space is not incidental but a central organizing theme and an expression of collective identity.

The Plaza de Mayo Madres.　The Plaza de Mayo Madres began to circle the main square in Buenos Aires in 1977—a square that symbolizes the Inquisition as well as the more contemporary convergence of governmental and populist politics in Argentina. Since 1977, they have circled the plaza every Thursday afternoon at 3:30, arm in arm, their heads covered with white handkerchiefs, demanding the "return alive of the [30,000] disappeared and punishment for the guilty" (*¡aparición con vida y castigo a los culpables!*). The Madres, representing the absence of their relatives by their presence, are held hostage by the national-security state to their disappeared relatives.

While cemeteries are bounded, "timed spaces of grief," the absence of the burial of a body creates painful contradictions: a loss with no end, a bodiless grave, an enclosed space waiting to be filled with a grief that has no closure. Denied an identity or even a name, the *desaparecidos* cannot "fill in" the graves, "making their absence present in Mother/Earth by filling in the eerie hole into which they fell" (Graziano 1992: 188).[18]

It is precisely this suspended animation—not alive but not pronounced dead—that has created a new subjective reality, a kind of mystique among some of the Madres. Many sense the "live presence" of their disappeared loved one standing and breathing next to them as they prepare food in the kitchen, reading over their shoulder in the living room, or circling with them, arm in arm, at the Plaza de Mayo (interviews with author, Buenos Aires, 1992):

> Graciela's presence is installed in my conscience. In which physical part of my body? I couldn't say precisely. But I discuss, reason, and sustain a continual dialogue with her which for others would be imaginary, but for me, it is not.... Her presence is implicit at all the battles we [madres] have had and will have; [she is there] in all the anger and hopelessness when we are confronted with the treachery and bungling. (Mellibovsky 1990: 23–24)

The singular presence of Madre-and-*desaparecido* is a rearrangement of the subject who refuses to die, a subject who has been reembodied and now cannot be killed and, as such, doubly challenges the juntas' "arranged absence" of the disappeared.[19]

The Greenham Common Women.   In August 1981, forty women, children, and men marched 120 miles from Cardiff, Wales, to the U.S. Air Force base at Greenham Common, 60 miles west of London, where 96 Cruise missiles were to be located. They called themselves the Women for Life on Earth peace march. Upon their arrival, they were not allowed to deliver a letter to the base commander, which read:

> We will not be the victims in a war which is not of our making. We wish neither to be the initiators nor the targets of a nuclear holocaust.... We are implacably opposed to the siting of U.S. Cruise missiles in this country. We represent thousands of ordinary people who are opposed to these weapons and we will use all our resources to prevent the siting of these missiles here. (Young 1990: 16)

Some of the protesters chained themselves to the fence (in conscious imitation of the suffragettes), and they set up a camp, which became women-only in February 1982 "to include women in political actions [but] not necessarily to exclude men." Like what the Madres did, this was a tactical decision made in the belief that the police would be led to be less violent — an assumption which they would discover to be unfounded (Kirk, author interview, 1987; Young 1990: 17 and 30; compare Schirmer 1988a). Supported by peace, church, Labor party, and feminist groups, the Women's Peace Encampment grew with "sites" at each of the gates along the 90-mile perimeter with its 10-foot-high barbed-wire fence. Events included die-ins, vigils, marches, and an embrace-the-base action that have involved thousands of women for over ten years.

The Body as Site of Resistance: Nonviolence and Women's Bodies-in-Protest. The Madres use symbols of the Catholic church and of motherhood to present themselves as apolitical and nonviolent; however, nonviolent direct action also entails a literal body politic. For the Madres, their bodily presence firmly and consistently counters the disappearance of the body from public space. As a result, their refusal to "disappear" from the public eye was itself seen as a threat to the juntas' attempts to empty the streets.

In the case of the women at Greenham Common, the body politic in public space was also critical.

> It is important to differentiate between the surface appearance — women lying down in the road or being dragged by the police — and the underlying reason for it. Some people take issue with what they see to be passive, "feminine" behavior, self-denigrating and subservient, which is not at all what the women involved in the actions feel. Though you appear to be surrendering your body, you are in complete control. You make a conscious decision to take part; you take the initiative and create the situation.... What many women are stressing is that acting in a nonviolent way involves a state of mind that challenges assumptions about power.... It is the underlying attitude of mind that is important.... Nonviolence is not just the absence of violence or simply a tactic, but a total approach to living.... Nonviolence involves the idea of power stemming from our only real resources — our feelings, ideas, and ultimately our bodies. (Cook and Kirk 1983: 70, 71, 76, 77; see also Kirk 1989)

Greenham women lying in trenches, weaving woolen webs across themselves, obstructing construction workers attempting to lay sewer pipes outside the main gate, or lying in front of bulldozers are just a few examples of this use of the body-in-protest.[20]

Shifting Boundaries of the State: The Illegality of Nonmovement. States can, by their own doing, create movements of dissent. In the case of the Plaza de Mayo Madres it was the Argentine repressive state that caused their "movement." For them to stand around would have been tantamount to holding a meeting, which at the time was illegal. Similarly, at Greenham Common,

> There are laws to cover virtually any situation: for example, simply standing still on the pavement can be deemed an offence. The authorities have tried to deal with us women at Greenham by attempting to evict us ... rely[ing] on very trivial legal technicalities. What is really on trial, however, is our freedom of speech and freedom to express political opinion ... ironically, exactly what the government claims to be defending with nuclear weapons. (Cook and Kirk 1983: 109)

Evictions of Greenham Common protesters best reflect the shifting boundaries of the state in England. Efforts by the district council of Newbury (where Greenham Common is located) concentrated on simple squatting charges, with the first attempt at eviction in May 1982. However, a strip of land alongside the main road near the air base is owned not by the council but the Ministry of Transport. While the council removed some campers and destroyed a large shelter, the women neatly circumvented the eviction order by packing up their belongings in shopping carts (a domestication of politics) and moving camp a few yards to the Ministry of Transport land. Then the council enforced its bylaws more strictly: no "structures" of any kind were allowed on the council land (the bailiffs used considerable force in evicting the women and their belongings), forcing women to live under plastic lean-tos (hidden in the woods) in the dead of winter (Young 1990: 25). The council then impolitically revoked the deed allowing public access to the common land, making the land out of bounds to everyone and thereby angering townspeople. Thus, while some women were jailed, the differential ownership of land and the disorganization of bureaucratic authority, not to speak of the limbo of legality, backfired, allowing, in the end, for more political space and more movement by the women. In both instances, the state unwittingly had become complicit in its own subversion.

Streets and Roadways as Political Arena.   Streets and roadways provide the spatial arena within which both groups move, slowly carving out an identity and a sense of political purpose virtually by their active use of public space. The women took of the streets and not just to the streets. As one Plaza de Mayo Madre stated, "We decided to take to the streets, and it was the streets that taught us. That was what gave us our political strength" (Simpson and Bennett 1985: 169).

Originally, the Interior Ministry had provided an office for the Madres in order to "process" (ignore) the hundreds of cases of disappearances. This office became the Madres' original meeting place. As they began their weekly vigils at the main square in the capital, state officials named them in relation to that space — the "mad women of the plaza" — a name that the women partially adopted.[21] Their specific public meeting place and fixed time provide them coherence and continuity, and to this day, they meet every Thursday at 3:30 in the central square. The confrontation of the Madres (who had a section in their newspaper, "Las Madres en la Calle" ["Mothers in the Street"]) with the police on 20 December 1977 is an example of the constantly shifting boundaries of the state and the way in which actions in public space come to define the nature of public politics:

> They met at the Plaza de San Martín to place flowers at the feet of
> the statue of the *Liberador,* hero of Argentinian and Latin American
> independence. They wanted to pay homage to him, defender of
> liberty and justice — two causes they claim as their own.... As the
> women approached the statue, flowers in hand, assault troops,
> bayonets at the ready, would not let them pass. The Madres did not
> insist. "Let's go to the Plaza de Mayo and place flowers before the
> presidential palace," the word passed from mouth to mouth. But the
> police followed. First they prohibited their access to the Calle
> Florida, the chic shopping street.... An hour passed in which the
> women kept being blocked by patrol cars and policemen. To make
> it more difficult for the police, the Madres went up one-way streets
> the wrong way, with police cars following, sirens blaring, but the

Madres were unable to pass through shoppers on the narrow streets. The women divided into two groups and finally succeeded in gaining the Calle Florida. Their arrival caused a sensation. Christmas shoppers and office workers getting off work stopped to watch the procession; shops were covered with decorations and music poured out of them. The procession of two hundred persons passed slowly, two by two. The two women at the head, both over fifty years old, carried two small signs: "I am looking for my son, Javier, disappeared on the first of...." "I have lost my two sons, kidnapped by *desconocidos*." Some shoppers hastened their step and looked aside. Some well-to-do ladies protested in a medium voice what a scandal it was to allow such demonstrations. Others drew closer and asked for explanations. In general, there was a sensation of discomfort at a time when one was preparing to celebrate Christmas.... At the end of the street, the route to the Plaza was cut off by the police. They again turned toward the San Martín monument, but police cut them off. The leaders advised the group, "This is enough. We could not leave our flowers at either place but we have been seen on the Calle Florida.... We will not risk an open confrontation with the police." They dispersed. (Bousquet 1982: 140)

The Madres were stunned at first by their ability to confront the police and then by the brutalities they were dealt. But although "keeping women in their place" meant keeping them off the streets and under control,[22] the junta was unable to control the Madres' public inversion of the state's claims to legitimacy: they refused to "disappear" and remain silenced.

At Greenham, roadways were first used by the handful of women who organized the Women for Life on Earth peace march from Cardiff to Greenham Common in August 1981 to protest NATO's decision to site Cruise missiles at Greenham. When the women, children, and a few men arrived from their march from Wales and complained of not being able to present a letter to the base commander at Greenham to protest the arrival of the missiles, a guard said to them, "Well, then, you can stay here [at the gate] as long as you like, but you won't get in to see the base commander." (In response to the U.S. 501st Tactical Missile Wing's billboard at Greenham, reading "Welcome: Comdr. Col. Thompson. Poised to Deter, Quick to React," the Women's Peace Camp drew up a sign that read "No Commanders. Poised with the Truth, Quick to Stop Pretending.") When women in Wales heard that the women had set up a peace camp outside the main gate, "we decided to live on the streets," passing out leaflets and talk-ing with everyone (Cook and Kirk 1983: 38).

Like the Madres, the Greenham Common women found city streets useful in making their politics public. On 7 June 1982, at the time of Pres-ident Reagan's visit to London, five streets around London's Stock Ex-change were used for a "die-in" that effectively blocked all traffic going through the financial district:

> The road each group of [seventy] women [altogether] would lie across had been decided beforehand, and when we arrived at the Stock Exchange, women quickly lay down to "die." In each group there were women handing out leaflets and trying to talk to passing office workers, explaining why the action was taking place: that the women were lying down to symbolize the one million who would be killed instantly in a nuclear attack on London.... Motorists shouted and swore at the women; one man snatched a woman's bundle of leaflets, tore them up and proceeded to stamp on them. The police, arriving on the scene late because of the traffic jams, found the whole situation rather confusing.... In the end, nine women were arrested, seemingly at random. (Cook and Kirk 1983: 40–42)

Both groups took to and of the streets to site their resistance bodily within the state's political architecture: either to pay homage to a statue rep-resenting freedom and justice, or to condemn a missile base and the Stock Exchange for weapons procurement.

Domesticating Government Space

Ironic Domesticity as the Iconography of Protest.   The Madres and the Greenham Common women transform public space by bringing objects of daily life to it. The Plaza de Mayo is flanked by monumental buildings that are incongruous with the private lives of domesticity: the presidential palace (the Casa Rosada), which was used by the juntas; the cathedral; and the Ministry of Social Welfare. This site of public masculinist power is de-mystified by older women, humbly circling the plaza wearing on their heads diapers first, and later white headscarves, embroidered with the names of their disappeared son or daughter or husband, together with worn photographs of their loved ones pinned to their breasts or placed on large placards at marches and demonstrations. These worn, fragile pictures, often carried next to the heart, reassert a timeless visibility:

> What has mobilized me is that [the junta] has eliminated a whole generation that should have followed us [Madres]; the [junta's] actions isolate me from the future, totally separate me from the continuity of life, and I want to recuperate this through Memory. (Mellibovsky 1990: 16)

The Madres have used the conservative image of women without husbands to care for them, together with photographs of children, to appeal to a "natural order" that the state does not respect. If this regime is not interested in international legitimacy, the diapers and pictures seem to plead, then it could at least honor the basis of society it claims to protect: mothers of families (*madres de familia*). But photographs also serve to reassert the presence of the disappeared in the mind of the public and to negate the "chronicle of announced death." Photographs exhibited publicly break the state's monopoly over memory and, together with the domestication of political space, serve, in turn, to substantiate these women's political shape and purpose.

Similarly, the Greenham Common women pinned photographs of young Hiroshima victims to their bodies: in February 1983, while then U.S. Vice-President Bush was dining with Prime Minister Margaret Thatcher, thirty women (representing the thirty thousand who had embraced the base on 12 December 1982) decorated themselves with symbols of their wish to live in a world free of nuclear weapons (thus bringing the Greenham fence to London) and lay down in Downing Street. Eleven women were arrested.

> I was covered with photographs of people and places I loved, a color chart, statements of Hiroshima victims and nightmares that women had of nuclear war. (Cook and Kirk 1983: 48)

Part of this "body image" is maternalized as a form of protection but serves also as a statement of irony. Two women from Yorkshire sent Mother's Day cards to Margaret Thatcher to remind her of her responsibility for their children's future, and in the summer of 1982, a Babies against the Bomb march was led by women in black mourning dresses pushing strollers, empty but for "tombstones" bearing the name of a child killed in Hiroshima or Nagasaki (Cook and Kirk 1983: 60).

"Transcending the Fence" at Greenham Common. At Greenham, the fence becomes the explicit formal boundary between the state and the public's welfare — where the state begins and ends. The fence acts as the interface between building and nature. For the embrace-the-base action of 12 December 1982, the fence was "domesticated," transformed by Greenham women from its destructive purpose into a creative work. The women and their thirty thousand supporters brought objects that expressed feelings about war: ribbons, children's toys, fruit, watches (to show time running out), recipes, clothing, a cigarette pack (which read "I will die in my own way, thanks"), a bottle of nailbiting lotion (with a sign stating "Cruise makes me nervous"); photos of relatives and diapers were attached (Young 1990: 17). The phrase "decorating the fence" was intentionally used to conjure up the traditional image of homemakers "making a space liveable, such as a living room" in contrast to the death space of the military installation. A second encirclement occurred a year later (after the arrival of the Cruise on 14 November 1983) at which fifty thousand women, with mirrors (in ironic allusion to women's supposed concern with vanity), reflected the base onto itself, "to give the military a new perspective" (Kirk, interview with author, 1987).

This domestic image was again captured in a demonstration outside the Bank of England in which women in waitress uniforms handed out "peace pies" to bankers and workers (Cook and Kirk 1983: 58, 64), pointing out the "household" names of companies (Singer, Goodyear) that supply parts for weapons systems. The Greenham fence was also domesticated (made nonviolent) when an old carpet was thrown over the barbed wire as a form of protection during a breaching of the fence on New Year's Day 1983. Sixty women went over the fence to dance atop the silos and draw attention to the missile silos that were well under construction.

> Ahead of us we saw the aluminum ladders. I remember seeing three on each side, leaning against the fence. It seemed ridiculously easy — there were streams of women going over the fence, over the carpet, making [the fence] so ineffectual. There was [even] a queue to go over.... Every now and again we'd link arms in a big circle and dance around the top of the silo ... and we planted a "Peace 83" banner on the sloping side. We arranged the concrete rubble and wooden planks into women's peace signs.... We were on top of the silos for about an hour and twenty minutes. The police

couldn't believe how many of us were there, celebrating the New Year! (Cook and Kirk 1983: 56)

Echoing the Madres' conscious concern with being seen by the police as nonviolent demonstrators, the Greenham Common activists agreed, in discussing "proper attire" for the direct action on New Year's Day 1983 that wearing dark clothing at night might allow them to be confused with "dark-masked IRA terrorists" (the image they imagined policemen to have of them); they might be taken for violent men and would be clandestine rather than visible. "So, the women wore brightly colored clothing to be clearly visible and to be incontrovertibly women"; they also dressed in Easter bunny outfits to dance atop the silos and thereby reveal "the ridiculousness of warmaking strategies" (Kirk, interview with author, 1987). The women's carnivalesque, nonviolent encampment of nonhierarchal "organized chaos" against the barbed wire, grey concrete, and hierarchy of uniformed soldiers was used by the women to place in stark contrast the two different value systems that were in confrontation across the perimeter fence (Young 1990: 36).

As during wartime, picnic baskets have served a useful purpose at Greenham. The first major cutting of the fence (through long discussions, the women came to change their views of the cutting from a violent to a nonviolent act of reclamation) took place on Halloween 1983. It was a Sunday, and about a thousand women arrived at the base with picnic baskets in which they carried food and wire clippers. The women dispersed all around the base and precisely at 4:00 began cutting the fence. The British and American military inside the base were on alert, expecting an "invasion" of the base by the women. However, the women's focus was on the fence itself, to cut it up into bits and make it less monolithic, not to enter the base. The soldiers thus couldn't arrest the women because they were not entering base property (in the United States this destruction of military property would be grounds for arrest), although the local police authorities on the outside arrested some 150 women. "This was the first time you could see the military without wire mesh, and it made them look more like people and more vulnerable," as one Greenham Common protester averred (Interview by the author, Greenham Common, 1987). Even some of the military couldn't reach the fence themselves from the inside because of the thick barbed wire (in some places it was ten layers deep),

so the women were able to get whole sections of the fence down
and sit on it. But because they were convinced we would enter,
they couldn't leave and thus had an all-night vigil. And they also
couldn't leave the fence because they also did not know if we
would not enter, either. (Kirk, interview with author, 1987)

The women thus momentarily demystified the military's seemingly monolithic control by "transcending the fence." In the end, over four of the nine
miles of fence was taken down by the women (Young 1990: 18).

The roadway on which camouflaged missile convoys exercised maneu-
vers, too, was domesticated. For example, in March 1987 a Cruise missile
truck convoy, returning from driving missiles around on the Salisbury Plain
to "distract the enemy," found the turning to the main gate at Greenham
blocked by a dilapidated sofa upon which three women sat chatting. When
the convoy arrived, one of the woman said in a very matter-of-fact tone
through a megaphone (parodying what the police would say to the women),
"As you will notice, this road is now occupied by women. The road is
now closed. The road is now closed. Please turn back and go away" (Kirk,
interview with author, 1987). The women tried to stop the camouflaged
convoy in order to spray-paint peace signs on its windows and sides.

This domestication of state institutions and transcendence of the fence
momentarily disarms the police and dislodges the binary assumptions of
nature/culture, public/private, and family/state and reverses the optic of
male authority/female passivity and of order/disorder:

The fence around Greenham Common represents the divisions of
public vs. private, culture vs. nature, order vs. disorder, leaders vs.
citizens, experts vs. laypersons.... The Greenham women have just
not shown any respect for the fence: they have gone over it, broken
through it and torn it down ... to challenge the distinction
between militaristic necessity and their own political judgment....
They have [thus] provided us with the beautiful metaphor of
"transcending the fence." (Scales 1989: 63)

Domestic imagery makes dissent appear part of quotidian practice.
Those who are not expert at dissent can still engage in it. It can, however,
also be appropriated by the state. For example, domestic metaphors used
by Argentine security forces made terror ordinary and commonplace: the
victim is *chupado,* or sucked out, disappeared without a trace, much as a
homemaker "tidies" and "cleans" a dirty house with a vacuum cleaner.[23]

At Greenham one police constable brought to a Greenham Common demonstration his own black and white banner, which read, "You are blocking the road. Please move on." This was in response to being completely ineffectual when singing and yelling kept his voice, enhanced by a megaphone, from being heard. As Gwyn Kirk pondered, "One has the domestic image of a police seamstress in the basement of police headquarters working furiously on a banner" (interview with author, 1987).

Motherhood as Protection and as Militancy.   When policemen began attacking Plaza de Mayo Madres in the square, the Madres asked, "Aren't you embarrassed to attack undefended mothers?... Don't you have children? Wouldn't you do what we are doing if you had a disappeared child?" (Bousquet 1982: 50).

As a protective strategy, the Madres made a conscious decision not to allow men to participate actively and publicly in their weekly vigil. A Madre explained:

> We decided when we were organizing, that young people and men
> should not be allowed to protest for reasons of security. To be
> young and male in Argentina carries a presumption of guilt; they
> are, a priori, suspected of holding subversive ideas, of belonging to
> a revolutionary movement. We decided we would be the standard
> bearers, we women of mature age, mothers of families, with all that
> represents in the Argentine tradition. (Bousquet 1982: 80)

These public actions moved women quickly away from their individual, immediate search for relatives toward a longer-term, broad-based protest on behalf of everyone who had disappeared in the country. One leader of the Plaza de Mayo Madres spoke at the weekly gathering in the plaza on New Year's Day 1987:

> Mothers, sisters, companions — companions in militancy because
> every one of us is a militant, a militant of life, but of serious life,
> giving and giving oneself ... we must permanently recover the
> dream of our children, not because we are their mothers but
> because we have become the mothers of the thirty thousand and
> the thirty thousand are all equal. (Madre deBonafini at the Plaza de
> Mayo, 1 January 1987; my transcription and translation)

Yet motherhood can also be used sarcastically for political effect. With the redemocratization of Argentina, the Madres have faced institutional closure. For example, in April 1985, they marched to the presidential palace, complaining of not having been able to meet with President Alfonsín for eight months since their first meeting with him soon after he took office. Subsecretary for Human Rights Rabossi claimed they were "seeking publicity," stating, "If I had been disappeared during *el proceso,* I would have chosen [Madre] deBonafini as a mother because she fought cleanly, without thinking of public office or reward." The Madres responded, "Where was Sr. Rabossi while the Madres were circling in the plaza, being persecuted, jailed, and kidnapped? Many of those who did not combat the genocide are today [government] functionaries.... Certainly, none of the Madres would choose Sr. Rabossi as a son" (Madres de Plaza de Mayo 1985).

At Greenham, too, women who had—or whose children had—nightmares of nuclear war were drawn out of their privatized lives, determined to gain a public voice and claim political space. They consciously established a women-only peace camp "not to exclude men, but to include women," and to give women the chance they felt they had not had in other peace groups to voice their dissent publicly and make decisions nonhierarchically. A specifically feminist stance on peace is emerging that accommodates maternal sentiment without succumbing to sentimentalism or "allowing a feminist agenda to be reduced to a concern for children" (Leonardo in Strange 1990: 219). Such a stance both analyzes the political roots of war and makes the connections between militarism and violence against women. While there has been concern among feminists about the sentimentalizing, and thus the depoliticizing, of militant motherhood as well as of feminism itself, it is striking to note the inability of these national-security states to rally either the Madres or the Greenham Common activists during the Malvinas/Falklands War on either side of the Atlantic. These mothers stood firm, despite enormous patriotic fervor and disfavor:

> Politically and socially, the [Madres] would stand alone on the side
> of the "traitors." The "war against subversion" would be sanctified
> as the necessary prelude to the war for the Malvinas. (Dabat and
> Lorenzano 1984: 76)

It was during this period of patriotic fervor that the Madres circled the plaza with a sign, "The Malvinas are Argentine and the disappeared are, too," while a group tried to interrupt their circling, yelling "Long live the country!" and handing out leaflets that read, "The friend of an enemy of the *patria* is our enemy." "This time the Plaza was everyone's," exclaimed the press (Graziano 1992: 47). Similarly, Greenham women marched against the use of F-111s from the Greenham air base to bomb Libya: they burned an American flag outside the base and presented a letter of protest to the base commander (Kirk, interview with author, 1987).

At such times, "the family" takes on a more public and massive presence to demand consensus and justice — and begins to lose its assumed private, apolitical (sentimentalized and individualized) character. It also raises the question as to whether space can be gendered.

Circles versus Grids: The Gendering of Space?   One interesting aspect of the actions by the Madres and the Greenham Common women is the recurrence of encirclement to counter the grid patterns of the government plaza and the military base. Interestingly, rather than marching in a straight line through the plaza up to the steps of the Casa Rosada, as many political party and trade union demonstrations in Buenos Aires have done, the Madres, in twos, arm-in-arm, circle the monument. At Greenham, thirty thousand women from all over Britain and Europe "embraced" the base on 12 December 1982. This, too, was in contrast to the linkup the Committee on Nuclear Disarmament had organized: a straight line along a road linking two military bases, with no view into the base and no direct confrontation with the military personnel. As one Greenham woman who participated in both protests recalled,

> People went away from the CND march feeling there to be no
> purpose, no center to the demo, while the encirclement was viewed
> as a great success politically both for us women and for those not
> involved with Greenham. We had a sense of purpose to it.
> (Interview with author at Greenham, 1987)

Similarly, at the Newbury Magistrates' Court proceedings in spring 1983, while the forty-four women who had danced on the missile silos were being tried, there was a massive demonstration outside the courthouse in the police station parking lot with hundreds of women "dancing, singing, crying, and pressing messages of support up against the windows of the courtroom. We know that it is difficult to perform illegal acts and so people need support." Once the women were sentenced and the police formed a large circle around those "accused," the other women in the courtroom stood on chairs behind the police and extended their hands over the heads of the policemen in order to keep physical contact and "to transcend the physical isolation" (Kirk, interview with author, 1987).

Whether these similar actions of encirclement are coincidental is difficult to say; nonetheless, they clearly indicate these groups' alternative spatial sense to patterns of traditional political public action, such as, for example, barricades. Their actions help invert the state's monopoly over public space.

The Barricades of Insurrection versus the Monuments of Protest. Traditionally, the physical appropriation of the street has been in the form of ambush and combat. For example, it has taken the form of an architecture of barricades — piles of casks and debris and cobblestones blocking public access (as in Paris in the 1830s). They were part of the transformation of a riot into an insurrection: "The barricade completed, the long wait for the counterattack began" (Vidler 1978: 82, 86).

The more contemporary protests discussed here, defined by these women as nonviolent direct action, are just as confrontational, defiant of authority, and unaccepting of boundaries or rules of the traditional notions of politics. Yet while the barricade acted as the pivotal instrument of political correctness and confrontation in the past, the military base fence and the government plaza — the structures of governance and not of insurrection — are now being used as confrontational platforms from which "women of the revolt and the troops of authority" are for a brief instant forced to recognize each other, even to speak and argue. Government space itself is inverted into spaces of dissent by the women. And rather than gunfire, "a civil war in a civic space," as Victor Hugo described Paris in the 1830s, there is the confrontation of voices speaking at these monuments of the state through megaphones (at both the Plaza de Mayo and Greenham Common), of the circling in twos (at the plaza), and of bodies blocking roadways (at Greenham). The corporeal nature of this confrontational nonviolent politics by women, sited on the existing architecture of governance, differs significantly from the armed, spontaneously crafted architecture of primarily male politics. Such a utilization of government architecture has the potential for reversing the optic of governance.

The Optic of Governance Reversed.   Contrary to the optic of government-as-social-order-and-civilization versus the all-pervasive violence of the mob-in-the-street, in these situations the image is reversed: the "public" takes and occupies state buildings, supreme courts, cathedrals, plazas, streets, missile silos, military gates, and missile-loaded vans in maintenance of the rule of law and justice, whereas the government represents the institutionalization of death. The "dumb eloquence of government"—the statutes, the fountains, the public squares, the missile silos, the layers of barbed wire fencing—are charged with collectivity and "transformed into a temporary stage on which [the actors] dramatize the power they still lack" (Berger 1968: 754–55).

The optic of governance was reversed in the courts also, with some of the Greenham Common women, on trial for "breaching the peace," addressing the Newbury magistrates with such statements as,

> What are you doing to keep the peace? The power you are using is supporting nuclear weapons. It supports binding women's voices, binding our minds and bodies in prison so our voices cannot be heard. So our warning of Death is being repressed. But we cannot be silenced.... I am asking you to keep the peace. *We* are not on trial. *You* are. (Cook and Kirk 1983: 124; my emphasis)[24]

As one Greenham Common protester who had been arrested stated without irony, "To take the oath is to tell the truth, and so when we took the stand we spoke of the evils of nuclear weapons" (interview with author, Greenham Common, 1987).

The irony is that the women who claim to be "saving and keeping the peace" may be charged with "breaching the peace" even though they are not being civilly disobedient, that is, stating by their actions that there should be no laws to keep the public order. Because courts are reluctant to rule on matters of "national security," the women are charged with being in violation of "technically unrelated laws" (Scales 1989: 41). Thus, the line between what is "lawful and orderly" and what is "lawless and disorderly," between what is "peaceful" and who is "breaching" it, is fluid, malleable, and dependent upon magistrates' interpretation.[25] The women, in refusing to conform either to the role of the submissive defendant or to the state's malleable definitions of peace, add to the subversion of court procedures and weaken the state's demands for an orderly public/space.

Similarly, at the trial of the generals, the Madres refused to accept the equation by the attorneys of "subversives" with the "disappeared." The national meeting of Madres on 23 June 1985 denounced the government interpretation that the repression suffered by the whole Argentine body was due to "terrorism of the left." The Madres accused the public prosecutor of the Federal Appeals Court of accepting the military's distinction between innocent and guilty victims:

> Dr. Strassera stated in his text, "I represent as much the Madres de Plaza de Mayo as the officials of the armed forces.... A lack of proof and judicial condemnations hinder one from distinguishing between the victims of those who were guerrillas and those who were not." The Madres respond that "it is impossible to represent both the victim and the victimizers, the repressed and the repressors.... We repudiate the use of such terms as 'terrorists,' 'delinquent-subversives,' and 'innocents' to refer to our children.... The distinction between innocent and guilty victims carries an implicit legitimation of the genocidal dictatorship. They are only victims.... We won't allow you to dirty their image."(Madres de Plaza de Mayo 1985)

Here the Madres not only challenge the definitions of both the military junta and the democratic Alfonsín government at the time, but they turn the very term used in defense of the dirty war against subversion by General Camps ("The sense of nationality ... became muddied and dirtied") against him and the national-security state itself. Nor would they publicly accept the species of amnesty passed by the Congress in 1987, the Law of Fullstop (*Punto Final*):

> We Madres have always been suspicious of the Alfonsín government's intentions, with the modification of the Military Justice Code, with trying all cases within the jurisdiction of the Supreme Military Council, and with accepting the majority of sentences handed down by the military court.... But now, with [this] *Punto Final,* we interpret this as a total moral and ethical abomination of justice. To place limits on the time when investigations may take place is never to know what happened to all those disappeared. (Collective interview with the Madres [*Linea Fundadora*] by author, Buenos Aires, January 1987)

Ironically, the one lesson Argentine officers say they have learned from the dirty war is never again to step outside the legal system to wage a war.

> We wouldn't have these damn headscarves [*pañuelos*; that is, Madres]
> fifteen years later if we [the military] had not used the tactic of
> disappearance, but rather we had worked within the legal-
> constitutional system to rid the country of the subversives—
> something we already had under control before the 1976 coup.
> (Argentine colonel, interview with author, 1992, Buenos Aires)

The irony is that the juntas' actions and means of gaining power generated
their own self-destruction and disempowerment, rather than the heroic
ending the military felt they deserved. In occupying (and painting a permanent circle of *pañuelos* on the pavement around) the plaza every Thursday, the Madres have created a spatialized political legacy. The dialectic of
the national-security state has, in turn, entailed unknowing complicity on
the military's part in its own subversion, in which the optic of governance
is reversed.

Conclusions

Although recent work on the "body politic" emphasizes how the state inscribes its power on the woman's body as a reflection of patriarchal order,
as "the social skin" of political life, the ways in which the Madres and
Greenham Common women utilize their "social skin" as a site for contesting and transforming these patriarchal meanings—and thus as resistance to the national-security state—attest to our need to reformulate our
visions both of political space and of women's agency, to create a spatialized discourse of empowerment.

Despite attempts by the national-security state with its architecture of
governance to contain and dispel disorder and to define the physicality of
legitimate politics as that which takes place off the streets, these "militants
for life" have boldly defied the "emptied streets" countenanced by counterinsurgency tactics of disappearance and torture, as well as potential nuclear bombing, by making public the concerns of survival, justice, and
truth. As defiant, disobedient female subjects of the state, their public actions have made more visible where the state's Map of Orderly Space begins and ends: at the immediate line where the military or police squad-
rons stand during their demonstrations in the plaza, at the fence, in the
roadways, and at the court bench. Their conscious use of bodies as public
sites of resistance represent more than the capture of political space and a

statement of political purpose: they also represent a temporary suspension of institutional control and a reversal of the optic of governance. It is the government, not the women, on trial for its paranoiac need for public secrecy concerning its past and future crimes.

By staging demonstrations on streets, in plazas, and atop missile silos, with flowers, banners, candles, photographs of their relatives, and songs, they counter the cult of death with a celebration of life. The transference of domestic imagery into the public domain — of children's toys on fences, of photographs of one's disappeared relative safety-pinned to one's breast, of embroidered diapers on the head — can break the binary spatial boundaries of private and public, as well as provide an "enlarged" moral alternative to national-security states. It is an alternative vision in which "family and justice" are not sacrificed for "security."

The erasure of women's public speech and presence in the modern state parallels the disappearance of victims of modern national security states, with their discourses of counterinsurgency and nuclear war, in one fundamental way: both are objectified and subjugated subjects. Yet, in utilizing their bodies as derisive and ironic metaphors to highlight viscerally the very lack of bodies in national security discourse, the Madres and the Greenham Common women have succeeded twofold. First, in countering the erasure of others (the disappeared of the past and those of present and future wars), they have reclaimed a presence from the absence. Second, as they increasingly participate in the public realm, they become political actors in their own right, entitled to act for themselves and for others. The double erasure of women-as-the-disappeared and women-of-the-disappeared by the modern state has led, paradoxically, to their own physical and political presence.

National-security states then have unwittingly become complicit in their own subversion in more than one sense. The juntas' actions and means of gaining power generated their self-destruction and disempowerment; similarly, in the discourse on nuclear war, the lack of consensus and disappearance of the body have created a dynamic of dissent. In addition, however, national-security states have stimulated, by their denial of movement, speech, and dissent, a public and particularly femininized body/speech critique that challenges and inverts the public masculinist scripts of war. It has provocatively disrupted comfortable affirmations that women remain outside the register of speech, and it has collapsed the rhetorical lines between public and private, between justice and family. By inventing new cultural formations and identities, by being architects of new political spaces and new lexicons with which to guide political behavior ("siting the active but nonviolent body"), and by inverting the old lexicons (in making the familiar, or domestic, strange), these women's initiatives have led the public into another space and time.

Notes

This essay is based on interviews with Greenham Common activists both at Greenham in 1987 and in Boston in 1987, and with Plaza de Mayo Madres in Buenos Aires in January 1987 and October-December 1992. Argentine military officers were also interviewed in October-December 1992 in Buenos Aires. As an International Peace and Security Fellow in 1991, I would like to thank the John D. and Catherine T. MacArthur Foundation for its generous support of the research for this article, and the Ella Lyman Cabot Trust at Harvard University for support of my research in Argentina in 1987.

    1. For a discussion of the masculine image of the state see Graziano (1992).

    2. See Landes (1988) for a discussion of these ideas.

    3. For an example of this discourse in the United States, see the Pentagon report *The Effects of Nuclear Weapons,* read widely by nuclear weapons scientists and defense planners (quoted in Gusterson 1991: 47).

    4. There are debates in Latin America between human rights organizations and militaries/governments as to the precise numbers of victims, as there are among nuclear historians as to the number of casualties caused by the atomic bombings in Japan. Although Bundy uses the figure 200,000 (1988: 80–81), and *The Japanese Times Weekly* cites 500,000 as the Japanese government's estimate (international edition, 24–30 August 1992: 2), official estimates provided by the United States Strategic Bombing Survey (*Summary Report* [*Pacific*], 20) gives the figure of 330,000 Japanese civilians (together with 300,000 German civilians) killed in stategic bombing raids during the final phases of World War II (cited in Sapolsky and Weiner 1992: 3 and footnote 9).

    5. Law 22.068, issued on 12 September 1979 by the ruling junta, declared dead those who had been reported missing during the previous five years. This law was strongly condemned by the Organization of American States for failing to address the question of whether people were alive or dead, and virtually no relatives have used it. Nonetheless, it was one of the first attempts by the military to annul the effects of its "disappearances" through legislation (compare Amnesty International 1985).

    6. The *Punto Final* law, passed on 23 December 1986, fixed a deadline for filing human rights suits against security forces; the Law of Due Obedience, passed on 4 June 1987, argued that no officer could be accused of having committed crimes if he had done so while following orders of his superiors (see Perelli in this volume).

    7. This law was enacted in England in 1920 to cover "prohibited places," which include military establishments and the U.K. Atomic Energy Authority establishments. There are several sections, carrying different maximum sentences ranging from fourteen years to life imprisonment.

    8. The doctrine was developed in a U.S. document commonly referred to as NSC-68,

as well as lessons learned from the French counterinsurgency experience in Algeria (see Perelli n.d.).

9. As in Nazi concentration camps, eradication of self was accomplished, according to survivors' testimonies, by stripping identities down to numbers: "The first thing they told me was to forget who I was, that from then on I would be known only by a number, that for me the outside world ended there" (CONADEP 1984: 182/164). One prisoner, even after being released, was so absent from herself that she believed she was dead and "remained for several minutes in a kind of paralyzed catatonia" — obediently "disappeared" (Graziano 1992: 99).

10. These first two terms come from interviews by the author with persons who were officials of the U.S. State Department during the Reagan administration and worked in El Salvador and Guatemala (and perhaps earlier in Vietnam). In interviews, they referred to Salvadoran death squad members as "tainted, not the type to be trusted," and to Guatemalan military intelligence / death squad members as being involved in "extracurricular activities."

11. In a 1990 interview, a former defense minister of Guatemala stated, "It's low intensity for the U.S. [military], but it's high intensity for us Guatemalans." This is rather disingenuous, given that the minister Gramajo, was one of the architects and the key coordinator of the massacre policy in the Guatemalan highlands between 1982 and 1983 (see Schirmer forthcoming).

12. Stated by Gen. Norman Schwarzkopf at his triumphal press briefing during the Gulf War (Gusterson 1991: 51).

13. Bundy wonders whether U.S. officials did not act on a calculation of human suffering in determining which cities to strike. The death toll from an attack on Kyoto might well have run higher if it weren't for "its broad avenues (which) limited the effects of fire" (Bundy 1988: 80).

14. Agreed to by NATO in 1979 and put into place in 1983, the "Euromissiles" were designed to be used by NATO forces for "limited first strikes" with high accuracy against Soviet military targets in a "protracted" and "winnable" nuclear war during the Reagan and Thatcher years.

15. "Attriting" is from a remark by General Schwarzkopf that as Gusterson states (1991: 50), reframes "mass murder as the completion of a bureaucratic task."

16. For background on the Plaza de Mayo Madres, see Perelli (this volume), Schirmer (1988a), and Fisher (1989), among others. Regarding the Greenham Common activists, see Snitow (1985), Blackwood (1985), and Kirk (1989), among many others.

17. While it is often used to denigrate women's actions, I use the term "spontaneous" here in Hannah Arendt's positive sense of "authentic politics," as opposed to a politics analogous to juridical relations (see Scales 1989 and Benhabib 1992).

18. Identities and names are being reconstructed with the help of forensic anthropologists (Cohen Salama 1992).

19. The Latin American term *¡Presente!* signifies a continual presence of a loved victim of the state despite their death. *¡Presente!* is a living memory of the past-into-the-future in defiance of the eerie absence-of-presence. A mass is held every 8 December at the Church of Santa Cruz in Buenos Aires, from which several Madres and nuns, after working on a full-page ad calling for "A Christmas for Peace," were abducted in 1977 by a "task force" and taken to the torture center at the Navy Mechanics School, tortured, and killed. As each woman's name is called out by the priest at this annual ritual of reaffirmation, the "spectators" become participants, responding "¡Presente!"

20. "Nonviolent direct action" or "citizen intervention" (Aldridge and Stark; quoted in

Scales 1989: 46) is preferred to "civil disobedience," as it defines the practice in terms of the actors' initiatives rather than in terms of the state or the law: "The meaning of the action is no longer dependent on whether the action will be seen as criminal," as technically legal or illegal (Scales 1989: 46–47).

21. While the Madres were dismissed as "mad women" (*las locas*) by the juntas — exhibiting madness in the midst of the normalcy and domestication of terror — the Greenham Common women were called "loonies," "strident feminists," "burly lesbians," "hefty ladies," and "Amazon waifs and strays" (like dogs) by the press, the military/police, and citizens (Cook and Kirk 1983: 95). However, when it was necessary to control the Madres, they became defined as "subversives" and "terrorist mothers" and were subjected to the same methods of elimination as had their disappeared relatives, with twelve members of the Plaza de Mayo Madres disappeared (see Schirmer 1988a).

22. The Plaza de Mayo Madres are only one of twenty-one Committees of Relatives of the Detained-Disappeared in eleven countries throughout Latin America. In Guatemala, for example, only a few days before two leaders of the Group of Mutual Support were found tortured and killed, the departmental governor of Guatemala City had warned that "The women of [the Groups of Mutual Support] will be put in their place.... Provoking public disorder is a subversive act" (quoted in Schirmer 1988a: 58).

23. See Perelli, this volume.

24. Feminist lawyers argued, citing the Genocide Act of 1969, that the women were justified in taking illegal actions to counter the far greater illegality of nuclear weapons. As one lawyer recounts, "The Greenham women ... gave all the wrong responses. They laughed, cheered and clapped. They didn't take half of it seriously.... We took control of that environment away from the men, however briefly.... Women scientists backed up our own [evidence] with the terrifying implications of their research" (Cook and Kirk 1983: 118).

25. This reluctance is clear in the suit brought by the women against the U.S. government for deploying first-use weapons on English soil, making the plaintiffs part of a population most likely to be first incinerated. In *Greenham Women against Cruise Missiles* v. *Reagan et al.* (2d Cir. 1985), the court stated that "if the merits [of the plaintiffs' pleadings] were reached, the court would have to determine whether the U.S. by deploying Cruise missiles is acting aggressively rather than defensively, increasing significantly the risk of incalculable death and destruction rather than decreasing such risk, and making war rather than promoting peace and stability.... The courts are simply incapable of determining the effect of the missile deployment on world peace.... Questions that are infinitely more complicated than those posed by the question 'How many angels can dance on the head of a pin?' are not ready for ready answers." Law, apparently, is "stuck in a prenuclear age" (Scales 1989: 67).

Bibliography

Alonso, Ana Maria. 1992. "Gender, Power, and Historical Memory: Discourses of *Serrano* Resistance." In *Feminists Theorize the Political,* ed. Judith Butler and Joan W. Scott. New York: Routledge. 404–25.

Amnesty International, 1987. *The Military Juntas and Human Rights: Report of the Trial of the Former Junta Members, 1985.* London: Amnesty International.

Arendt, Hannah. 1968. *The Origins of Totalitarianism.* New York: Harcourt Brace Jovanovich.

Benhabib, Seyla. 1992. *Situating the Self.* New York: Routledge.

Berger, John. 1968. "The Nature of Mass Demonstrations." *New Society* 23 (May): 754–55.

Blackwood, Caroline. 1985. *On the Perimeter.* New York: Penguin Books.

Bousquet, Jean-Pierre. 1983. *Las locas de la Plaza de Mayo.* Buenos Aires: El Cid Editores.

Bryson, Norman. 1984. *Tradition and Desire: From David to Delacroix.* Cambridge: Cambridge University Press.

Bundy, McGeorge. 1988. *Danger and Survival: Choices about the Bomb in the First Fifty Years.* New York: Harper and Row.

Butler, Judith. 1991. "Contingent Foundations: Feminism and the Question of 'Postmodernism.'" *Praxis International* 11 (2 July): 151–65.

Bynum, Caroline Walker. 1992. *Fragmentation and Redemption: Essays on Gender and the Human Body in Medieval Religion.* New York: Zone Books.

Cixous, Hélène. 1976. "The Laugh of Medusa." *Signs* 1 (4, Summer): 875–93.

Cohen Salama, Mauricio. 1992. *Tumbas anónimas: Informe sobre la identificación de restos de victimas de la represión ilegal.* Buenos Aires: Catalogos Editora.

CONADEP (Comisión Nacional de Investigación de Desaparición de Personas). 1984. *Nunca mas.* Buenos Aires: Editorial Universitaria de Buenos Aires.

Cook, Alice, and Gwyn Kirk. 1983. *Greenham Women Everywhere.* Boston: South End Press.

Dabat, Alejandro, and Luis Lorenzano. 1984. *Argentina: The Malvinas and the End of Military Rule.* Trans. Ralph Johnstone. London: Verso.

Debray, Regis. 1977. *The Revolution on Trial.* London: Penguin Books.

Fisher, Jo. 1989. *Mothers of the Disappeared.* Boston: South End Press.

Foucault, Michel. 1977. *Discipline and Punishment.* Harmondsworth, Middlesex, U.K.: Penguin Books.

———. 1980. "Questions on Geography." In *Power/Knowledge,* ed. Colin George. New York: Pantheon Books.

Graham, Ruth. 1976. "Rousseau's Sexism Revolutionized." In *"Woman in the Eighteenth Century" and Other Essays,* ed. Paul Fritz and Richard Morton. Toronto: Hakkert. 127–39.

Graziano, Frank. 1992. *Divine Violence: Spectacle, Psychosexuality, and Radical Christianity in the Argentine "Dirty War."* Boulder, Colo.: Westview Press.

Gusterson, Hugh. 1991. "Nuclear War, the Gulf War, and the Disappearing Body." *Journal of Urban and Cultural Studies* 2 (1): 45–55.

Kirk, Gwyn. 1989. "Our Greenham Common: Feminism and Nonviolence." In *Rocking the Ship of State: Toward a Feminist Peace Politics,* ed. Adrienne Harris and Ynestra King. Boulder, Colo.: Westview. 115–32.

Landes, Joan. 1988. *Women and the Public Sphere in the Age of the French Revolution.* Ithaca, N.Y.: Cornell University Press.

Madres de Plaza de Mayo. 1985. "Las evasivas de Alfonsín." *Madres de Plaza de Mayo* (newspaper), 8 July (no. 8): 2.

Massera, Alte. Emilio E. 1979. *El camino a la democracía.* Buenos Aires: El Cid Editores.

Mellibovsky, Matilde. 1990. *Circulo de amor sobre la muerte.* Buenos Aires: Ediciones del Pensamiento Nacional.

Offe, Claus. 1984. "Collective Identity and Social Movements." Paper presented at the Center for European Studies, Harvard University.

Partnoy, Alicia. 1986. *The Little School: Tales of Disappearance and Survival in Argentina.* San Francisco: Cleis Press.

Perelli, Carina. n.d. "From Counterrevolutionary Warfare to Political Awakening: The Uruguayan and Argentine Armed Forces in the Seventies." Unpublished manuscript.

Sapolsky, Harvey M., and Sharon K. Weiner. 1992. "War without Killing." *Breakthroughs* 2 (2, Winter): 1–5.

Scales, Ann C. 1989. "Militarism, Male Dominance, and Law: Feminist Jurisprudence as Oxymoron?" *Harvard Women's Law Journal* 12 (Spring): 25–73.

Schirmer, Jennifer. 1988a. " 'Those Who Die for Life Cannot Be Called Dead': Women and Human Rights Protest in Latin America." *Harvard Human Rights Yearbook* 1 (Spring): 41–76.

———. 1988b. "The Dilemma of Cultural Diversity and Equivalency in Universal Human Rights Standards." In *Human Rights and Anthropology,* ed. Theodore E. Downing and Gilbert Kushner. Cambridge, Mass.: Cultural Survival. 91–106.

———. Forthcoming. *A Violence Called Democracy: The Guatemalan Military Project, 1982–1992.*

Simpson, John, and Jana Bennett. 1985. *The Disappeared and the Mothers of the Plaza.* New York: St. Martin's Press.

Snitow, Ann. 1985. "Holding the Line at Greenham." *Mother Jones* (February/March): 30–47.

Strange, Carolyn. 1990. "Mothers on the March: Maternalism in Women's Protest for Peace in North America and Western Europe, 1900–1985." In *Women and Social Protest,* ed. Guida West and Rhoda Lois Blumberg. New York: Oxford University Press. 205–24.

Vidler, Anthony. 1978. "The Scenes of the Street: Transformations in Ideal and Reality, 1750–1871." In *On Streets,* ed. Stanford Anderson. Cambridge: MIT Press. 26–111.

Young, Alison. 1990. *Femininity in Dissent.* London: Routledge.

8

Living Ancestors

Nationalism and the Past in Postcolonial Trinidad and Tobago

Daniel A. Segal

Nationalism and the "Old" and "New" Worlds

NATIONALISMS OF THE so-called Old World typically proclaim that their respective nations are primordial and transhistorical. And since our scholarship generally takes European history to be exemplary and universal, such claims to primordiality have often been cast as a defining characteristic of nationalist ideologies. Concomitantly, most scholars have framed New World nationalisms as problematic cases, rather than normative ones, precisely because the New World is inscribed with signs of polygenesis—notably syncretism, diffusion, and so-called miscegenation. It is not simply that diversity is hypervisible in the New World, for this is equally true in Central and Eastern Europe, but that New World nationalisms have, more often than not, embraced ancestral diversity as a defining national characteristic. While there is nothing inevitable about this, neither is it accidental. In the case of the Americas, the historical consciousness of both "discovery" and subsequent recent migrations figures polygenesis as fundamental to the contemporary society, and thus as something likely to be at least partially valorized. Certainly, it is an error—one that depends upon the privileging of European history as exemplary—to believe that the affirmation of multiple origins precludes the emergence of a powerful nationalism. Simply consider the United States.[1]

In U.S. nationalism, we find a particular organization of time accompanying affirmations of multiple origins: chronologically dispersed moments of entry into "America" are constructed as the synchronizing, and thus unifying, event of "immigration." Each moment of entry, no matter its historical date or circumstances, is figured as a new beginning endowing each immigrant group with a common, national past. In this nationalist perspective, once people have become "Americans," they come to possess the nation's past (its "discovery," its "founding," its "forefathers"), regardless of when, or from where, they arrived. This has the effect of dividing history into two—creating a past that is complete and geographically distant and a past that is a dimension of the present and geographically here.

Moreover, the past that is complete (the past of the "Old World") becomes the depository of the primordial separateness, or disassociation, of America's immigrant groups vis-à-vis each other. National unity is constituted not by a claim to primordial unity, as is typical of European nationalisms, but by locating prenational disassociation of immigrants in a past that is fully past. To declare "America" a new beginning is to declare closure on the time before "America"—on the time before immigration.[2]

In observing that U.S. nationalism has often affirmed and valorized the nation's multiple origins, I am not suggesting that U.S. nationalism has been universally inclusive. Indeed, nationalist affirmations of ancestral pluralism have frequently been tied to definitions of the United States as a white country. What characterizes the powerful nationalism of the United States is not any lack of racism, but that it asserts the unity of the nation by constituting closure on past disassociation, rather than by proclaiming the nation to be primordial. Just which ancestral differences are placed into this completed past—and who therefore counts as fully "American"— has always been a highly contested issue in U.S. history. But "the American People" is imagined not as always having existed, but as having been forged in historical, rather than prehistorical, time.[3]

To argue that U.S. nationalism locates the prior disassociation of nationalized immigrants in a past that is complete is not to argue that this past is fully forgotten or always neglected. Indeed, there are moments of nostalgia for precisely the distinctions that are proclaimed over and done, but this nostalgia honors the closure on prior disassociation. For instance, ethnic festivals in late-twentieth-century U.S. cities provide objectified displays of the peoples who have entered into U.S. nation. Nostalgia thus serves a nationalist periodization of time by constituting immigrant differences as mementos of a "world we have lost" that can nonetheless be consumed in the present.[4]

In sum, the case of U.S. nationalism shows us that powerful images of national unity do not require a belief in the primordial existence of a nation. Prenational disassociation can be acknowledged, if it is contained in a past that is bounded as a bygone era. What can be said in general about powerful nationalisms is that they discount and efface the prior disassociation of the set of persons they include in their nationality. This can be done either by representing the unity of the nation as primordial and transhistorical, or by constructing temporal closure on prior disassociation — and no doubt by other symbolic strategies as well.

Nationalism and the Past in Postcolonial Trinidad

This essay is primarily concerned with another example of nationalism in the Americas, that of postcolonial Trinidad and Tobago.[5] As one would expect, Trinidadian nationalism posits the existence of a shared national character uniting Trinidadians.[6] Yet even proudly patriotic representations of the Trinidadian nation end up suggesting that its ancestral elements, and their disassociation vis-à-vis each other at the moment of their arrival in the New World, persist in Trinidad now. These representations do not, then, fulfill the nationalist purpose of effacing and discounting the prior disassociation of Trinidad's ancestral constituents. In representations of the nation, present-day Trinidadian society is populated by collective characters from the colonial past, each of whom is defined both by ancestry (or "race") and an affixed position in the plantation economy. The three most prominent of these figures of living ancestors are "Europeans" ("masters"), "Africans" ("slaves"), and "East Indians" ("indentured laborers").[7]

This account of Trinidadian nationalism argues that the often perceived "pluralism" of Trinidadian society is an effect of a particular memorialization of the past, rather than of some unusual degree of social heterogeneity within contemporary society. My views thus challenge one of the prominent social scientific theories of Caribbean societies, M. G. Smith's "plural society" thesis. According to Smith (1965), Caribbean societies are characterized by an abnormal degree of social pluralism resulting from the persistence of ancestral lifeways. From my perspective, Smith's theory is itself an instance of the historical consciousness that fragments perceptions and constructions of nations in the post-colonial Caribbean. This is a case not of imagined community, but of imagined pluralism.[8]

The Positive Vision of the Trinidadian Nation.   It is important to note that the appearance of past pluralism within the nation does not occur solely, or even primarily, in representations of social disorder or conflict. On the contrary, even the most confidently patriotic accounts of national harmony depict Trinidad as plural rather than one and inherently whole. In positive visions of the nation, the standard image of Trinidad is that of a "cosmopolitan" society, one in which diverse peoples live side by side — a "United Nations in miniature," as one respondent told me.

This rhetorical figure is codified and elaborated in texts designed to introduce and promote the nation to foreigners. For example, a brochure from the state-run Tourist Board, circulated in the mid-1980s, offers this introduction to the country:

> Roughly rectangular in shape, about 50 miles long (80 km) by
> 37 miles wide (59 km), Trinidad boasts over a million inhabitants,
> including Africans, British, Spanish, Portuguese, Chinese, French
> and East Indians — both Moslem and Hindu. They give Trinidad an
> air of cosmopolitan excitement and a variety of fascinating cultures
> for you to enjoy. (Trinidad and Tobago n.d.: unpaginated)

This pitch is not only for tourists. In *Investment Opportunities in Industry,* the government's Industrial Development Corporation (IDC) "welcomes foreign investors" in much the same way. Once again, an initial presentation of geography and demography marks the passage as a summary of basic facts:

> Situated at the southeastern end of the Caribbean archipelago ...
> Trinidad and Tobago has a population of 1,149,300....
>   Trinidad has one of the most cosmopolitan communities in the
> Caribbean. People of African descent account for 40.8 per cent of
> the population and East Indians 40.7 per cent. The remainder is
> divided among people of Mixed Races (16.3 per cent); European,
> and Chinese descent. The Europeans are chiefly of British, French,
> Spanish or Portuguese origin....

English is the predominant language in this highly literate
society (adult literacy 95 per cent). (Trinidad and Tobago 1984:
unpaginated).⁹

Finally, in *The Trinidad Carnival,* Errol Hill provides a similar introduction
for foreign scholars:

Trinidad [is] possibly the most cosmopolitan country for its size
anywhere in the world ... with a population descended from
natives of black Africa, India, China, several European countries,
[and] the Middle East. (1972: 3)

These disparate texts contain a common argument. Its conclusion is
that present-day Trinidad is "cosmopolitan," and its evidence is the history of plural ancestries. The implicit warrant necessary for this evidence
to support this conclusion is that the ancestral kinds that immigrated into
Trinidad are present in the nation now. In short, ancestral heterogeneity is
assumed to be equivalent to contemporary heterogeneity. In this historical
consciousness, the diversity of the past is not past, but is "yet still in the
present, not simply as past causes of present conditions, but actually present" (Alexander 1977: 432).

The image of past diversity within the present-day nation is not simply a tale told to lure foreigners. Social diversity may find a place in tourist
brochures as an appealing commodity, but there is no similar rationale for
the inclusion of these images in the IDC's guide for international investors. Indeed, from a business point of view, heterogeneity is likely to be
unsettling. Anticipating this difficulty, the IDC's brochure follows its account of diversity with an assurance that its foreign, Anglophone readers
will be able to communicate in "cosmopolitan" Trinidad. The text's specter
of ancestral Babel is, moreover, purely a rhetorical effect of the image of
Trinidad as "cosmopolitan," for contemporary Trinidad is highly monoglot.
It is thus noteworthy that the IDC's response to the disturbing possibility
of ancestral multilingualism is qualified and understated: "English is the
predominant language." In short, the text's avowed purpose—to make
foreign investors feel comfortable—is superseded by its nationalist consciousness of the presence of ancestral kinds.¹⁰

Finally, two of these three texts contain yet another indication that they
are shaped more by their Trinidadian producers than by their intended audience. In both the IDC's and the Tourist Board's brochures, Trinidadians
whose ancestors came from South Asia are referred to by the term "East

Indian." A common West Indian term, "East Indian" is likely to be opaque to most North American and British tourists.

All three of these texts share a positive vision of Trinidad's ancestral pluralism: the term "cosmopolitan" bespeaks toleration. It claims that Trinidad's ancestral kinds live harmoniously with one another. This view, presented implicitly in the three previous examples, is neatly articulated by an editorial entitled "Problem of Race" that appeared in the daily *Express* in 1985. Throughout the text, the editors use the terms "race," "ethnicity," and "culture" interchangeably to refer to ancestral kinds—which is to say that ethnicity and culture are, like race, treated as inherited phenomena. The editorial begins with the observation that the ancestral pluralism of Trinidad's population exists not only in the past and present, but in perpetuity:

> Race, of course, will always remain one of the most sensitive issues
> in our society, composed as it is of people from many different
> ethnic origins. (*Express,* 13 June 1985: 8)

The text then affirms a positive vision of "tolerance" and "harmony" among Trinidad's plural races:

> Our approach to the question of racial and cultural variety has
> always been to accentuate the positive, to emphasize the
> exceptional degree of tolerance and harmony we have achieved as
> the world's most diverse people. (Ibid.)

What is being celebrated here is not the creation of unity from heterogeneity—not the capacity to invent a new identity out of many old identities—but the coexistence of diverse ancestral kinds in "harmony." Furthermore, though "the people" of Trinidad are described as both harmonious and diverse, these two properties are not accorded the same ontological status. Trinidad's social "harmony" is something contingent. Indeed, the *Express* presents its perception of national "harmony" as an "approach" the newspaper has adopted—an instance of patriotic boosterism—rather than an objective fact. Diversity, by contrast, is figured as something inherent in the composition of the Trinidadian "people." It is a property that exists not as a result of social conditions that might give way at some point in the future, but as a result of "ethnic origins" that are immutable.

Though the positive vision of Trinidad's pluralism insists upon the presence of diversity, the four sources quoted above are, even in their entirety, virtually silent about how the ancestral kinds present in contemporary society differ from one another. In short, the texts refrain from discussing the very diversity they celebrate. This tension of silence within the positive vision of Trinidadian society is well illustrated by the comments of a prominent "East Indian" government minister. As an East Indian in a government perceived as "African," he had lived, throughout his long political career, as a public symbol of the government's avowed multiracialism. Not surprisingly, his responses to my questions about diversity in Trinidad are deft and nuanced:

ETHNOGRAPHER: Do you perceive many ethnic differences between the East Indian community and the African?

GOVERNMENT MINISTER: No, not again. I don't think so. That is only in politics. In politics you hear that, but in the day-to-day life of the community, everybody lives happily together.

ETHNOGRAPHER: Socially and culturally you see the communities as quite similar?

GOVERNMENT MINISTER: But no, you have two — you have cultural differences. People misunderstand and say it is race, but a Hindu does not eat beef, and ... a Muslim does not eat pork, nor consume alcohol ... so there are cultural differences to that extent.... But I don't think that these differences are based on any racial or other things, but people have to practice their religion ... and the others don't follow it, so to that extent there are differences.

ETHNOGRAPHER: This is an unrepresentative sampling, but at most of the Muslims whose houses I've been at [in Trinidad], there is liquor.

GOVERNMENT MINISTER: Yes, I have heard this, and I know it happens. In fact, quite a few Muslims drink, but they are violating the laws of the religion. Quite a few Muslims eat pork; they are violating the laws of the religion. A Hindu ought not to eat beef and pork, and a lot of Hindus in Trinidad eat pork and eat beef too. Look at one here. [The minister points at an East Indian staff member who has entered his office.] I've always quarreled with him about it.

In these comments, the minister's initial answer denies that there are significant "differences" between Afro-Trinidadians and Indo-Trinidadians. Yet his next response rejects the view that they are "quite similar." The minister reconciles the apparent contradiction by stating that although there are "cultural differences," these are not a matter of "race." But how, in these comments, do the terms differ? What distinction is being drawn by the minister? Let us note that the minister believes that cultural norms and obligations are inherited in conjunction with ancestral identities: he regards religious taboos on food as inescapable. The difference is not that "culture" is free of essentializing. Rather, in the minister's comments, the terms differ primarily in their referential pragmatics: "cultural differences" are illustrated by the contrast between Muslims and Hindus, not by the contrast between East Indians and Africans. In effect, then, the rhetorical move from "race" to "culture" involves a switch from discussing Africans and East Indians to discussing Muslims and Hindus. Here the beginning of the minister's second response is crucial. He starts to say "But no, you have two—" but finishes by altering his phrasing: "You have cultural differences." In the context of the prior dialogue, "two" refers specifically to Afro-Trinidadians and Indo-Trinidadians. "Cultural differences," by contrast, has no predetermined referent. It thus enables a switch in examples, and this switch allows the minister to maintain the positive vision of Trinidad as diverse but not divided. Whereas the initial example of Indo- and Afro-Trinidadians is associated with conflicted positions in the plantation political economy, the replacement example is depoliticized and defused, since Hindu and Muslim are symbolically linked in Trinidad as two varieties of East Indian.[11] Furthermore, the minister's rhetorical switch serves to deflect attention from another example associated with the divisions of plantation society—that of Africans and Europeans. Identified in religious terms (as suggested by the Hindu and Muslim example), both are Christians. In sum, in the minister's answer, "cultural differences" are represented by religious identities, and these are unlike "race" in their symbolic separation from the conflicts of the plantation political economy.

Yet we must recall that the racial distinctions the Minister displaces are precisely those that are routinely deployed to demonstrate Trinidad's "cosmopolitanism." The positive vision of the Trinidadian nation is thus unstable. It affirms the presence of racial elements that are seen, ultimately, as discordant and for this reason are moved to the margins of discussion. The positive image of the Trinidad nation as "cosmopolitan" thus contains (in both senses) its own antithesis: a negative vision of Trinidad as a nation fragmented by the continued presence of ancestral disassociation.

The Negative Vision of the Nation: Narrations of Conflict.   In representations of the Trinidadian nation as a site of conflict and disorder, the nation is populated by a set of codified and reified collective characters: specifically, the enclassed races and raced classes of plantation society. Discourse about the nation as fragmented by pluralism brings into the present a colonial past, regarded as the formative moment of contemporary society, when racial ancestry and class supposedly corresponded. Each character in this historical tableau is defined by an ancestral land and a point of entry into the political economy of the plantation — or, more precisely, by a system of correspondences between them. In this memorialized past, "African" meant "slave," "white" meant "master," and "East Indian" meant "indentured laborer" — as well as the vice-versas.

To illustrate and expand on this analysis of the negative vision of the Trinidadian nation, I examine here narrations of the public controversy over the funeral in 1985 of Rudolph Charles, one of Trinidad's most prominent leaders of a steel band or "pan." Pan is identified in Trinidad both as a product of the Afro-Trinidadian proletariat of Port-of-Spain and as the cultural property of the nation (compare Aho 1986 and Brereton 1981: 224–27). Rudolph Charles was the leader of a steel band called Desperadoes, a name that accurately suggests the band's attachment to one of the city's poorest and "blackest" neighborhoods, Laventille Hill. At Charles's funeral, social disorder was visible: mourners transgressed authorized spaces, and their voices transgressed authorized silences. In the accounts of the funeral that were published in Trinidad's two daily papers, the *Express* and the *Guardian,* the funeral became a historical pageant of conflict between "races" that had entered into plantation society in distinctive and ascribed social positions.

Charles's funeral was not a simple affair. The service took place in Port-of-Spain's Cathedral of the Immaculate Conception, away from Laventille Hill. The body was taken from the cathedral to a cremation site on the banks of the Caroni River, some ten miles from Port-of-Spain. Throughout, Charles's body lay in a coffin constructed from two chrome-plated steel drums (see Figure 1). During the days between Charles's death and the funeral, this singular casket had become widely known as "the casket pan" or "the silver chariot." In addition to relatives and close friends of Charles, the funeral was attended by political leaders and representatives of the Desperadoes' corporate sponsor (the West Indian Tobacco Company, or WITCO) as well as "thousands of people, most of them from the Laventille community" (*Trinidadian Guardian,* 5 April 1985: 1). The cause of Charles's death was itself a matter of controversy. Officially, he was re-

Figure 1. The "pan casket" containing the body of Rudolph Charles being followed by a crowd outside of Port-of-Spain's Cathedral of the Immaculate Conception. Photograph courtesy of the *Trinidadian Guardian*.

ported to have died of coronary failure, but widespread rumor attributed his death to a cocaine overdose.

Accounts of the funeral can be placed into three categories. In one view, expressed in the news reports and editorials of the two daily papers, as well as in the news coverage on Trinidad and Tobago television, Charles was represented as a "hero" of the Trinidadian nation as a whole. The editorial in the *Express* announced "We Mourn a National Hero" (5 April 1985: 8), and the *Guardian*'s news story made repeated connections between Charles and Trinidad's first prime minister, the late Eric Williams. Under a photo of the body resting "in state," for instance, the *Guardian* reported "Panman's Funeral Seen as the Largest since That of Late Prime Minister," and added:

> Charles died on the same date as Dr. Williams—March 29—and like the late Prime Minister, his body was also cremated.
> Charles was one of the lucky persons to get an audience with Dr. Williams. (5 April 1985: 1)

In both this report and the *Express* editorial, Laventille was represented simply as the local "community" to which Charles happened to be attached—"where he was born" (*Guardian*)—and not as a place with a particular racial identity. Moreover, these reports focused on the officially scheduled events of the funeral: the religious rites, the music, and the eulogies. By contrast, they said little about the audience or the actions of the people in it. Disorder at the service was described in a markedly low-key manner. Only in the continuation of its report, on an interior page, did the *Express* note that "There were small scuffles as people tried to get a look at the body" (5 April 1985: 18).

A second view was strongly critical of public behavior at the funeral. The most notorious expression of this opinion was a commentary in the *Express* under the byline of Nylah Ali. This essay began by raising doubts about the praises given Charles and casting aspersions on his followers:

> If Rudolph Charles was the disciplinarian that people say he was, then he would have been most disappointed in the behavior of the majority of the congregation that attended his funeral service at the Cathedral of the Immaculate Conception yesterday morning. (5 April 1985: 2)

The "crowd," Ali complained, occupied "the center aisle" in front of the casket "despite pleas from" the officiating priest, Father Harvey, and responded inappropriately when he addressed them:

> "We do not want this to be a bacchanal, but a celebration of life," said Fr. Harvey as he began the service. But in contrast to his message, the congregation applauded his brief comments.
> Applause also greeted the eulogists ... and [the calypsonian] Sparrow,[12] and then the very bacchanal Fr. Harvey warned against broke out following the latter's rendition of *My way.* (Ibid.)

In Ali's account, the social particularities of the mourners were not ignored, but derisively marked:

> [The funeral] was a Carnival of colour, including the disturbing sight of a woman dressed in fluorescent yellow. (Ibid.)

In contrast to this "disturbing" sight, Ali provided an account of behavior befitting the memory of a deceased artistic genius:

> One person who attended yesterday's service said she recalled
> attending the service of George Balanchine, the famed
> choreographer of the New York City Ballet, which was four hours
> long and just as crowded, yet was disciplined despite the emotions
> of those present. (Ibid.)

Here, Ali uses the implicit flattery of likening the death of Charles to the
death of a "famed" producer of "high culture" (ballet in New York) as a
rhetorical position from which to castigate again the behavior of Charles's
mourners. The essay ends with a similar pragmatic use of Shakespeare:

> With respect and reverence for Charles, for the service he never
> had . . . a quote must be borrowed from that other master, William
> Shakespeare, in his tragic play *Hamlet*: "Good night, Sweet Prince,
> Let flights of angels sing thee to thy rest." (Ibid.)

In sum, Ali's text systematically contrasts an uncivilized world of unruly
behavior with a world of respectability that honors Balanchine and Shakespeare. Though the text does not use terms that are explicitly racial, this
contrast is nonetheless raced. The text presumes that readers will know
that most of the mourners were black Trinidadians; it represents these
mourners with allusions to Carnival ("Carnival of colour," "bacchanal")
that are, by common association, also allusions to Afro-Trinidadians; and it
systematically sets the behavior of the mourners against images of a white
metropolitan cultural elite (Balanchine's mourners, Shakespeare).

It was, moreover, in explicitly racial terms that others responded to
Ali's commentary and defended the mourners from Laventille. Some three
weeks after Ali's piece appeared, the *Express* published a three-part essay
by Meryl James Bryan, "Hill People Captured the Cathedral When Their
General Was Buried." (Bryan 1985). Bryan's essay opens by invoking the
authority of "social theorists" who have found that Trinidad society is characterized by "cultural dualism," and then proceeds to narrate Charles's funeral as a "struggle for the soul of our society" between Trinidad's "two
contradictory cultural strains":

> *The masses* flooded *the cathedral. Africa* met Europe; and the melee
> started. The sponsor had reserved about one third of the church for
> "dignitaries and WITCO people.". . . .
>
>   The Hill people weren't buying that. . . . [They] crowded the
> aisles; some jumped through the Cathedral windows, the Cathedral
> doors having been locked. . . .

> One 50ish ... woman ... sporting a green pants and T-shirt
> that loudly and most appropriately proclaimed: "Pan Nite and Day"
> could take it no more. She defiantly pushed through the barrier of
> the charming WITCO P.R.O. [Public Relations Officer] ... [and]
> made her position clear: "Is we dead; and we church." (Bryan 1985,
> 29 April: 13; my emphasis)[13]

In this narrative, the behavior Ali deemed unruly—even including the
appearance of flamboyant clothes at a funeral—becomes a moment of resistance by the (African) oppressed against the (European) elite, or, alter-
natively, (oppressed) Africa against (elitist) Europe. Throughout Bryan's text,
the terms and indexicals of race and class are used as if there is a one-to-
one correspondence between them, and Bryan locates the origins of this
social order in what she calls "Plantation Society" (Bryan 1985, 1 May: 41).

In this discourse, race brings into the present an imagined past—
specifically, a moment of societal formation—when race and class were
supposedly paradigmatic equivalents. As a result, race fragments the social
whole by figuring positions of relative domination as elemental races—in
effect, configuring class relations as relations between naturally solidary
and individuated ancestral kinds.

This racialist reification of class is particularly evident in Bryan's han-
dling of the relationship between Africans and East Indians. Consider, for
example, her discussion of Charles's cremation. Whereas for the *Guardian*
cremation linked Charles to Eric Williams, in Bryan's text cremation introduces a discussion of the relationship between "Afro-Trinidadians" and
"Indo-Trinidadians":

> Ironically, Rudolph Charles, the General of one of urban
> Trinidad's most African populations and an undisputed leader of the
> steelband movement, was cremated, Hindu-style, on the banks of
> the Caroni River.
> Perhaps, just as his life symbolized unity and continuity to the
> people of Laventille, ... his burial ... holds the promise of unity
> and solidarity between Afro-Trinidadians and Indo-Trinidadians.
> (Bryan 1985, 1 May: 39)

Here, despite an endorsement of the "unity and solidarity" of Trinidad's
oppressed, the text nonetheless affirms the presence of two distinct and essentialized, raced "underclasses." Note, for instance, that Charles's association with a Hindu practice is seen as "ironic," that is, as surprising given his

"African" identity. Moreover, Charles's cremation is identified as "Hindu-style" without any evidence that Hindu rituals were observed. It is not that the cremation is demonstrated to have been "Hindu-style," but that as a cremation it is assumed to be Hindu and, by extension, Indian. In this text, the ancestral identity of persons or institutions is not a contingent property that must be documented, but something inherent that can be presumed.

Finally, that Bryan perceives the prior disassociation of Africans and Indians as an aspect of contemporary Trinidad is revealed by a fundamental tension in her text. On the one hand, her text speaks of two underclasses ("Afro-Trinidadians" and "Indo-Trinidadians"), but on the other hand, it states that what characterizes Trinidad today is the conflict between its "two contradictory cultural strains" — "African" and "European." Implicitly, then, the third "strain," the "East Indian," is assumed to be outside of the nation, entering into it only in "ironic" combination with the "African." Once again, the plantation past is yet still in the present, for the figure of Indo-Trinidadians as outsiders — as *East* and not *West* Indians — rests upon a historical memory of South Asian immigrants as indentured laborers present in the West Indies on contracts of a finite term, at the end of which, it was supposed, they would return to their natal land.[14]

Concluding Observations: On Powerful and Weak Nationalisms

We have seen that the positive and negative visions of Trinidad converge, for in both the nation is populated by ancestral kinds that remain as distinct elements, or collective characters, notwithstanding their social mixing in the New World. Nationalist presentations of a unitary Trinidadian identity are thus socially weak relative to the persistence of prenational disassociation.

Yet, contrary to what nationalist ideology would lead us to expect, there is no evidence that this weakness is dysfunctional. Postcolonial Trinidad has not been characterized by social fragmentation. Ancestral distinctions have often been construed as contemporary pluralism (or "dualism"), but they have not been particularly divisive in social life. But just as we should resist a nationalist evaluation of the absence of closure on prior disassociation, so, too, we should be wary of thinking that a "weak national-ism" is somehow outside of nationalist hegemony or socially liberatory.

Powerful nationalisms efface and discount the prenational disassocia-tion of their "people," either by figuring national unity as something pri-mordial or by placing disassociation into a past that is enclosed and com-plete. But in either case, powerful nationalisms place prenational distinctions under erasure, and thereby imagine that their nation was founded as an as-sociation of like individuals rather than socially differentiated persons. This notion produces characteristic mythologies of equal opportunity and concomitant denials of the persistence of institutions of status or rank. Moreover, as has frequently been noted, powerful nationalisms decrease the visibility of class relations. On the one hand, class differences within a nation are submerged by a common nationality; on the other hand, class relations that span national identities are understood not as a feature of a geographically dispersed political-economic order but as relations between distinct "societies," "races," or "cultures." In the late twentieth century, for instance, many among Europe's bourgeoisie have come to believe that their societies lack a proletariat, but this is so because their laborers have, to a great extent, been remade as "foreign." There is, as a result, the ab-surd spectacle of bourgeois surprise when it is found that some of these "foreigners" (that is, workers) are at home in Europe.

By contrast, weak nationalisms locate the disassociation of national citizens in a past that is continuous with the present. Ancestral differences are imagined as ever-enduring and omnipresent. Moreover, in the case of Trinidad, ancestral differences are congealed with the class positions of an imagined past, when social stratification was supposedly without ambigu-ity, complexity, or fluidity. But regrettably, and painfully, this coincident reification of ancestry and class is no more a source of liberatory insight into present-day social relations than is the historical consciousness of powerful nationalisms.

Notes

An earlier version of this paper was presented at the University of Chicago. I benefited from the discussion that followed my presentation there, particularly from the formal response prepared by Alaina Lemon. I am grateful as well to Raymond T. Smith, Richard Handler, and Jonathan Boyarin for their very helpful comments.

1. This paper builds upon the social-constructionist approach to nationalism developed by Handler (1988), Handler and Segal (1993), Segal (1988, 1991, n.d.), and Segal and Handler (1992). My work has been more concerned than that of Handler (1988) with the relative power of different nationalisms. McConnell (1992: 221–23) reviews the literature that holds that U.S. and European nationalisms are fundamentally incomparable. I am not, of course, suggesting that constructions of primordiality are found only in European nationalisms; see, for instance, Fujitani's fine discussion of the nineteenth-century invention of Japan's primordial existence (1993). On the historical commemoration of the "discovery" of the "New World," see Segal (1994a).

2. Concerning the Statue of Liberty, Boyarin has written: "The Statue of Liberty, then, stands for the levelizing inclusion of a certain set of internally differentiated immigrations" (1992: 15). Marling (1988) reports evidence of how various waves of immigrants acquired George Washington as their "founding father."

3. On the importance of race in U.S. nationalist discourse, see Segal (1991), Saxton (1990), Smith-Rosenberg (1992), and Strong and Van Winkle (1993). Quite obviously, the definition of U.S. nationality in terms of historically remembered "immigration" has served, and still serves, to marginalize Native Americans.

4. Hyphenated identities, such as Italian-American, involve this same division of time. Note, for instance, that their order is not reversible, for the first element serves to memorialize ancestors and the second serves to affirm present-day allegiance. If hyphenation indicated a combination of coeval identities, then "Italian-American" and "American-Italian" would be equivalents. The memorialization of ancestors is, however, highly selective. To identify a person as Italian-American is to record and remember that her or his ancestors left (what eventually became) Italy. Yet many other aspects of genealogical predecessors are neglected. It would be socially bizarre for someone to declare herself or himself a "peasant-American," notwithstanding the great number of "Americans" who have ancestors who were peasants. Few of the descendants of peasants feel the historical struggles of peasants as their own, for this is a historical identity that has been enclosed and terminated by a host of myths of history, including both Old and New World nationalisms. For more on hyphenated identities and the commemoration of ancestry, see Urciuoli (1993: 2).

5. This essay relies primarily on ethnographic research conducted in Trinidad from September 1984 to August 1985; the analysis is informed by additional fieldwork during August–September 1982, December 1986, and February–March 1992. My research in 1984–85 was funded by a fellowship from the Organization of American States, and during this time I received valuable support from the Institute for Social and Economic Research at the University of the West Indies. For both, I am most grateful. For a general overview of Trinidad's society, culture, and history, see Segal (1994b).

6. The single word "Trinidad" is commonly used in place of "Trinidad and Tobago."

7. A similar argument about "race" and historical consciousness in preindependence Trinidad is developed in Segal (1993). My analysis there and in this essay is indebted to Alexander's analysis of race-talk in Jamaica (1977 and 1984).

8. The view of Caribbean societies as *sociologically* plural is widely held in the Caribbean, particularly among the bourgeoisie. M. G. Smith's work formalized this view. By contrast, much of R. T. Smith's work has aimed at demonstrating the absence of sociological "pluralism" in Caribbean societies (1960, 1967, 1976, for example, and Smith and Jayawardena 1959). Discussions of the "plural society" debate include Austin (1983), Craig (1982), Hoetnik (1967), and McKenzie (1966). The phrase "imagined communities" is, of course, from Benedict Anderson (1991).

9. This pamphlet does not contain bibliographic information. I have relied on evidence within the pamphlet and on interviews to establish this publication date.

10. Note, moreover, that while the IDC's text creates the phantasm of multiple ancestral languages, it makes no mention of the range of English dialects that are, in fact, a component of contemporary Trinidad.

11. There are also Afro-Trinidadians who are Muslims, but in most situations the unmarked racial identity of "Muslim" is "East Indian."

12. "Sparrow" is the sobriquet of the preeminent calypsonian of the last thirty or so years. On the history of calypso, see Rohlehr (1990) and Warner (1982); for more on Sparrow, see James ([1961] 1977).

13. "Pan Nite and Day" was the slogan for a large steel band festival of the previous October. "We" in this passage operates as the possessive form. This usage thus marks the quoted speech as "dialect" in opposition to the English associated with, among others, the public relations officers of Trinidad's corporations.

14. On the meanings of "East Indian" identity see Naipaul ([1965] 1973) and Segal (1993).

Bibliography

Aho, William. 1986. "Steelband Music in Trinidad and Tobago: The Creation of a People's Music." Unpublished manuscript.

Alexander, Jack. 1977. "The Culture of Race in Middle-Class Kingston." *American Ethnologist* 4: 413–35.

———. 1984. "Love, Race, Slavery, and Sexuality in Jamaican Images of the Family." In *Kinship Ideology and Practice in Latin America,* ed. Raymond T. Smith. Chapel Hill: University of North Carolina Press. 147–80.

Anderson, Benedict. 1991. *Imagined Communities: Reflections on the Origin and Spread of Nationalism.* Rev. ed. London: Verso.

Austin, Diane. 1983. "Culture and Ideology in the English-Speaking Caribbean: A View from Jamaica." *American Ethnologist* 10 (2): 223–40.

Boyarin, Jonathan. 1992. *Storm from Paradise: The Politics of Jewish Memory.* Minneapolis: University of Minnesota Press.

Brereton, Bridget. 1981. *A History of Modern Trinidad, 1783–1962.* Kingston: Heinemann.

Bryan, Meryl James. 1985. "Hill People Captured the Cathedral When Their General Was Buried." *Express,* 29 April: 13; 30 April: 31; 1 May: 38–39. Port-of-Spain.

Craig, Susan. 1982. "Sociological Theorizing in the English-Speaking Caribbean: A Review." In *Contemporary Caribbean: A Sociological Reader,* ed. Susan Craig. Trinidad: Susan Craig. 143–80.

Fujitani, Takashi. 1993. "Inventing, Forgetting, Remembering: Toward a Historical Ethnography of the Nation-State." In *Cultural Nationalism in East Asia,* ed. H. Befo. Berkeley: Institute for East Asian Studies, University of California. 77–106.

Handler, Richard. 1988. *Nationalism and the Politics of Culture in Quebec.* Madison: University of Wisconsin Press.

——— and Daniel Segal. 1993. "Introduction" (to special issue: *Nations, Metropoles, Colonies*). *Social Analysis* 34: 3–8.

Hill, Errol. 1972. *The Trinidad Carnival: Mandate for a National Theatre.* Austin: University of Texas Press.

Hoetnik, Harmannus. 1967. "The Concept of Pluralism as Envisaged by M. G. Smith." *Caribbean Studies* 7 (1): 36–43.

James, C. L. R. [1961] 1977. "The Mighty Sparrow." In *The Future in the Present*. London: Allison and Busby. 191–201.

Lewis, S., and T. G. Mathews, eds. 1967. *Caribbean Integration: Papers on Social, Political, and Economic Integration*. Río Piedras, Puerto Rico: Institute for Caribbean Studies, University of Puerto Rico.

McConnell, Stuart. 1992. *Glorious Contentment: The Grand Army of the Republic, 1865–1900*. Chapel Hill: University of North Carolina Press.

McKenzie, Herman. 1966. "The Plural Society Debate: Some Comments on a Recent Contribution." *Social and Economic Studies* 15 (1): 53–60.

Marling, Karal Ann. 1988. *George Washington Slept Here: Colonial Revivals and American Culture, 1876–1986*. Cambridge: Harvard University Press.

Naipaul, V. S. [1965] 1973. "East Indian." In *The Overcrowded Barracoon*. New York: Alfred A. Knopf. 30–38.

Rohlehr, Gordon. 1990. *Calypso and Society in Pre-Independence Trinidad*. Port-of-Spain: Gordon Rohlehr.

Ryan, Selwyn. 1972. *Race and Nationalism in Trinidad and Tobago*. Toronto: University of Toronto Press.

Saxton, Alexander. 1990. *The Rise and Fall of the White Republic: Class Politics and Mass Culture in Nineteenth Century America*. London: Verso.

Segal, Daniel. 1988. "Nationalism, Comparatively Speaking." *Journal of Historical Sociology* 1 (3): 300–321.

———. 1991. "'The European': Allegories of Racial Purity." *Anthropology Today* 7 (5): 7–9.

———. 1993. "'Race' and 'Colour' in Pre-Independence Trinidad and Tobago." In *Trinidad Ethnicity*, ed. K. Yelvington. London: Macmillan. 81–115.

———. 1994a. "'Discovery' in the Text: The Objectification of 'Races' and the Meaning of 'America' in Undergraduate History Textbooks." In *Commemoration, Resistance, and Revitalization: Reflections on the Columbian Quincentenary and Other Commemorative Events*, ed. P. Strong. Durham, N.C.: Duke University Press. Forthcoming.

———. 1994b. "Trinidad and Tobago." In *The Encyclopedia of World Cultures*. Boston: G. K. Hall. Forthcoming.

———. N.d. "Carnival and the Absence of Nationalist Substantiation in Trinidad and Tobago." Unpublished manuscript.

——— and Richard Handler. 1992. "How European Is Nationalism?" *Social Analysis* 32: 52–64.

Smith, M. G. 1965. *The Plural Society in the West Indies*. Berkeley and Los Angeles: University of California Press.

Smith, Raymond T. 1960. "Review of Social and Cultural Pluralism and Integration in West Indian Societies." *American Anthropologist* 63: 155–57.

———. 1967. "Social Stratification, Cultural Pluralism and Integration in West Indian Societies." In *Caribbean Integration: Papers on Social, Political, and Economic Integration*, ed. S. Lewis and T. G. Mathews. Río Piedras, Puerto Rico: Institute for Caribbean Studies, University of Puerto Rico. 226–58.

———. 1976. "Race, Class, and Political Conflict in a Postcolonial Society." In *Small States and Segmented Societies*, ed. S. Neuman. New York: Praeger Publishers. 198–226.

——— and Chandra Jayawardena. 1959. "Marriage and the Family amongst East Indians in British Guiana." *Social and Economic Studies* 8 (4): 321–75.

Smith-Rosenberg, Carol. 1992. "Dis-Covering the Subject of the 'Great Constitutional Discussion.'" *The Journal of American History* 79: 841–73.

Strong, Pauline Turner, and Barrik Van Winkle. 1993. "Tribe and Nation: American Indians and American Nationalism." *Social Analysis* 34: 9–26.

Trinidad and Tobago. 1984. *Investment Opportunities in Industry*. Port-of-Spain: Industrial Development Corporation.

————. N.d. *General Information*. Trinidad and Tobago Tourist Board.

Urciuoli, Bonnie. 1993. "Containing Diversity: Good Citizenship as the Basis for the Acceptable Enactment of Difference in the U.S." Paper presented at Democracy and Difference, Bloomington, Indiana, 22 April.

Warner, Keith. 1982. *The Trinidad Calypso: A Study of the Calypso as Oral Literature*. Port-of-Spain: Heinemann.

Afterword: Political Memories in Space and Time

Charles Tilly

Artisans versus Partisans

Antoine de Crouzet, great judge of Montpellier, spent a busy 30 June 1645. As he reported in his deposition,

> [I] received word from various places that many women of the city as well as the city's artisans and farmers had gathered in a group of two or three hundred to complain of a certain tax levied on artisans of guilds and brotherhoods for the Happy Accession to the Crown, and other taxes and imposts, and that they went, carrying axes, knives, halberds, and swords, to the Swan Inn, seeking the tax farmers who were staying there. (Bibliothèque Nationale Fonds Français 18432)

Crouzet and his clerk sped to the spot, where the inn's "host" and "hostess" told them that the women had left after demanding the sieur Romanet, reputed to be the culpable tax farmer:

> After searching the whole inn without finding him, they used their axes to break open a chest in Romanet's room, taking all the papers and leaving the inn as they shouted loudly that someone should kill all the *partisans* and sack and burn their houses. (Ibid.; see also Coquelle 1908, Le Roy Ladune 1966, and Beik 1974 and 1985)

241

In those days, a *partisan* belonged to a *parti* that divided up responsibility, and profits, for a given source of government revenue; a *partisan* was a kind of tax farmer. On 29 June a group of children had stoned a tax farmer's son at a public ceremony; when the boy's parents had tried to punish the rock throwers' ringleader the next day, mothers of the children in question had devastated the parents' house (Beik 1974: 245–46). During the four-day rebellion that thus began, clusters of women, artisans, and harvest workers molested the property, persons, and relatives of tax collectors, parading naked corpses of their vituperated victims through Montpellier's streets.

During the four days of violence, about twenty-five people, evenly split between townspeople and authorities, died; eventually two women were executed for their participation in the attacks. Announced Chancellor Pierre Séguier to the seven-year-old king, Louis XIV (or rather to his regent mother and her advisor-cum-lover Cardinal Mazarin),

> The crime of Montpellier's inhabitants is serious. . . . It does not
> deserve your clemency. The dregs of the people and the weaker sex
> had the nerve to take arms; to seize the city gates; to break into the
> houses of the king's officers or tax commissioners; to mark for
> pillage the houses of those inhabitants they suspected of being tax
> farmers and condemn them to death; to attack a duke, peer,
> marshal of France, and governor of the province in the city that
> engages the better part of his friendships, clientele, and personal
> routines, endangering his life; to burn, sack, and massacre as the
> tocsin sounded; to run down an intendant; not to fear the cannons
> of a royal fortress, but on the contrary to push them aside and battle
> its soldiers. (Bibliothèque Nationale Fonds Français 18432)

Predictably, Séguier recommended severe repression.

For an example to all of France, well he might. In those years of rising taxation for France's expenses in what later came to be known as the Thirty Years War, violent attacks on tax farmers repeatedly, over much of France, escalated into revolts against royal authority (Tilly 1986: chaps. 4 and 5). Montpellier's rebellion of June-July 1645 aimed at the *Joyeux Avènement,* a one-time tax imposed on the pretext of Louis XIV's accession to the throne. As usual, royal agents had farmed the tax out to a financier who advanced money to the Crown in return for the right to collect considerably more than the sum advanced and to receive royal backing—including military force, if necessary—in making his collections.

At Louis XIII's death in 1643, which brought the always risky succession of a child, Languedoc's powerholders (like those of most other regions) had tried to win back some of the autonomy they had lost under that aggressive king and his ruthless minister Richelieu. The Estates of Languedoc had tried to suspend the *Joyeux Avènement,* which essentially required corporate entities such as guilds to buy new guarantees of their privileges from the incoming regime. In those days when intendants stood halfway between the peripatetic troubleshooters they had been under Richelieu and the regional administrators they would become under Colbert, Languedoc boasted two competing intendants who differed in their styles, policies, and Parisian patrons. They disagreed about, among many other things, how to collect the new impost.

In short, Languedoc's ordinary people had some reason to think that they would find authorities vulnerable, acquiescent, or even secretly cooperative in the face of popular resistance to new taxes. By seizing and scattering Romanet's papers, the invaders were desecrating the official memory of the tax-farming arrangement in favor of their own memory of times before the war when much more modest taxes had been authorized by the municipality and the Estates of Languedoc, not to mention their recollection of the great days of 1632 when popular resistance to war-inspired taxation had precipitated a threat to Louis XIII's very crown. In 1632 the king's brother Gaston d'Orléans led a revolt and the duke of Montmorency, Languedoc's hereditary military governor, joined him. Montmorency lost his life for that indiscretion, but his beheading did not dim the memory of 1632 as a moment of concerted resistance to royal greed.

I do not claim that Montpellier's struggles of 1645 provide a paradigm for the politics of memory, or that my quick observations constitute a model for the study of that politics; a closer look at the city's history in that turbulent time would surely identify complexities I have not mentioned. It is relevant to my tale, for example, that a century earlier the people of Languedoc had converted massively to Protestantism, and that as recently as the 1620s Louis XIII had been conducting military expeditions to subdue largely autonomous Protestant strongholds within the province.

I do claim, however, that seventeenth-century resistance to the *Joyeux Avènement* raises a number of the same questions as the more contemporary analyses in the rest of this volume. Which spaces provided the moral frame for women's action in June 1645: all of France, Languedoc, Montpellier, the women's own neighborhoods, the bourgeois quarters in which the tax farmers lived? To which times did the vengeance refer: just the moment of that particular tax, or a long accumulation of interactions with an expanding state? What political grounds did Montpellier's guilds and brotherhoods have for their actions: what rights, previous agreements, established procedures? To pose the questions is to recognize three crucial features of memory's politics: (1) that definitions of justice attach people to particular settings in space and time; (2) that, at least implicitly, people always have a choice among the mnemonic and moral frames they adopt in pursuing justice; and (3) that an observer—historian, ethnographer, or fellow citizen—cannot account for the shared interests on which people will act without investigating what mnemonic and moral frames they actually had available.

This volume's essays amply illustrate these features of memory's politics. Jonathan Boyarin's introduction seeks not only to survey how the available frames are changing but also to recommend new ways of synthesizing them. Carina Perelli emphasizes the politics of Argentine memories under military rule, showing how authorities and citizens struggled over what reconstructions of the past were permissible. In Lisa Yoneyama's essay on Hiroshima we see Japanese people actively choosing how they will remember nuclear devastation. Charles Hale troubles us by uncovering the acute and life-threatening competition among different definitions of identity and right in Nicaragua, forcing us to ask, in effect, "Who *are* the subalterns, who the powerholders?" Jonathan Boyarin's discussion of Hegel draws out unexpected parallels to Zionist thought, which in turn help identify the effects of assuming that nation-states are the ideal, and ultimately inevitable, instruments of human government. For Akhil Gupta, the observation of Indian beliefs in reincarnation leads to the discovery of circular temporalities in ostensibly rational capitalist social life. In Greenham Common and the Plaza de Mayo, Jennifer Schirmer finds a challenge to the state regulation of public space and hence to the relative priority of memories and moral codes. Daniel Segal, finally, dissects Trinidad's official pluralism, seeing government-propagated understandings of ethnic history as simultaneously powerful and ridiculous.

Not that all these authors have the same views of space, time, and the politics of memory. Daniel Segal's conception of Caribbean ethnicity, for example, entails much greater plasticity, contingency, and mystification than Charles Hale's. The papers have in common a conviction that memory *has* a politics, and that effective rights depend on shared memories.

Instead of attempting to scan the preceding papers for agreements and disagreements in these regards, my contribution pursues those insights in a
loosely related set of political phenomena: contentious repertoires, citizenship, and nationalism.

Ordinary people of the seventeeth century did not leave detailed independent reports of their memories; the great bulk of the available evidence
concerning popular reconstruction of the past in seventeenth-century
France comes from authorities, elite observers, and confessions exacted under duress. Through those distant, distorting filters, nevertheless, the actions and demands of ordinary people bespeak a strong sense of rights,
justice, and shared experience. Montpellier's women, after all, mimicked
official procedure in sending a drummer through the city's streets to assemble crowds for the (successful) liberation of prisoners taken by authorities during the first days' pillaging; the attacks on *partisans* themselves involved not only the stripping of victims but also the ceremonious burning
of their wealth in the streets. They invoked the rites of popular retribution.

For several centuries before 1850, Western Europeans and North
Americans commonly wrought justice on ordinary people's exploiters by
entering their houses en masse, drinking their liquor, gathering up pre-
cious goods, and staging public bonfires of the goods in nearby streets. If
the owners were so imprudent as to remain at home, the avengers ravaged
them personally as well. In response to the Stamp Act of 1765, Bostonians
entered the residence of Lieutenant-Governor Thomas Hutchinson,

> which in a few hours they reduced to a mere skeleton; all the
> furniture, plate, glasses, china, wearing apparel, his valuable and
> costly library, the files and records of office, fell a prey to their
> destructive rage. (*Gentleman's Magazine and Historical Chronicle*
> [London] 1765: 474)

During London's turmoil of June 1780 (the so-called Gordon Riots, after
Lord George Gordon, head of the Protestant Association), crowds repeat-
edly gave similar treatments to chapels and houses of prominent Catholics,
whom they regarded as threats to Protestant hegemony. At the trial of
George Staples for his part in the destruction of a house in Moorfields (7
June), witness John Williams reported that

> he saw the prisoner at Mr. Malo's house; that he had a stick in his
> hand, and was breaking the window frames; that a great number of
> people were at this time throwing furniture out into the street; he

knew the prisoner before this, had seen him very often crying muffins; while the witness stood, the prisoner brought a bottle to the window, drank out of it, and gave it to the mob on the out side of the house; after this, the prisoner set to work again, and soon after brought a second bottle, and did the same as before. ... John Figgit, the person who gave information against the prisoner, said he was present at the commencement of the tumult, and that the prisoner was very active destroying the wainscoting, and throwing it into the flames. (*London Chronicle,* 6 July 1780: 20)

Despite roisterous drinking, the "pulling down" (as eighteenth-century Englishmen called it) of a private dwelling, chapel, jail, poorhouse, mill, or other dishonored building generally involved careful selection of targets, public destruction of the property, and relatively little purloining of valuables for personal profit.

Contentious Repertoires

This well-known performance coupled with a number of others: Rough Music or charivari; machine breaking; seizures of hoarded grain or high-priced bread for public sale; expulsions of tax collectors, scabs, and other malefactors; invasions of enclosed fields; group hunting on posted lands; forced liberation of prisoners from jail; and still other forms of retribution and assertion of rights. Each one had a standard form with many variants. Together, the performances constituted a repertoire of public contention, a set of stylized collective conversations with objects of reprobation that featured dramatic representation of complaints, direct retaliation for misdeeds, and sometimes even immediate righting of the wrong.

Although this particular repertoire belonged distinctively to early modern Western Europeans and their cousins in British North America, those Europeans were not in the least distinctive in having their own repertoires of contention. Every population that exercises collective rights and privileges maintains some such repertoire of claim-making performances. Today, for example, those Europeans' descendants have at their disposal such routines as electoral campaigns, social movements, demonstrations, petition drives, and collective lawsuits. Like their ancestors' house smashing, these performances are collective, political, interactive, cultural, and historical:

collective in belonging to whole populations rather than to single individuals,

political in exercising power and engaging holders of concentrated power,

interactive in linking claim makers with objects of claims,

cultural in resting on shared understandings, and

historical in accumulating and modifying incrementally from one performance to the next.

Contentious repertoires share these properties with political discourse; indeed, discourse and contention overlap and reinforce each other. Their collective, political, interactive, cultural, and historical character means they amply exemplify the politics of memory.

The case of contentious repertoires, however, reveals the dual content of memory's politics. For the "politics of memory" refers to both (a) the process by which accumulated, shared historical experience constrains today's political action and (b) the contestation or coercion that occurs over the proper interpretation of that historical experience. In this volume, most of my fellow authors emphasize the second meaning, but we can focus their arguments by dwelling for a while on the first. My own exploration of contentious repertoires in Great Britain between 1758 and 1834 confirms that the forms of public claim making changed incrementally as a function of successes and failures; varied considerably by group, locality, issue, and period; excluded many other forms that were technically possible; articulated closely with social ties outside the world of contention; and fell into familiar clusters within which participants constantly strategized and innovated (see, for example, Tilly 1982, 1983, 1989b, and 1993a).

What of memory? Repertoires of contention join shared memories of the past with shared visions of the future. From the past people take not only a history of their relations to potential objects of their claims and a more general sense of their own common identity but also histories of the particular forms of claim making they have at their disposal: lawsuits, humble appeals to patrons, expulsions, pulling down of houses, and more. These pasts frame collective ideas of what actions are generally possible, permissible, and desirable. But constructions of the future also matter, as people scan the present for opportunities and threats, thereby arriving at estimates of the likely outcomes under current circumstances for various possible, permissible, and desirable actions.

In the short run, potential participants in collective action estimate

the likelihood that other potential participants will cooperate with sufficient effectiveness to accomplish their goals instead of defecting or acting
ineffectually. Considering the long run, they also estimate the probable
effects of an array of possible completed actions on themselves, their fellows, and the objects of their claims, choosing appropriate actions (or inaction) accordingly. The evidence for these estimates emerges from collective
evaluation of previous experience. Political entrepreneurs and charismatic
leaders significantly influence the evaluations. Memory and forecast merge.

The process repeats itself, moreover, as strategic interaction with other
groups occurs: participants on all sides of the claim making recast past,
present, and future through readings of their own and other people's actions. Strategic action, with its multiple successes and failures, thereby produces modifications in contentious repertoires. In Great Britain, just such
a process swept away the pulling down of houses, the invasion of enclosed
fields, and associated actions in favor of demonstrations, public meetings,
electoral campaigns, and their companion forms of contention.

In this sort of transformation, two histories intertwine. One history
proceeds at a fair distance from popular struggle and collective action, as
international wars change the organizational structures of states, employers'
adoption of new technologies alters the conditions of work, migration
shifts the locations and social ties of populations, prevailing theories of social causation shift, and so on through a variety of changes we call "structural" precisely because from the viewpoint of any individual or small
group they seem exterior and inexorable. With respect to the history of
contention we can think of them as changes in *political opportunity structure.*

The other history takes place within the stream of contention itself:
the outcome of one round of claim making modifies the conditions for
the next round; innovation within one round becomes model or prece-
dent for the next round; social relations established or changed within
contentious encounters endure beyond them; third parties change their
positions with respect to the protagonists; all participants gain experience
that shapes, inhibits, or facilitates their next participation; all concerned
incorporate interpretations of what happened into their own variants of
collective memory; the very incentives for action or inaction shift as a
consequence of accumulated experience.

The two histories obviously interact: innovative tactics by demonstrators, for example, induce police to invent new tactics of crowd control,
which cause reorganization of police hierarchies and training, which in

turn alters the political opportunity structure at the next round of contention. Contenders likewise undergo continuous structural changes such as aging, insertion in careers, geographic mobility, and shifts in friendship patterns, which in turn influence their capacities and propensities for collective action. Ultimately the distinction between "external" and "internal" histories blurs as the two intertwine. For analytic convenience, nevertheless, it helps to recognize a continuum of changes from one to the other.

A precisely parallel process to the one producing alterations in contentious repertoires transforms political rights. By rights I mean no more than enforceable claims, claims that third parties to the relationship in question reliably intervene to support and certify as just. Rights become *political* to the extent that they bear on powerholders, especially agents of government. Thus in democratic regimes citizens' political rights typically include remonstrance against government malfeasance, public assembly, voting, and judicial due process. But agents of states also have rights, for example, to collect taxes, conscript soldiers, and patrol public places. Rights on one side imply obligations on the other.

Mutual claim making among powerholders and ordinary people takes place within the frames of shared memory, including memories of rights that are sufficiently well established that third parties step in to support their enforcement. Struggle and bargaining alter those rights. The alteration usually takes place incrementally in the course of day-to-day struggles, but sometimes occurs abruptly in the context of revolution. Revolutions entail, among other things, rapid redefinitions of relations between past and future, between shared memories and shared expectations. In the process old claims lose their enforceability; objects of claims who previously acquiesced refuse to comply as third parties cease to intervene on the claimants' behalf. Thus in the European revolutions of 1848, kings' claims to rule suddenly lost their force as the assertion that adult males should elect representatives and rulers abruptly gained effect.

Citizenship and Nationalism

Citizenship and nationalism illustrate the creation of political rights at two different scales: national and international.[1] Citizenship consists of a cluster of rights and obligations binding subjects of a state, considered as a category, to agents of that same state. Before 1800 or so, almost all the world's large states ruled indirectly through privileged intermediaries like the military governor Montmorency of Languedoc, who enjoyed great autonomy within his own zone of control so long as he did the king's bidding on a national scale. Although one might make a case that eighteenth-century France extended citizenship to nobles, priests, and central-government bureaucrats, the term fits Old Regime experience awkwardly.

Starting with extensive elections of regional commissions in 1787 and accelerating with the elections for the Estates General of 1789, however, the country rapidly created direct mutual obligations between state agents and a majority of France's household heads, defined ordinarily as the oldest resident male. New rights and obligations included not only voting and participation in public assemblies, but also military service, officeholding, standard judicial procedures, and much more. The bulk of the French Revolution's popular struggle pivoted precisely on the scope and character of the mutual obligations entailed by citizenship.

Each redefinition of citizenship, indeed, resulted from struggle at a national scale, including struggles over who belonged to the nation: the repeated alterations of suffrage, the tying of political participation to military service, the dispossession of the Roman Catholic church, the banning of émigrés, and much more. More generally, the successive rulers of the revolutionary state found themselves engaged in two momentous efforts: (1) to supplant the Old Regime system of indirect rule through the installation of a centralized system that could rely on its own network (chiefly mercantile and administrative bourgeoisie) of reliable supporters; and (2) to draw the means of great wars against the major European powers from an often reluctant population, many of whom had thought that the revolution would bring escape from the terrible burdens imposed by prerevolutionary wars.

The two efforts led to struggle and bargaining with large segments of the national population. The result: changing definitions of citizenship for both ordinary citizens and agents of the state, by no means all of them to the satisfaction of either side. The new rights made it impossible for the monarchies that succeeded Napoleon, for all their Old Regime pedigrees, to restore anything like the prerevolutionary system of indirect rule.

On a European scale, French conquests and popular struggles during the Napoleonic Wars established rudiments of citizenship in country after country. Even in Great Britain, where authorities spent much of their domestic effort condemning the French example, fighting off movements for revolution or reform, and restricting civil liberties, the net effect of political change between 1789 and 1815 was to strengthen effective rights of citizens to petition, associate, and assemble (Tilly 1991b). The nineteenth century brought extension and crystallization of citizenship throughout Europe, not to mention its major colonies and regions of emigration. By 1900, much of the world gave lip service, or more, to the ideas and practices of citizenship. Where those ideas and practices included relatively broad and equal definitions of citizenship, binding consultation of citizens with respect to the personnel and policies of government, and protection of citizens from arbitrary state action, we can even speak of democracy (Tilly 1993c and forthcoming [a]).

The extension of citizenship occurred in a deeply historical process. Each struggle and bargain developed within the framework of previously established rights to struggle and bargain; each struggle and its settlement, furthermore, altered those rights to some degree. Collective memory constrained struggle but also changed as a consequence of struggle. Similarly, visions of the future shifted as a direct consequence of claims and counterclaims by ordinary people and powerholders.

Nationalism followed a related course. Nationalism makes the claim that nations — large, culturally homogeneous, connected populations of common origin and destination — exist, and states should correspond to nations. Such a correspondence can form in two different ways: through a state's creation of a nation, or through a nation's acquisition of a state. *State-led* nationalism advocates the first path, which often involves subordination of "minority" cultures to some putative "majority" culture; nineteenth-century Germans, Italians, and Russians, indeed, all fought over which versions of German, Italian, or Russian culture should have priority within the states that bore their names. But once one of the versions began to win, state agents built that definition into official languages, monuments, museums, schools, histories, ceremonies, iconographies, currencies, postage stamps, and a wide variety of other cultural forms. *State-seeking* nationalism advocates the second path, which usually requires enlisting outside aid in carving a new state or autonomous province out of a previously existing state, empire, or set of colonies. Innumerable putative nations had lived under indirect rule for ten thousand years before 1800. In Europe, strenuous demands for political autonomy in the name of a nation had recurred before then under two circumstances: when empires had sought to impose official religions on dissenting minorities, and when empires sought to strengthen central control over populations that had previously enjoyed substantial autonomy through weak imperial administration or indirect rule. But as political programs and demands, nationalism of either variety remained rare.

With the era of the French Revolution, however, both state-led and state-seeking nationalism became standard features of national politics in Europe and its extensions. Indeed, state-led nationalism generated state-seeking nationalism. It did so by justifying the principle of national self-determination, by threatening previously autonomous minorities within the national territory, and by offering new allies to rebels against imperial control. Spain lost the bulk of its American empire under the impact of French conquests in Iberia. The defeat of Napoleonic France, in its turn, gave the victorious allies an opportunity to redraw the European map in the image of presumed nations, a rationale that justified the French-aided secession of Belgium in 1830 from the recently created kingdom of the Netherlands. State-led and state-seeking nationalisms cascaded.

During the nineteenth century, while European powers were creating spectacularly heterogeneous empires in Asia and Africa, the European portion of the Ottoman Empire, under pressure from Russia and Austria-Hungary, was splintering, giving rise to widespread demands for national self-determination. Later the Russian and Austro-Hungarian empires recapitulated parts of the Ottoman experience. Indeed, the recent fragmentation of the Soviet Union shared some features with those earlier bursts of state-seeking nationalism; ethnically labeled but heterogeneous political units, such as Georgia and Azerbaijan, that had gained coherence as administrative units of a federal state received the encouragement of outside powers in demanding independence on behalf of ostensibly unified nations.

Other analysts of nationalism have amply demonstrated the importance of social construction and myth making in the justification of both kinds of nationalism.[2] Here, too, collective memory constrained struggle, but also changed as a result of struggle; Romanians defined who they were in the course of fighting against Ottoman rule and comparing themselves with presumptive nations to their north and west. Collective memory and current struggles also interacted with visions of the future, as definitions of what was possible—in this case, what groups of people might achieve political autonomy under what conditions—shifted incessantly. Past, present, and future shaped each other in another deeply historical process.

Conclusions

The histories of contentious repertoires, citizenship, and nationalism overlap and share important features: altering through an interaction between internal struggles and changes in political opportunity structure over which the internal struggles have relatively little influence; displaying the incessant interplay of shared memory, visions of the future, and collective action; depending on common interpretations of the past for definitions of what is permissible, desirable, and feasible; and following trajectories in which each series of steps limits those that follow. The histories in question are systematic, causal, and knowable. They do not consist of arbitrary, unverifiable interpretations whose persuasiveness depends merely on their present rhetorical force. Nevertheless, we have no way of understanding or explaining those histories without examining the processes by which shared memories form, change, and interact with collective struggles.

The politics of memory therefore comes in at least two magnifications. On a large scale we see the whole political process of mutual influence among shared memories, definitions of the future, and collective action. At an increased magnification, we see the contestation that surrounds every effort to create, define, or impose a common memory—to form a coherent discourse about the origins of a people, the sources of citizens' rights, the lessons of previous challenges. If we looked at many different magnifications, we might well discover something like a series of fractals, each subdivision of a structure revealing smaller elements having identical structures, every level from a continent to a pair of interacting individuals showing us the incessant interplay of contested pasts and problematic futures through uncertain collective action. Most of this book emphasizes the contest and the contestability of shared memory, but in so doing it contributes to an enriched, coherent, and verifiable history of politics.

Notes

Because it draws heavily on my previous and current research, documenting this paper presented me with a dilemma: either stuff the notes to bursting or cite myself excessively. I chose the latter course, not with the claim that my previous writings contain the definitive word on this paper's topics but because they include voluminous bibliographies.

1. For bibliography, see Tilly 1989b, 1990, 1992a, 1992c, and forthcoming (b).

2. Recent writing on the subject in a variety of idioms includes Anderson (1991); Armstrong (1982); Bruckmüller (1990); Comaroff (1991); Connor (1987); Dann and Dinwiddy (1988); Gellner (1983); Greenfeld (1992); Hass (1986); Hobsbawm (1990); Horowitz (1985); Hroch (1985); Kearney (1991); Laitin (1991); Laitin, Petersen, and Slocum (1992); Lerner (1991); Löwy (1989); Mellor (1989); Noiriel (1988, 1991); Østergard (1992); Segal (1988); Tacke (1993); Thompson (1989); Tilly (1991a, 1992b, 1993b); Topalov (1991); Waldmann (1989); and Zaslavsky (1992).

Bibliography

Anderson, Benedict. 1991. *Imagined Communities: Reflections on the Spread of Nationalism.* 2d ed. London: Verso.

Armstrong, John A. 1982. *Nations before Nationalism.* Chapel Hill: University of North Carolina Press.

Beik, William H. 1974. "Two Intendants Face a Popular Revolt: Social Unrest and the Structure of Absolutism in 1645." *Canadian Journal of History* 9: 243–62.

———. 1985. *Absolutism and Society in Seventeenth-Century France.* Cambridge: Cambridge University Press.

Bruckmüller, Ernst. 1990. "Ein 'deutsches' Bürgertum? Zu Fragen nationaler Differenzierung der bürgerlichen Schichten in der Habsburgermonarchie vom Vormärz bis um 1860." *Geschichte und Gesellschaft* 16: 343–54.

Comaroff, John. 1991. "Humanity, Ethnicity, Nationality: Conceptual and Comparative Perspectives on the U.S.S.R." *Theory and Society* 20: 661–88.

Connor, Walker. 1987. "Ethnonationalism." In *Understanding Political Development,* ed. Myron Weiner and Samuel P. Huntington. Boston: Little, Brown. 196–220.

Coquelle. 1908. "La sédition de Montpellier en 1645, d'après des documents inédits des Archives des Affaires Etrangères." *Annales du Midi* 20: 66–78.

Dann, Otto, and John Dinwiddy, eds. 1988. *Nationalism in the Age of the French Revolution.* London: Hambledon.

Gellner, Ernest. 1983. *Nations and Nationalism.* Ithaca, N.Y.: Cornell University Press.

Greenfeld, Liah. 1992. *Nationalism: Five Roads to Modernity.* Cambridge: Harvard University Press.

Haas, Ernest. 1986. "What Is Nationalism and Why Should We Study It?" *International Organization* 40: 707–44.

Hobsbawm, E. J. 1990. *Nations and Nationalism since 1789: Programme, Mythe, Reality.* Cambridge: Cambridge University Press.

Horowitz, Donald L. 1985. *Ethnic Groups in Conflict.* Berkeley and Los Angeles: University of California Press.

Hroch, Miroslav. 1985. *Social Preconditions of National Revival in Europe: A Comparative Analy-*

sis of the Social Composition of Patriotic Groups among the Smaller European Nations. Cambridge: Cambridge University Press.

Kearney, Michael. 1991. "Borders and Boundaries of State and Self at the End of Empire." *Journal of Historical Sociology* 4: 52–72.

Laitin, David D. 1991. "The National Uprisings in the Soviet Union." *World Politics* 44: 139–77.

———, Roger Petersen, and John W. Slocum. 1992. "Language and the State: Russia and the Soviet Union in Comparative Perspective." In *Thinking Theoretically about Soviet Nationalities: History and Comparison in the Study of the USSR.* New York: Columbia University Press. 129–68.

Le Roy Ladurie, Emmanuel. 1966. *Les paysans de Languedoc.* Vol. 1. Paris: SEVPEN. 496–98.

Lerner, Adam J., ed. 1991. Special issue: *Reimagining the Nation. Millennium* 20.

Löwy, Michel. 1989. "Internationalisme, nationalisme et anti-impérialisme." *Critique Communiste* 87: 31–42.

Mellor, Roy E. H. 1989. *Nation, State, and Territory: A Political Geography.* London: Routledge.

Noiriel, Gérard. 1988. *Le creuset français: Historie de l'immigration, xixe–xxe siècles.* Paris: Editions du Seuil.

———. 1991. *La tyrannie du national: Le droit d'asile en Europe, 1793–1993.* Paris: Calmann-Lévy.

Østergard, Uffe. 1992. "Peasants and Danes: The Danish National Identity and Political Culture." *Comparative Studies in Society and History* 34: 3–27.

Segal, Daniel A. 1988. "Nationalism, Comparatively Speaking." *Journal of Historical Sociology* 1: 301–21.

Tacke, Charlotte. 1993. "Les lieux de mémoire et la mémoire des lieux: Mythes et monuments entre nation et région en France et en Allemagne au xixe siècle." In *Culture et société dans l'Europe modern et contemporain,* ed. Dominique Julia. Florence: European University Institute. 133–66.

Thompson, Richard H. 1989. *Theories of Ethnicity: A Critical Appraisal.* New York: Greenwood.

Tilly, Charles. 1982. "Britain Creates the Social Movement." In *Social Conflict and the Political Order in Modern Britain,* ed. James Cronin and Jonathan Schneer. London: Croom Helm.

———. 1983. "Speaking Your Mind without Elections, Surveys, or Social Movements." *Public Opinion Quarterly* 47: 461–78.

———. 1986. *The Contentious French.* Cambridge, Mass.: Belknap Press.

———. 1989a. "Collective Violence in European Perspective." In *Violence in America,* ed. Ted Robert Gurr, vol. 2. Newbury Park, Calif.: Sage Publications. 62–100.

———. 1989b. "State and Counterrevolution in France." *Social Research* 56: 71–97.

———. 1990. *Coercion, Capital, and European States, A.D. 990–1990.* Rev. ed., 1992. Oxford: Blackwell.

———. 1991a. "Ethnic Conflict in the Soviet Union." *Theory and Society* 20: 569–80.

———. 1991b. "Revolution, War, and Other Struggles in Great Britain, 1789–1815." Center for Studies of Social Change, New School for Social Research, Working Paper 127.

———. 1992a. "Cities, Bourgeois, and Revolution in France." In *Liberté, égalité, fraternité: Bicentenaire de la grande Révolution français,* ed. M'hammed Sabur. University of Joensuu Publications in Social Sciences, no. 14. Joensuu, Finland: Joensuun Yliopisto. 28–68.

————. 1992b. "Futures of European States." *Social Research* 59: 705–17.

————. 1992c. "Where Do Rights Come From?" In *Contributions to the Comparative Study of Development,* ed. Lars Mjøset. Oslo: Institute for Social Research. 9–36.

————. 1993a. "Contentious Repertoires in Great Britain, 1758–1834." *Social Science History* 17: 253–80.

————. 1993b. *European Revolutions, 1492–1992.* Oxford: Blackwell.

————. 1993c. "Of Oilfields, Lakes, and Democracy." Center for Studies of Social Change, New School for Social Research, Working Paper 152.

————. Forthcoming (a). "Democracy Is a Lake" (revised version of 1993c). In *The Social Construction of Democracy,* ed. Herrick Chapman and Reid Andrews. New York: New York University Press.

————. Forthcoming (b). "States and Nationalism in Europe, 1492–1991." *Theory and Society.*

Topalov, Christian. 1991. "Patriotismes et citoyennetés." *Genèses* 3: 162–76.

Waldmann, Peter. 1989. *Ethnischer Radikalismus: Ursachen und Folgen gewaltsamer Minderheitenkonflikte.* Opladen, Germany: Westdeutscher Verlag.

Williams, Brackette F. 1989. "A Class Act: Anthropology and the Race to Nation across Ethnic Terrain." *Annual Review of Anthropology* 18: 401–44.

Zaslavsky, Victor. 1992. "Nationalism and Democratic Transition in Postcommunist Societies." *Daedalus* 121 (2): 97–122.

Contributors

JONATHAN BOYARIN, an anthropologist, has studied and taught at the New School for Social Research. He has done fieldwork on Jews and others in Paris, Jerusalem, and New York and has been active in the Jewish peace movement. His work over the past two decades has sought to link the fields of Yiddish culture, critical theory, and the transformations of modern identity. He is coeditor and translator of *From a Ruined Garden: The Memorial Books of Polish Jewry,* editor of *The Ethnography of Reading* and of *A Storyteller's Worlds: The Education of Shlomo Noble in Europe and America,* and author of *Polish Jews in Paris: The Ethnography of Memory* and of *Storm from Paradise: The Politics of Jewish Memory* (Minnesota 1992).

AKHIL GUPTA is assistant professor in the anthropology department at Stanford University. He previously taught at the University of Washington, Seattle.

CHARLES R. HALE worked for five years doing anthropological research with the Center for Research and Documentation on the Atlantic Coast (CIDCA) in Managua and Bluefields, Nicaragua. His book on ethnic politics during the Sandinista era, titled *Resistance and Contradiction,* is forthcoming. He is currently an assistant professor of anthropology at the University of California at Davis.

257

CARINA PERELLI, a political scientist, is director of Peitho, Sociedad de Análisis Político in Montevideo, and international consultant in the areas of transitions, democratization, and elections, as well as an expert in the area of civil-military relations. She has written extensively on these subjects and has contributed to the study of the culture of fear in situations of extreme repression. She is now working on the aftermaths of the culture of fear in Latin America.

JENNIFER SCHIRMER is the 1994–96 Luce Fellow at the Center for the Study of Values in Public Life at Harvard Divinity School, and research affiliate at the Center for European Studies at Harvard. Her research and publications include an analysis of the dynamic between women's protest and national security regimes, and a political ethnography on military ideology and thinking in Guatemala, *A Violence Called Democracy: The Guatemalan Military Project, 1982–1992.*

DANIEL A. SEGAL teaches anthropology and world history at Pitzer College in Claremont, California. He is the author, with Richard Handler, of *Jane Austen and the Fiction of Culture: An Essay on the Narration of Social Realities* and the editor of *Crossing Cultures: Essays in the Displacement of Western Civilization.* He has been curator of an exhibition of contemporary Caribbean art.

CHARLES TILLY teaches and directs the Center for Studies of Social Change at the New School for Social Research in New York City. His most recent books are *Coercion, Capital, and European States, A.D. 990–1990* and *European Revolutions, 1492–1992.*

LISA YONEYAMA is a kibei nisei who was born in Urbana, Illinois, and raised in Kyoto. She is currently an assistant professor of cultural studies and Japanese studies in the Literature Department at the University of California at San Diego. Her interests include the United States and Japan, cultural history, minority discourse, the issues of gender and militarism, and Asian American studies.

Index

Compiled by Eileen Quam and Theresa Wolner